Educational Broadcasting in Nigeria in the Age of Artificial Intelligence

"Artificial Intelligence (AI) has seized the whole gamut of the human sensorium. The race to ace its mastery is fierce. This book is the silver bullet to win the race. The book brims with panoptic insight on the rubrics of AI. For the intelligentsia and broadcasters, this is an incomparable resource. The tenor is lucid, eloquent and enticing!"

—Prof. Fred A. Amadi, *Department of Journalism and Media Studies, Rivers State University, Port Harcourt, Rivers State, Nigeria*

"*Educational Broadcasting in Nigeria in the Age of Artificial Intelligence* is timely and insightful, and each chapter expertly navigates the ever evolving terrain, addressing crucial gaps in research and scholarship. A must-read for educators, policymakers, and researchers seeking to understand the future of educational media in an AI-driven world. There is no use fighting AI. Our task should be to understand it and deploy it maximally to advantage our research given its enormous potential. Those who fail to recognize AI's enormous potential will be left behind."

—Prof. Adelaja Odukoya, *Dean, Faculty of Social Science, University of Lagos, Akoka-Lagos, Nigeria*

Unwana Samuel Akpan
Editor

Educational Broadcasting in Nigeria in the Age of Artificial Intelligence

palgrave
macmillan

Editor
Unwana Samuel Akpan
Department of Mass Communication
University of Lagos
Lagos, Nigeria

ISBN 978-3-031-68529-3 ISBN 978-3-031-68530-9 (eBook)
https://doi.org/10.1007/978-3-031-68530-9

Cover credit: Visions of America/Joe Sohm

This Palgrave Macmillan imprint is published by the registered company Springer Nature Switzerland AG
The registered company address is: Gewerbestrasse 11, 6330 Cham, Switzerland

This edited volume pays tribute to Prof. Comfort Memfin Ekpo, a preeminent figure in the field of educational technology in Africa. The dedication is a recognition of her extensive contributions spanning decades, encompassing impactful teaching, scholarly endeavors, and influential leadership within the academic sector.

Foreword

Professor Comfort Memfin Ekpo is an outstanding scholar and leader in the Nigerian university system whom I was privileged to know when she was serving as the first female Vice Chancellor of the University of Uyo, and the second female Vice Chancellor (after Prof. Grace Alele William of the University of Benin) in the Federal University system. I was then serving as a two-time Vice Chancellor, doing pioneering work at Federal University Dutsin-Ma, Katsina State. We often interacted at different fora as Vice Chancellors, and I found her intelligent, insightful, and outstanding in her contributions towards addressing the challenges in the university system. I was therefore excited and honoured to be invited to write the foreword to the compilation, written to honour her and her legacy in scholarship, leadership and exemplary career, titled "*Educational Broadcasting in Nigeria in the Age of Artificial Intelligence*"

I appreciate all the contributing scholars and editors for bringing their different unique insights to celebrate Professor C. M. Ekpo.

In the educational technology sector, the emergence of artificial intelligence (AI) is nothing short of revolutionary. As scholars, Professor Comfort Memfin Ekpo, and I could not have foreseen a future where a digital tool like AI would not only aid in the mastery of essay writing but also assist in organizing the flow of thoughts in any article. Today, we find ourselves in an era where the capabilities of AI transcend human imagination.

The benefits of AI permeate various sectors, and its potential in educational broadcasting would be profound if properly harnessed. This book underscores the importance of leveraging AI to enhance research and programming in educational broadcasting. It is a call to action, urging scholars, researchers, universities, and publishers to embrace this transformative technology for the advancement of research, teaching, learning, and the overall development of humankind.

As we navigate the uncharted waters of the digital age, it is essential to recognize that AI is here to stay. Rather than resist its inexorable influence, we encourage scholars to harness its power, unlocking new avenues for exploration and advancement in educational broadcasting and beyond.

The volume stands as a collective effort, featuring contributions from established and budding scholars across Nigeria. Their articles constitute a robust body of work that will undoubtedly motivate and propel the field of educational broadcasting research forward.

I wholeheartedly recommend this book to scholars, broadcast stations, researchers, and policymakers. It is a comprehensive resource that not only pays homage to a distinguished academic, but also serves as a guide to navigating the evolving sector of educational broadcasting in the age of AI.

His royal Majesty, Professor James O. I. Ayatse, CFR.
Tor Tiv.
Charmain, Benue State Council of Traditional Rulers.
Chancellor of University of Benin & Chancellor, Abia State University, Uturu.
Former Vice Chancellor, University of Agriculture (now Joseph Sarwuan Tarka University) Makurdi, Benue State, Nigeria.
Former Pioneer Vice Chancellor, Federal University Dutsin-Ma, Katsina State.

Preface

The primary objective of this edited volume stems from a collective endeavour to honour the distinguished legacy of Dr. Comfort Memfin Ekpo, a trailblazing professor of Educational Technology in Africa, who is also the second female Vice Chancellor to head a federal university in Nigeria, after Prof. Grace Alele William, of University of Benin, Nigeria. Prof. Comfort Ekpo is also the first female professor and Vice Chancellor in the prestigious University of Uyo, Nigeria.

Furthermore, our aim in assembling this anthology is to present a comprehensive and compelling body of literature addressing the intersection of educational broadcasting and artificial intelligence in Nigeria. Prof. Comfort Ekpo's influence serves as the catalyst for exploring the unexplored discourses in educational technology.

Moreover, this volume is motivated by the dearth of prominent literature on how AI influences and will continue to shape education in Nigeria, with a particular focus on educational broadcasting production, research, teaching, and learning. The articles, carefully curated from both established and budding Nigerian scholars across the nation, provide diverse perspectives on this crucial subject.

Consider this compilation as a toolkit, offering valuable insights on leveraging AI for educational broadcasting while steadfastly upholding ethical standards. As we navigate the uncharted waters of technological evolution, I strongly believe that this volume will serve as a guide for harnessing the benefits of AI in education, ensuring a sustainable and ethically grounded future for educational broadcasting in Nigeria.

This volume is thematically divided into two sections, with an introduction. The first section is tagged, "Educational Broadcasting, Production, Research, Teaching, Learning, and AI." Chapter 1 under this section looks at "Artificial Intelligence (AI) Dynamics in Educational Broadcasting Research and Production in Nigeria: Riding the Wave or Drowning in the Looming Tsunami of Change?", while Chapter 2 asks "How Symbiotic is the Union Between Artificial Intelligence and Educational Broadcasting?", while in Chapter 3, "Artificial Intelligence and the Transformation of Broadcasting: Implications for Nigerian Broadcast Professionals" is explored. The author in Chapter 4 looks at "Artificial Intelligence and Automated Educational Broadcasting in Nigeria: A Futuristic Technesis for Today's Consideration", and in Chapter 5, the authors situate their discussion around "Enhancing the Teaching and Learning of Educational Broadcasting Through Artificial Intelligence" in Chapter 6, the "Prospects and Challenges of Artificial Intelligence in Children's Radio Programmes in Rivers State, Nigeria", are explored. "Challenges of Educational Broadcasting in a Digitized Age of Artificial Intelligence (AI)" is the title of Chapter 7, where the author took time to enumerate the challenges faced by educational broadcasting in the age of AI, and in Chapter 8, the authors examine the "Potentials of Digitized and AI Enhanced Educational Broadcasting", while in Chapter 9, the author discusses "Artificial Intelligence in Educational Broadcasting: Tool for Dissemination of Effective Pedagogy across Scholastic Levels in Nigeria." In Chapter 10, titled, "Leveraging on 4IR for an Effective Educational Broadcasting in Nigeria", the author advises on how to deploy AI in educational broadcasting in Nigeria, and in Chapter 11, "Adapting Radio Broadcasting as a Tool Against Teachers Tendency for Resisting AI Technology", is discussed. In Chapter 12, "Artificial Intelligence (AI) Influence in Educational Media Broadcast in Individualized Instruction in The 21st Century", is looked at, and in Chapter 13, the author examines "Promoting Educational Broadcasting in the Digital Era for Effective Teaching and Learning in Nigerian Schools", while "Artificial Intelligence and Educational Broadcasting: Digitizing Higher Education (HE) in Nigeria Context", is looked at in Chapter 14.

Section two, which is the last section, is on "AI and Educational Instructions." Chapter 15 under this section is on "Artificial Intelligence in Educational Technology: Panacea to Efficient Instructional Delivery", the authors in Chapter 16 investigate "Artificial Intelligence (Speechify App) for Dyslexia on Students' Performance and Retention in Reading in Port Harcourt Metropolis, Rivers State, Nigeria", while "Modern Aspects of Communication for Pedagogic Knowledge and Skills Development in Human Kinetics, Sports and Health Education Students in Lagos State University, Lagos, Nigeria", is explored in Chapter 17.

Lagos, Nigeria Unwana Samuel Akpan, Ph.D.

Acknowledgements

First and foremost, my appreciation goes to God who made this volume a reality. I would also like to express my deepest gratitude to all those who contributed one way or the other to the publication of this book. Putting together an edited book is a journey that cannot be undertaken alone, and I am fortunate to have had the support and assistance of so many wonderful people along the way, especially my associate editor, Dr. Stella Nwosu, and the chapter authors whose insights have brought this book to life.

Second, I want to thank my family for their unwavering support and encouragement throughout this endeavor. Your belief in me has been my greatest motivation.

I am indebted to my dedicated acquisitions editor, whose keen insights and thoughtful guidance helped shape this manuscript into its final form. Your expertise and patience were invaluable.

I would like to extend my appreciation to my research assistants for their diligent research and assistance in gathering information for this book. Their dedication to detail greatly enhanced the quality of the content.

To my friends and colleagues who provided feedback, encouragement, and a listening ear during the ups and downs of the writing process, I am truly grateful. Your input was invaluable in refining the ideas within these pages.

Lastly, to the readers, it is my hope that this book will enrich your knowledge and inspire new perspectives.

With heartfelt appreciation,

Unwana Samuel Akpan, Ph.D.

Introduction

Educational Broadcasting and Artificial Intelligence: Challenges and Opportunities for Theory and Praxis in Nigeria

This volume stands as a testament to the illustrious career of Prof. Comfort Memfin Ekpo, a luminary in the field of Educational Technology research. Widely recognized as one of Africa's foremost scholars in Educational Technology Scholarship, Prof. Comfort Ekpo has made significant contributions to the field, with an extensive portfolio of publications that reflect her dedication to advancing educational practices.

Remarkably, Prof. Comfort Ekpo holds the distinction of being the second female vice-chancellor to head a federal university in Nigeria, after Prof. Grace Alele William. Furthermore, she holds the honor of being the first female professor and vice-chancellor at the prestigious University of Uyo, Nigeria. Her leadership, scholarship, and research have left an indelible mark on the educational sector in Nigeria.

Motivated by Prof. Comfort Ekpo's legacy, the editor/author envisioned this volume as a platform to gather insights from both established and emerging scholars across Nigeria on how Artificial Intelligence has impacted, and would continue to impact educational broadcasting production, research, teaching, and learning. The primary focus is to examine the profound impact of Artificial Intelligence (AI) on the education sector, particularly within the educational broadcasting research track in Nigeria. The goal also is to navigate the challenges and opportunities presented by AI, ensuring that its integration aligns with ethical standards and educational excellence.

In the chapters of this book, distinguished contributors draw upon their extensive academic experiences to offer diverse perspectives on the pitfalls, benefits, concerns, and best practices related to AI in educational broadcasting production, research, teaching, and learning. The insights presented herein serve as a guide for educators, policymakers, and stakeholders as they navigate the dynamic territory of AI in education.

In recent times, educational broadcasting production, and technological advancement in Artificial Intelligence (AI) stand as a transformative force with immense potential. As we explore the pages of this groundbreaking book, it becomes evident that the synergy between AI and educational broadcasting can revolutionize research, teaching, practice, and learning experience in Nigeria.

Africa, as a continent, is on the cusp of a digital revolution, and Nigeria, with its burgeoning population, holds a pivotal role in shaping the future of education through technological innovation. Recognizing the paramount importance of AI, there is an urgent need for governments across Africa, including Nigeria, to foster and encourage research in this emerging digital tool.

Remarkably, despite the burgeoning discourse on AI globally (O'Connor, 2022; Bogost, 2023; Pichai, 2023), there is a noticeable absence of literature addressing the specific impact of AI on educational broadcasting within the Nigerian context. This book seeks to bridge that gap, offering a comprehensive exploration of the intersection between AI and educational broadcasting in Nigeria.

In light of the transformative potential of AI, I earnestly call upon the Nigerian government to prioritize and commission research in this vital area. By doing so, the government can ensure that the benefits of AI are harnessed ethically and morally, aligning with the principles of equitable access to knowledge and educational opportunities.

It is essential to recognize that AI is not merely a passing trend but a transformative force that is here to stay. The education sector, particularly the educational broadcasting research track, must embrace AI cautiously, ensuring that its integration aligns with the ethical foundations of the profession. This volume serves as a call to action for governments in Africa to champion and support research initiatives in the realm of AI, fostering a conducive environment for the exploration and application of this emerging digital tool.

In a plea to governments, the authors underscore the importance of commissioning research in the burgeoning field of AI, recognizing its potential to reshape education and propel nations toward digital literacy and development.

Furthermore, we extend a passionate plea to the scholarly community in Africa to engage in large-scale research endeavors, exploring how AI can enhance various sectors of the economy. Embracing AI in research, teaching, and learning will propel African countries to the forefront of digital technology, fostering skills development and sustainable growth.

I express my gratitude to the distinguished chapter authors, and my associate editor, Dr. Stella Nwosu, who all dedicated their time and expertise to contribute valuable insights to this volume. Together, we have collectively navigated the uncharted territories of AI in educational broadcasting, laying the foundation for a future where knowledge knows no bounds.

Unwana Samuel Akpan, Ph.D.

References

Bogost, I. (2023). ChatGPT is about to dump more work on everyone. *The Atlantic. Archived from the original.*

O'Connor, S. (2022). Open artificial intelligence platforms in nursing education: Tools for academic progress or abuse?. *Nurse education in practice*, *66*, 103537–103537.

Pichai S. (2023). An important next step on our AI journey: Google. https://blog.google/technology/ai/bard-google-ai-search-updates/.

Contents

Notes on Contributors

Keziah Akuoma Achuonye is a professor of Curriculum Studies/ Instructional Technology with over 30 years of teaching, supervision, and research experience at the Ignatius Ajuru University of Education, Port Harcourt, Rivers State, Nigeria.

James John Adebayo holds a Ph.D., and teaches in the Department of Mass Communication, Faculty of Communication and Media Studies, Federal University Oye-Ekiti, Nigeria. His research interest is on health communication, advertising and public relations, cum media studies. He has researched extensively on health communication issues in Nigeria and Africa.

Olorunfemi Adedeji is a new media and communications expert, with an interest in game development, emerging technology, robotics, and immersive media. As a new media artist passionate about exploring the intersections of technology, art, and entertainment, Olorunfemi is constantly seeking new and innovative ways to create experiences that captivate and engage audiences. With a background in advertising, journalism, and educational technology (12 cumulative years), he has a diverse set of skills that he brings to every project he works on. Whether he is developing games, experimenting with emerging technologies, developing external communications strategy for an organization or exploring the potential of robotics and immersive media, his goal is always to create something that is both visually stunning and intellectually stimulating. He believes that the future of art and entertainment lies in the creative use of technology, and is excited to be a part of that future. His skills include: 3D/2D Animation, Immersive Media (Games, VR/AR Development) Instructional Design, NAO Humanoid Robot Programming (Python, C#, QiChat), Advertising, Journalism and Educational Technology. He holds degrees in Visual Art/Education. Presently, he is pursuing an MA in Instructional Design, and also an M.Ed Student of Educational Technology, at the University of Port Harcourt. He is currently Knowledge and Communications Manager, IITA, Yola and editor newmedia.ng.

Dr. Harriet Akudo Agbarakwe is a senior lecturer, in the Department of Curriculum Studies and Educational Technology at University of Port Harcourt. She is also the Assistant Director, Open Distance and eLearning Centre (ODeL), University of Port Harcourt. She majors in instructional systems design, course development and also serves as a curriculum implementer specialist. She had her Bachelor of Science (B.Sc.) in Science Education (Biology option) from University of Science and Technology now Rivers State University in 2003, Master of Education in Educational Technology, 2011, and Doctor of Philosophy in Curriculum Studies and Educational Technology (Educational Technology, 2016) from University of Port Harcourt. Her research findings have contributed immensely to teaching, learning and performance enhancement in education, clinical training and Human capacity. These were achieved through the design, development and deployment of innovative teaching methods, enhanced students engagement and performance during instruction. The outcomes proved to a great extent that the learner is "The Centre of learning" hence the need for designing authentic, self-directed and motivated meaningful learning experiences for enhanced learning outcomes using emerging technologies and pedagogies.

Dr. Unwana Samuel Akpan is a multidisciplinary media scholar-practitioner with over two decades of broadcast experience. He has been a visiting scholar at the Department of Communication, Culture and Media Studies (CCMS), where he completed his Postdoctoral Studies in the School of Communication and Media Studies, Howard University, Washington DC, USA. He is the Editor of the University of Lagos Communication Review. He started his career with The Federal Radio Corporation of Nigeria, and was deployed to The National Broadcast Academy, its training arm, after obtaining his Ph.D. in Mass Communication. He's presently a lecturer in the Department of Mass Communication, University of Lagos, Akoka, Nigeria. He has been a visiting scholar in the Department of Communication, Culture and Media Studies, Howard University, Washington DC, USA, where he completed his Postdoctoral Research. He has publications in the form of book chapters and research articles in prominent national and international journals. He has delivered several research papers at international conferences, and has published journal articles, book chapters and books in both prominent local and international journals and publishers such as Lexington, *Palgrave Macmillan (Springer Nature), Routledge (Taylor and Francis), Peter Lang*. His classes are where research, teaching and learning interface, and he's dedicated to making students succeed in the classroom and beyond. His research and teaching investigate and explore Broadcast Contents, Sport Communication, African Communication Systems, Diaspora Communication Studies, Media Aesthetic.

Dr. Teresa Chinasa Anyanwu is an associate professor, Department of Social Science Education, lmo State University, Owerri.

Oluwakemi Aweda-Akinuliola is a lecturer at the Department of Mass Communication, University of Lagos, Nigeria. She has both M.Sc. and B.Sc. degrees from the University of Lagos, Department of Mass communication. She is currently a Ph.D. student at the same institution. Her research interests are in Broadcasting, Gender and Communication, Online journalism, and Children in Communication.

Dr. Adeyinka Joseph Babajide is a lecturer in the Department of Communication and Language Arts Education, College of Languages and Communication Arts Education, Lagos State University of Education, Lagos State, Nigeria. He holds a doctorate degree (Ph.D.) in Communication Studies; Master's Degree in each discipline of Communication Studies, Business Administration and Marketing; Post-Graduate Diploma in Education (PGDE); Bachelor of Science in Mass Communication (Second Class Upper Division); Higher National Diploma in Business Administration and Management (HND); National Diploma in Banking and Finance (ND); and Proficiency Certificate in Information and Communications Technology Programme. His Ph.D. thesis was ranked the Best in School of Communication, Lagos State University, Ojo for 2020 Academic Session and consequently was nominated for 2021 ASR Best-Africa Based Dissertation Award. He has almost

20 years experience in corporate communication, business communication and procedural communication from his service as Administrator at the then Adeniran Ogunsanya College of Education, Lagos State, Nigeria, where he rose to the position of Principal Assistant Registrar (PAR). Simultaneously, he lectured and supervised projects, students on teaching practice and Students Industrial and Work Experience Scheme (SIWES) at the College of Education on a part-time basis for almost two decades. However, Adeniran Ogunsanya College of Education, Lagos State, Nigeria and Michael Otedola College of Primary Education were merged to form Lagos State University of Education, Lagos State, Nigeria on 2nd February, 2022 and he was appointed as full-time lecturer. He was the Speech Writer for the legacy College, Adeniran Ogunsanya College of Education, for over a decade. He is the pioneer Speech Writer for the new University, Lagos State University of Education. He published fifteen (15) articles: 2 in international academic journals and 13 in national academic journals while at Adeniran Ogunsanya College of Education. After his appointment as a lecturer, he has published two (2) research publications in peer-reviewed books and learned journals; one in international academic journal and the other in national academic journal. Dr. Babajide is a Fellow, Institute of Corporate Administration of Nigeria; Member, Teachers Registration Council of Nigeria (TCRN); and Associate, Nigerian Institute of Public Relations. He is a researcher with a strong background in conception and execution of research proposals. He is effective at identifying and investigating learners' challenges and methodically solving teething troubles in their teaching/learning process. He is a morally sound man who believes in hard work, dedication, diligence, honesty and discipline as a set of tools not only to drive attainment of uncommon success in teaching-learning, but also to supersede the peak of preselected objectives.

Dr. Chinwe Joyce Chukwuemeka is a respected academic and researcher in the field of Language Education in the Department of Curriculum Studies and Educational Technology. She holds a Ph.D. in Language Education from a prestigious university and has published numerous articles in top-tier academic journals. Her research focuses on Language and the brain, utilization of digital tools for language learning, special educational needs with a particular emphasis on the use of artificial intelligence. Dr. Chukwuemeka is also a dedicated educator, having taught courses on different aspects of English language and research methods at both the undergraduate and graduate levels. In addition to her academic work, she is committed to promoting diversity and inclusion in higher education and regularly provides assistance to students with learning disabilities. Dr. Chinwe's passion for advancing knowledge and understanding in her field is evident in all aspects of her work, making her a valuable contributor to the academic community.

Thelma U. Ekukinam is associate professor of Educational Technology. She holds a Doctoral and Masters Degree in Educational Technology with a first degree in English Education. Her research interest is on the utilization of local resources for teaching and learning and most especially improving the performance of teachers. She is a member of the Reading Association of Nigeria (RAN) which has impacted positively on children's reading habits, a pioneer researcher in the Read and Write Now project (RAWN). Dr. Ekukinam is a certified trainer in Jolly Phonics and Jolly Grammar. Currently lecturing at the University of Uyo.

Osakpolor Emwinromwankhoe lectures at the Department of Mass Communication, Ambrose Alli University, Ekpoma, Edo State, Nigeria. His research cuts across broadcasting, Nollywood studies, gender and feminist studies, new media, and development communication. He is published in a good number of local, national and international journals as well as in acclaimed books, including *CINEJ Cinema Journal* and *The Quint: An Interdisciplinary Journal from the North*. He is a doctoral student at the University of Benin where his thesis focusing on gendered Nollywood narratives is undergoing finishing touches.

Gertrude Kanayo Ezekoka is a professor of Educational Technology in the Faculty of Education, Imo State University. She is currently the Director of the GST unit and Head of the Educational Technology unit in the Faculty of Education. Prof. Ezekoka is a quality product of the Nigerian Educational System being a unique alumnus of University of Benin, University of Port Harcourt and Imo State University, Owerri. She holds the following qualifications: Ph.D. in Educational Technology (2004), M.Sc. Ed in Science Education (2015), M.Ed in Educational Technology (1996), PGDE (1988), and B.Sc. Zoology (1983). Prof. Ezekoka has served the University in various capacities with valuable contributions. These include: Director of GST unit, Head of Educational Technology unit; Chairman of Ph.D. Proposal and Seminar committee, Faculty Representative to School of PG Studies, Supervisor of University Examination

Committee, Member of University Admission Committee, etc. Prof. Ezekoka teaches Undergraduate and Postgraduate courses in Educational Technology and Science Education. She has successfully supervised 25 Masters students and co-supervised and produced 21 Ph.D. holders, and is a Mentor to many students. She has more than 42 publications of journal articles, books and book chapters nationally and internationally. Gertrude belongs to some Professional and non Professional organizations such as Educational Media and Technology Association of Nigeria (EMTAN), National Association of Women in Academics, (NAWACS), Science Teachers Association of Nigeria (STAN) and Academic Staff Union of Universities (ASUU). Prof. loves worshiping God, jogging, traveling, music and relaxing with friends.

Prof. Bidemi Bilkis Lafiaji-Okuneye is the current and pioneer Vice Chancellor of the Lagos State University of Education, Oto/Ijanikin, Lagos. She was born in Surulere, Lagos and is an indigene of Lagos state from the Lafiaji and Iginla Dynasties. She attended St. Paul Anglican Primary School, Ishaga, Isolo, Gbeleyi Primary School, Ishaga, Isolo and Metropolitan College, Isolo for her post-primary education. Her tertiary education started with a Diploma in Physical and Health Education at the prestigious Lagos State University. She obtained her first degree in the same university in 1995 where she graduated with a second-class upper division. She came top of her class and that earned her Graduate Assistantship position in the Department of Physical and Health Education. She is the first product of the Department to be retained as a Lecturer. Her Master Degree Certificate in Health Education was obtained at the University of Lagos while her Ph.D. Degree Certificate was awarded by the University of Ibadan in 2005. Her Teaching career started in 1997 at the Lagos State University, Ojo. She rose through the ranks to become a Professor in the Health Education Unit of the Department. She has served the University in various capacities amongst which are; the Ag. Dean of Student Affairs, Hall Warden, LASU Female Hostel, Sub-Dean, Faculty of Education, Chairman of various committees, Subject Coordinator, Sandwich Degree Programme, Class Advisor, University Honorary Badminton Coach, Examination Officer, Staff Secretary of the Department, Branch Treasurer, Academic Staff Union of Universities, Member of Staff School Management Committee, Assistant Director, LASU Directorate of Advancement and Editor-in-Chief, Educational Perspectives (Official Journal of the Faculty of Education, Lagos

State University). Prof. BIdemi Bilkis Lafiaji-Okuneye was an international handball player who represented Nigeria in many championships and competitions outside the shores of the country including Sweden, Denmark, France and Norway. She was the number one goalkeeper of the defunct Jegede Babes. She is a member of many professional bodies like International Council of Health, Physical Education, Recreation, Sports and Dance (ICPHER S.D); Nigeria Association of Physical, Health Education, Recreation, Sports and Dance (NAPHER-SD); National Association Sports Science and Medicine (NASSM) and Nigeria School Health Association (NSHA). Prof. B. B. Lafiaji-Okuneye has earned many awards of excellence from organizations, groups and stakeholders across diverse works and calling. At the then Adeniran Ogunsanya College of Education, she holds the distinction of being the first and only professor to have been appointed as a provost. Through her commitment, dedication and unique leadership style, she played a crucial role in the transmutation of Adeniran Ogunsanya College of Education to Lagos University of Education. She equally put the needed framework in place to facilitate the approval of 66 programmes by the National Universities Commission (NUC) culminating into the admission of the pioneer set of undergraduates. She is happily married to Prof. Rafiu Olaoluwa Okuneye and they are blessed with children.

Dr. Iniobong Courage Nda is a senior lecturer in the Faculty of Communication and Media Studies, University of Uyo, Akwa Ibom State, Nigeria, where she has taught communication and media studies since 2012. As a scholar who has garnered practical expertise from both the print (The Sensor Newspaper) and broadcast media (The Nigerian Television Authority, NTA) respectively, Dr. Nda has been able to integrate her field experience with the classroom demands for effective and efficient teaching of mass communication and has published her researches in several national and international journals including contributing chapters to books. She is an active member of the African Council of Communication Education, (ACCE), Nigerian Institute of Management, (NIM), and the Nigerian Union of Journalists (NUJ). Her research interests are in Business/Organizational, Health and Development Communication.

Mishack Ndukwu is a Ph.D. student at Imo State University, Owerri, Nigeria, where he also lectures with the Department of Film and Multimedia Studies. He has several journal articles and book chapter contributions to his credit and he is the State treasurer of Association of Communication Scholars and Professionals of Nigeria (ACSPN) Imo State chapter.

Dr. Adeline O. Nkwam-Uwaoma lectures in the Department of Film and Multimedia Studies, Faculty of Communication and media Studies, Imo State University, Owerri, Nigeria, which she joined after working for more than two decades as a broadcaster at the Imo Broadcasting Corporation, (IBC) Owerri, where she rose to the rank of Deputy Director, News and Current Affairs. She has several publications to her credit, is a member of several professional bodies and is happily married with children.

Ucheyamere C. Nkwam-Uwaoma is a Ph.D. student at Bournemouth University, United Kingdom and also a visiting lecturer at the University of Southampton's Winchester School of Art, United Kingdom. He has several publications to his credit and is a member of professional bodies.

Dr. Stella N. Nwosu possesses a B.Sc. degree in Chemistry (First Class), a Postgraduate Diploma in Education (PGDE), a Masters in Educational Technology and a Ph.D. in Educational Technology. Her research interests include Instructional Systems Designing, Differentiated Instructional Strategies and teacher professional development. Dr. Nwosu has over 23 years experience in science teaching, and is currently involved in Continuing Professional Development of secondary and tertiary education teachers. She is a lecturer and a staff in the Institute of Education and Professional Development, Faculty of Education, University of Uyo, in Akwa Ibom State, Nigeria; where she also serves as the research project Coordinator and Secretary of the Institute of Education Research Committee among other duties.

Ubong Andem Obong is a doctoral candidate at the Faculty of Communication & Media Studies, University of Uyo, Nigeria. As a lecturer at the Faculty of Communication & Media Studies, Taraba State University, Jalingo, Nigeria, he teaches and researches on broadcasting, behavioural change communication, emerging media studies, and critical discourse in film and creative screen productions. He is the principal investigator and lead exponent of the Research Lab for Critical Discourse in Nollywood Films (RL4CDINF) and has contributed seminal works in films, broadcasting, and emerging media studies in reputable journals across the globe.

Emmanuel Nnabuchi Okwumabua is a professional graduate teacher with over 15 years experience as the media director of Virtues International Academy, Port Harcourt, Rivers State, Nigeria.

Dr. Festus Oladimeji Olafare is an educational/instructional technology specialist with focus on design and development of content and material. He has his/her undergraduate degree in Educational Technology, graduated from the University of Ilorin in 2006; master's in educational technology in Instructional Technology from the University of Ilorin in 2011; and a Ph.D. in Educational Technology from the University of Ilorin in 2014. Over the 6 years experience, conducted research in Instructional Technology (Usage of ICT for instruction and assessment), mentored 12 students, Olafare worked in Information and Communication Technology for instruction and achieved Association for Integration of Technology in Education (AITIE) membership of professional and academic groups.

Dr. Idongesit Akan Udi is a senior lecturer in the Department of Educational Technology, University of Uyo, Nigeria. She holds an NCE in Education, B.A. and MFA in Fine Arts and a Ph.D. in Educational Technology. Her research interests are Instructional System Design in the area of enhancing and improvement of classroom instructional delivery using technological tools. She is passionate about wholesome development and acquisition of artistic skills for the acquisition of teacher education competencies through the use of new technology which is the fundamental of all teaching and learning. She has participated in some grant winning research and several other researches. These include; Educational Research Network for West Africa and Central Africa (As Team Head, ERNWACA, 2012–2013) and as Team Member ERNWACA, 2014–2015; Institutional Based Research Fund (IBRF) 2011–2014 (Merged) TetFund as Principal Investigator- (Project Period, 2016–2017); as Co-Researcher IBRF (2021–Date). She has published 26 journals, 4 book chapters, 1 monograph, 1 book of abstract, 2 conference proceedings and 24 exhibition articles. She has attended several international conferences and workshops both locally and internationally and has also served in several capacities as the need may be, thank you. She is a member of various Professional Bodies including, Educational Media and Technology Association of Nigeria (EMTAN) and many others.

Prof. Beshel Cletus Ushie is a core teacher both in training and practice having attended virtually all levels of formal education in Nigeria. He has Ph.D. & Msc in Educational Technology; BEd (Elementary Education); NCE (History/Religious Studies and Teachers Grade 11. He has facilitated learning at the Primary, Secondary, Teachers College, College of Education and Universities for more than Two score years+. Currently, a professor of Educational Technology in the University of Calabar. His publication profile has more than 80 articles that span across local and international journals.

List of Figures

List of Tables

PART I

Educational Broadcasting, Production, Research, Teaching, Learning, and AI

CHAPTER 1

Artificial Intelligence (AI) Dynamics in Educational Broadcasting Research and Production in Nigeria: Riding the Wave or Drowning in the Looming Tsunami of Change?

Unwana Samuel Akpan

Introduction

As a broadcast professional who has been in the industry for decades, I have discovered through experiential knowledge and existential realities in the sector that broadcasting is first business before it is anything else (Akpan, 2020), and I have repeatedly asserted this in various fora or forums for those who care to listen. If we all agree that broadcasting must first be business before it is anything else, then any smart businessman would acquire and explore any technology that would assist him/her to

U. S. Akpan (✉)
University of Lagos, Akoka-Lagos, Nigeria
e-mail: unwanaa@yahoo.co.uk

U. S. Akpan (ed.), *Educational Broadcasting in Nigeria in the Age of Artificial Intelligence*,
https://doi.org/10.1007/978-3-031-68530-9_1

accomplish tasks efficiently, effortlessly, and affordably, without compromising on quality and standards. The big question is, could this new technology that might help broadcast professionals perform their tasks better be Artificial Intelligence (AI)?

The first time I ever learned about ChatGPT, powered by Artificial Intelligence (AI) at a conference in 2023, I just said within me, "truly, plagiarism has found worse bedfellows in AI." Whether it is a "Greek gift" or not, this "digital gift" called AI, from the digital natives to humanity appears "*tsunamic*," and is pet-like. It is no longer in contention that AI in its various forms masterly and virtuosically assists man in most chores that might be tasking and time-consuming. If it is generally accepted, as it is in recorded history that right from the time man started inhabiting the world—from stone age of human civilization in Africa to the annals of Western civilization, that man has always searched for technology that would help make his chores easier, it is therefore true that man would continue to conceive and invent technologies that would ease his work burden. Then one might begin to ask, does it mean that Artificial Intelligence (AI) has come to stay, and goes no way? In another development, AI has raised ethical concerns in academic circles, and these concerns I believe are based on originality of contents, and fears that the digital tool might pale human creativity into history. Paul Graham, the cofounder of Y Combinator, wrote on his X formerly Twitter, social media handle, "AI is the exact opposite of a solution in search of a problem. It's the solution to far more problems than its developers even knew existed." John Tamny who writes for the Forbes reveals that though AI pioneer Sam Altman was admitted to an elite university, Stanford, he concentrated on birthing something for the future that provides solutions to the everyday digital needs of man:

> In Altman's case, and surely he's not unique among Stanford matriculates, he couldn't even be bothered to complete college. And he couldn't because he was too focused on creating an all-new future rather than learning about the past from professors with skills and knowledge that would logically be a fraction of his own. Which is the point, or should be. We needn't fear what they're teaching today, not teaching, or what they're learning or not learning. We don't need to simply because the Americans who drive all progress are too busy creating all-new knowledge to bother with what's known now, and this new knowledge will similarly free the proverbial man-on-the-street from having to waste time learning things

> that, even if they were once useful are surely not useful now. (Forbes, 2024, para. 1)

AI's solution-providing potentials, effects, and accessibility are striking virtually every sector on an unprecedented rate. At the moment its rampaging effects are felt everywhere, including broadcasting.

The Chat Generative Pretrained Transformer popularly known as (ChatGPT), an artificial intelligence (AI) chatbot tool created and developed by OpenAI, was officially and brazenly released on November 30, 2022 to the general public to be used for free (at least for now), and as of today has amassed universal attention, especially among college students and undergrads. Though it was made available for free, there are other AI versions that are not free. Since the free version was released to the generality of the public, it has quickly gained popularity, and the demands for it, especially among college students and undergrads has skyrocketed, surpassing 100 million users by January 2023, stamping and solidifying its status as the fastest-growing digital consumer application as of today (Milmo, 2023). The quirky proficiency of ChatGPT and similar generative AI tools to produce text indistinguishable from human literary endeavors has sparked both approbation and reproval. This polarity of opinions has sparked discourses surrounding the implications and impact of this cutting-edge technology, and where this might be leading us to. In the higher education sector, quality assurance leaders and social critics are brawling with challenges posed by these emerging AI technologies within the university system. Simultaneously, there are new vistas cum opportunities that arise, presenting a bilateral scenario for academic institutions. This paper aims to succinctly outline and examine these challenges and opportunities, offering an embryonic route forward in steering the mercurial digital topography of AI in educational broadcasting research and production.

Historical Perspective

Over the past decade, the sphere of artificial intelligence (AI) has undergone remarkable progress, leading to the development of diverse AI-based tools across various sectors, including academia (Allen et al., 2018; Gallego et al., 2021; Rakha et al., 2021). Despite these advancements, there is a notable absence of literature exploring the implications of AI in educational broadcasting, particularly in a country like Nigeria, which is still navigating the transition from analog to digital broadcasting.

Generative AI (GAI), a new technology leveraging large language models, has garnered towering attention, strikingly with the introduction of generative pre-trained transformers (GPT), typified by ChatGPT, launched by OpenAI on November 30, 2022 (OpenAI, 2023). Just within two months, ChatGPT accumulated a lurching 100 million monthly users, setting a record as the fastest technology preference in history (Hu, 2023). This impetus has inspired and motivated other leading technology players in the field, such as Google with Bard and MedPalm, and Microsoft with Bing Chat, to develop related products (Newman, 2023; Pichai, 2023; Singhal et al., 2023).

The inrush of this cutting-edge technology called AI, has kindled an upsurge of interest within the academic community, leading to an accelerated investigation of potential applications and implications of the emerging technology. The intersection of AI and education, particularly in the context of educational broadcasting, holds the promise of metamorphic changes, raising critical questions about adaptability and integration, especially in developing nations like Nigeria.

AI and Global Scholarship

To date, over 650 research articles and editorials have investigated the usage and challenges of General Artificial Intelligence (GAI), with many leveraging GAI in their own research and writing endeavors (Ganjavi et al., 2024). In drafting research reports, studies frequently highlight GAI's potential to enhance grammar and vocabulary, translate text into multiple languages, generate innovative program ideas, synthesize vast amounts of information, propose historical statistical data, code, and create novel textual content, and this can be applied to educational broadcasting research. This versatile tool is seen as streamlining the broadcasting process overall (Bhatia & Kulkarni, 2023; Graf & Bernardi, 2023; Lecler et al., 2023; Macdonald et al., 2023; Ollivier et al., 2023).

In academia, scholars are warned about GAI's lack of accountability for its output, presenting risks such as inaccuracy, bias, and plagiarism. In the broadcast sector, where inaccuracies are deemed unacceptable, these pitfalls are particularly concerning. Global scholarship is grappling with the reality of AI's emergence as a digital tool that has come to erode human literal prowess. In December 2022, Nature published the inaugural article addressing concerns surrounding the application of ChatGPT and GAI in academic writing, throwing light on the continuing discourse within scholarly circles. In recent times, notable academic journals and publishers have responded to the increasing integration of Generative Artificial Intelligence (GAI) in research by amending their editorial policies and author guidelines. For instance, Science, in January 2023, took a stringent stance, explicitly forbidding the usage of GAI for text, figures, images, or graphics generation in writing tasks. The violation of this policy is deemed as scientific misconduct (COPE, 2023; Moussa & Teixeira da Silva, 2023; Sample, 2023; Stokel-Walker, 2022).

Contrastingly, some other journals have adopted a more subtle permissive approach, allowing the integration of GAI in research with certain restrictions and emphasizing the necessity of complete disclosure if it was used. The Committee on Publication Ethics (COPE), a collective comprising editors, publishers, universities, and research institutes, released a position statement in February 2023 regarding AI tools in research publications. COPE highlighted that AI tools cannot fulfill the requirements for authorship as they lack the ability to take responsibility for the submitted work. While acknowledging the use of AI, COPE suggested ways for disclosure, underscoring the need for ultimate accountability of authors for work generated by AI tools.

Despite the endorsement and approval of COPE's AI statement by certain journals and editorial associations, such as the Journal of the American Medical Association and the World Association of Medical Editors (WAME), it falls short of providing a comprehensive framework for responsible GAI software usage in academic contexts, including educational broadcasting. First, it is obvious that the current COPE's statement lacks the capability in addressing potential pitfalls associated with GAI tools, and second lacks a standardized disclosure statement, leading to a diverse range of ad-hoc guidelines developed by individual journals and publishers to navigate the intricacies of AI integration in academic engagements.

AI: General Concerns

The deployment of AI into highly human-sensitive and sophisticated sectors is gradually gaining traction and momentum, and this leaves the question if AI should be incorporated into educational broadcasting. For instance, Daily Trust Newspaper (2024), recently revealed that "Israel's army has deployed some AI-enabled military technology in combat for the first time in Gaza, raising fears about the use of autonomous weapons in modern warfare." According to the newspaper report:

> The army has hinted at what the new tech is being used for, with spokesman Daniel Hagari saying last month that Israel's forces were operating "above and underground simultaneously."' A senior defense official told AFP the tech was destroying enemy drones and mapping Hamas's vast tunnel network in Gaza. New defense technologies including artificial intelligence-powered gunsights and robotic drones form a bright spot in an otherwise dire period for Israel's tech industry. (Daily Trust Newspaper, 2024, para. 3)

The Daily Trust Newspaper reported that the day-to-day increase in civilian casualties calls for the urgent need for enhanced oversight in the deployment of advanced defense technologies, Mary Wareham, an arms expert at Human Rights Watch, told AFP. The arms expert at Human Rights Watch, brings to attention the severity of the present situation in Gaza, ascribing some of the suffering to the impact of emerging technologies such as AI.

Expressing her concerns, Wareham stressed the deleterious effects of new technologies on the surging death toll. She highlighted the need to address these issues in order to mitigate the consequences of evolving defense tech. According to her: "Now we're facing the worst possible situation of death and suffering that we're seeing today – some of that is being brought about by the new tech," Mary Wareham, expressed her concerns" (Daily Trust Newspaper, 2024, para. 3).

In the wake of the International Court of Justice's ruling on South Africa's case against Israel, where concerns of potential genocide against Palestinians were raised, even before then, over 150 countries endorsed a UN resolution in December calling for a cease fire. This resolution acknowledged "serious challenges and concerns" associated with modern military technologies, distinctly stressing issues related to 'artificial intelligence and autonomy in weapons systems.' The global consensus reflects increasing apprehension about the ethical implications and risks posed by these advancements in the defense/military sector. As the arms conflict gets under way, the usage of affordable unmanned aerial vehicles, (UAVs) commonly known as drones, has strikingly influenced the dynamics of warfare in Gaza, thereby making attacks from the air easier and cheaper.

Notably, on October 7, Hamas employed drones to deploy explosives, prompting Israel to adopt innovative technology to shoot them down. Israel's response to the October 7th attack involves the use of AI-enabled optic sights, developed by the Israeli startup Smart Shooter. These sights are integrated with weapons such as rifles and machine guns, providing an effective means to counter drone threats. As per a report from the Daily Trust Newspaper in (2024), a senior defense official highlighted the significance of this technology, stating that it assists soldiers in intercepting drones, which are frequently employed by Hamas in their operations. According to a Daily Trust Newspaper report (2024, para. 2), "It helps our soldiers to intercept drones because Hamas uses a lot of drones," said the senior defense official.

Generative AI Tools and Plagiarism Concerns in Educational Broadcasting Research

AI devices like ChatGPT present a key concern due to their enormous capabilities to produce text blocks that are so fluent that closely mimic human-authored content. This fluency and quality raise worries regarding potential misapplication in fraudulent activities and plagiarism in the educational broadcasting research, as inaccuracies are an unpardonable offense in broadcasting.

The challenge posed comes from the laboriousness in distinguishing ChatGPT-generated text from human-generated text, even when putting the texts through the specialized AI-text detection software. Responding to this issue, OpenAI has launched its own AI detection software. However, it is remarkable that this detection software, while aiming to address concerns, is not foolproof. An exemplifying example is a quiz where it erroneously identified initial passages from the Bible as likely being AI-generated (Bogost, 2023). This underscores the ongoing difficulties of achieving complete accuracy and exactness in distinguishing between AI-generated and human-generated textual materials.

In academia, the prevalent issues of plagiarism have become increasingly perturbing. Remarkably, the arrival of ChatGPT's potentiality to masterfully craft essay answers for examination questions, seemingly well-researched and referenced, has led some academics to question the continued feasibility of essays as a reliable assessment method for brilliance and theme understanding. The surreptitious potential for plagiarism, difficult to uncover in these machine-generated answers, further complicates the educational broadcasting research track. Nsikak Idiong, an associate professor of political communication at the University of Uyo has recently expressed his concerns on AI, in regards to fake news and deepfakes. On his Facebook page, he reiterated:

> If you care about truth, about the veracity of information, and about the reliability of news, then you should be concerned about the dangers posed by artificial intelligence. Today I read a report that's so blatantly erroneous and yet so masterfully written that if I didn't know the persons and subject matter involved I would have been guilty of the fallacy of biased generalization, or worse! In the age of the Internet and of AI, every information is potentially fake news. Worse still, deep fakes abound everywhere, and they are almost indistinguishable from reality. The Bible in 1 John 4:1 says "Beloved, believe not every spirit, but test the spirits to know whether they are from God." I would paraphrase that and say: Friends, believe not everything you read or view on the Internet. In 2024, test every information to know whether it's true, so that you don't fall prey to calumniators and to purveyors of fake news.

Responding to the post on Idiong's Facebook page, Charles Obot, a professor of broadcasting disappointingly avers, "To me, the greater 'victim' of Artificial Intelligence (AI) is academics- assignments, dissertations and theses. While lecturers who are not painstaking are accomplices." Another academic media studies, Oyokunyi Ita, while responding to the post said, "That is why I am teaching my project supervisees ethical use of generative AIs before they start writing. AIs are here to help only when used properly. There are globally accepted ways of using AI in education." In a related opinion, another scholar of media studies said, "AI is good! It's just the users that are not good users. Just like Google and other search engines before AI. The problem is that the user doesn't know how to use it, what to take and what not to take. They just take everything it gives."

Professor Charles Obot put a similar post on his Facebook timeline expressing concerns for AI and academic works. There were different shades of views. A Facebook respondent on Professor Charles Obot's wall, Russellz Attah Jnr, Sir, admits:

> AI is deceptive and treacherous in its offerings...it appears beneficial on the surface but comes with hidden risks or consequences. On one hand, AI offers significant promise in terms of advancing technology, automating tasks, and improving various aspects of everyday life. Yet, there are also legitimate concerns about the ethical implications of AI, including issues around privacy, job displacement, algorithmic biases.

Another respondent, Oyokunyi It's, asserted:

> My dear Prof, AI problem is bigger than plagiarism in the sense that a student may plagiarize but copying and pasting some seemly sensible notes, but AI gives you unlimited option since it is not topic specific, location specific and even ideas specific so it gives you a potpourri of options. The trouble is that the lazy, incompetent and foolish students will now copy AI in all its manifestation of glory and stupidity. This year all my project students who have submitted chapter 1 have fallen victim to the errors of Ai and that helps define the nature of students I am supervising.

For Edikan Ukpong, he pointed out, "that is why I am teaching my first project supervisees ethical use of generative AIs before they start writing. AIs are here to help only when used properly. There are globally accepted ways of using AI in education."

Reuben Cletus, another respondent, believes that "AI is good!It's just the user that's…Just like Google and other search engines before AI. The problem is that the user doesn't know how to use it, what to take and what not to take. They just take everything it gives."

For Aniediabasi Etuk, "there is more to AI than we can see now. The dark side of it is yet to unfold in its fullness. I am not even sure if regulation of AI application and usage would address the danger it possesses. This is not just in education but in all works and spheres of life where its application is enforced."

These concerns extend beyond traditional academic essays, impacting the authenticity and creativity of educational broadcast scripts. The subtle coalescing of AI-generated content in such scripts not only poses a challenge, as the line between genuine human artistic display and machine-generated text becomes obscured, but prevents creativity and artistic originality. A recent study showed the enormity of this issue, disclosing that ChatGPT independently achieved a passing score of 60% on the United States Medical Licensing Exam (Kung et al., 2023), a groundbreaking achievement in the absence of human input. Surprisingly, this landmark demonstrated not only the capacity for rote memorization but also the ability to display valid clinical reasoning and insights.

Also, the advancement of AI models, illustrated by Google's MedPaLM, has unveiled considerable progress, achieving a stunning 85% on the same medical examination (Matias & Corrado, 2023). This trajectory emphasizes the continual rarefaction of AI language models, amplifying the challenges posed by their integration into academic assessments and educational content creation such as educational broadcasting. More recently, Microsoft's advanced language model, GPT-4, excelled by achieving an 86.7% score in the same exam, surpassing other models in performance (Nori et al., 2023). It is noteworthy to consider that an AI model like ChatGPT successfully passing a medical school graduating exam raises concerns about the emerging educational broadcasting research track (Mbakwe et al., 2023).

AI and Broadcast Scripts

ChatGPT exhibits the capability to review existing literature and masterfully compose academic papers comparable in quality and thematic arrangement to those authored by human researchers. However, the important question arises: can AI generate educational programs scripts of high quality that are suitable for public consumption and adept at portraying cultural existential realities? The answer is yes, looking at this groundbreaking record. A recent study showed that reviewers could accurately identify only 68% of scientific abstracts generated by ChatGPT (Gao et al., 2022). Despite this, ChatGPT's proficiency in generating scientific titles, objectives, and articles has led to the AI tool being acknowledged as a coauthor in at least four articles published in January 2023 (Loh, 2024). In Loh (2024) revelation, it was disclosed that 'Nurse Education in Practice,' a peer-reviewed journal, featured an article where ChatGPT was acknowledged as a co-author. The article's subject prompted the human author to compose an editorial using the AI chatbot, exploring its potential application in nursing education (O'Connor, 2022; Stokel-Walker, 2023), and this could be the new norm in educational broadcasting. These revelations provoked shades of instant responses from scientific meeting organizers and journal publishers, prompting amendments to guidelines for presenters and authors. Recently, the International Conference on Machine Learning has now prohibited papers found to be containing text from AI software like ChatGPT (Gottlieb et al., 2023; Ravi et al., 2023).

Reputable publishing houses, including Springer Nature, the JAMA Network, and Elsevier (publisher of the Lancet family of journals), have reviewed their policies (Editorials, 2023; Flanagin et al., 2023; Liebrenz et al., 2023). These publishers no longer accept any AI tool as a credited author on a research paper, arguing that authorship entails answerability and that digital softwares such as AI tools cannot be held responsible for submitted work. They insist on the necessity of highlighting and acknowledging any AI tool's involvement in any essay while also advising authors on how to disclose AI use. They also emphasize that authors are entirely accountable for the work produced by AI tools. Taking an even stricter stance, the Science family of journals argues that an AI tool cannot be considered an author because it can not be answerable to queries (Thorp, 2023). They precisely assert that textual contents, figures, images, or graphics must not be generated by an AI software, reinforcing their commitment to traditional human authorship and content creation. It therefore means producers/content creators can consult AI for scripting (writing their programs scripts) and generating topics of discussion for each program.

What AI Might Not Naturally Achieve in Educational Broadcasting

Unfortunately, AI might not be able to survey the current cultural and traditional happenings in the environment in order to incorporate these happenings into the program scripts.

AI might not be able to think critically to script educational broadcasting scripts that can meet the yearnings of the everyday needs of some local communities in unreached and ungoverned territories.

AI might take everyone's job, but would never be able to fit into the shoes of the programs producer/contents provider, and the makeup artiste, because these roles demand human artistic and aesthetic reasoning.

AI might not be able to assume the role of a makeup artist.

Conclusion and Recommendations

The benefits of Generative AI in educational broadcasting production, research, teaching, and learning. AI should be like the proverbial African child, which should not be thrown away with the dirty water. AI models like ChatGPT have the potential to revolutionize the educational broadcasting craft for producers, presenters, and directors. Prior to the existence of ChatGPT, its predecessors were already instrumental for researchers, aiding in organizing thoughts, crafting programming code, and summarizing research literature. The structured organization of thoughts within a programmme's script not only enhances the overall flow but also facilitates effective comprehension for the audience.

As this cutting-edge technology continues to rampage across sectors, educational technology researchers may find applications in designing innovative broadcasting experiments, facilitating educational broadcasting peer reviews, and influencing editorial decisions in academic journals, ultimately expediting the scientific discovery process and facilitating the translation of research findings into practical applications. The multi-layered capabilities of AI models like ChatGPT offer a promising route for advancing educational broadcasting production, research, teaching, and learning endeavors.

References

Akpan, U. (2020). Elite local leagues and transnational broadcast of European football. In C. Onwumechili (Ed.), *Africa's elite football: Structure, politics, and everyday challenges* (pp. 34–44). Routledge.

Allen, B., Jr., Seltzer, S. E., Langlotz, C. P., et al. (2018). A road map for translational research on artificial intelligence in medical imaging: From the 2018 National Institutes of Health/RSNA/ACR/The Academy Workshop. *Journal of the American College of Radiology, 16*(9), 1179–1189. https://doi.org/10.1016/j.jacr.2019.04.014pmid:31151893

Bhatia, G., & Kulkarni, A. (2023). ChatGPT as co-author: Are researchers impressed or distressed? *Asian Journal of Psychiatry, 84*, 103564.

Bogost, I. (2023). ChatGPT is about to dump more work on everyone. *The Atlantic. Archived from the original.*

COPE. (2023). *Authorship and AI tools: COPE position statement*. https://publicationethics.org/cope-position-statements/ai-author#:~:text=COPE%20position%20statement&text=COPE%20joins%20organisations%2C%20such%20as,responsibility%20for%20the%20submitted%20work

Daily Trust Newspaper. (2024). Fears as Israel deploys new military AI in Gaza War. https://dailytrust.com/just-in-fears-as-israel-deploys-new-military-ai-in-gaza-war/

Editorials, N. (2023). Tools such as ChatGPT threaten transparent science; here are our ground rules for their use. *Nature, 613*(612), 10–1038.

Flanagin, A., Bibbins-Domingo, K., Berkwits, M., & Christiansen, S. L. (2023). Nonhuman "authors" and implications for the integrity of scientific publication and medical knowledge. *JAMA, 329*(8), 637–639. https://doi.org/10.1001/jama.2023.1344pmid:36719674

Gallego, V., Naveiro, R., Roca, C., Rios Insua, D., & Campillo, N. E. (2021). AI in drug development: A multidisciplinary perspective. *Molecular Diversity, 25*, 1461–1479. https://doi.org/10.1007/s11030-021-10266-8pmid:34251580

Ganjavi, C., Eppler, M., Pekcan, A., Biedermann, B., Abreu, A., Collins, G., Gill, I., & Cacciamani, G. (2024). Publishers' and journals' instructions to authors on use of generative artificial intelligence in academic and scientific publishing: Bibliometric analysis. *The BMJ*. https://doi.org/10.1136/bmj-2023-077192

Gao, C. A., Howard, F. M., Markov, N. S., Dyer, E. C., Ramesh, S., Luo, Y., & Pearson, A. T. (2022). Comparing scientific abstracts generated by ChatGPT to original abstracts using an artificial intelligence output detector, plagiarism detector, and blinded human reviewers. *BioRxiv, 4*(12), 1055.

Graf, A., & Bernardi, R. E. (2023). ChatGPT in research: Balancing ethics, transparency and advancement. *Neuroscience, 515*, 71–73.

Graham, P. (2023). *A.I. the exact opposite of a solution in search of a problem: The solution to far more problems than its developers even knew existed.* https://twitter.com/paulg/status/1689874390442561536?t=SZkVo2JqHuW8Bo88HxbsIQ&s=19

Gottlieb, M., Kline, J. A., Schneider, A. J., & Coates, W. C. (2023). ChatGPT and conversational artificial intelligence: Friend, foe, or future of research? *The American Journal of Emergency Medicine, 70*, 81–83.

Hu K. (2023). *ChatGPT sets record for fastest-growing user base—Analyst note Reuters.* https://www.reuters.com/technology/chatgpt-sets-record-fastest-growing-user-base-analyst-note-2023-02-01/

Idiong, N. (2024). Facebook post on AI. https://m.facebook.com/story.php?story_fbid=pfbid0ErCFfq5g4PTfYmZ765FFir3aN6jCDC6w8oCLaPaycCAEXivsLj9REV3Howu2CQYsl&id=100000907115225&mibextid=Nif5oz

Kung, T. H., Cheatham, M., Medenilla, A., Sillos, C., De Leon, L., Elepaño, C., ... & Tseng, V. (2023). Performance of ChatGPT on USMLE: Potential for AI-assisted medical education using large language models. *PLoS Digital Health, 2*(2), e0000198.

Lecler, A., Duron, L., & Soyer, P. (2023). Revolutionizing radiology with GPT-based models: Current applications, future possibilities and limitations of ChatGPT. *Diagnostic and Interventional Imaging, 104*(6), 269–274.

Liebrenz, M., Schleifer, R., Buadze, A., Bhugra, D., & Smith, A. (2023). Generating scholarly content with ChatGPT: Ethical challenges for medical publishing. *The Lancet Digital Health, 5*(3), e105–e106.

Loh, E. (2024). ChatGPT and generative AI chatbots: Challenges and opportunities for science, medicine and medical leaders. *BMJ Leader.* https://bmjleader.bmj.com/content/early/2023/05/02/leader-2023-000797

Macdonald, C., Adeloye, D., Sheikh, A., & Rudan, I. (2023). Can ChatGPT draft a research article? An example of population-level vaccine effectiveness analysis. *Journal of Global Health, 13.*

Matias, Y., & Corrado, G. (2023). Our latest health AI research updates. *The Keyword.*

Mbakwe, A. B., Lourentzou, I., Celi, L. A., Mechanic, O. J., & Dagan, A. (2023). ChatGPT passing USMLE shines a spotlight on the flaws of medical education. *PLOS Digital Health, 2*(2), e0000205.

Milmo, D. (2023). ChatGPT reached 100 million users two months after Launch. *The Guardian.* 2023. https://www.theguardian.com/technology/2023/feb/02/chatgpt-100-million-users-open-ai-fastest-growing-app

Moussa, S., & Teixeira da Silva, J. A. (2023). Testing the robustness of COPE's characterization of predatory publishing on a COPE member publisher (Academic and Business Research Institute). *Publishing Research Quarterly, 39*(4), 337–367.

Newman, J. (2023). 33 *AI tools you can try for free at Fast Company.* https://www.fastcompany.com/90856183/30-ai-tools-you-can-try-for-free

Nori, H., King, N., McKinney, S. M., Carignan, D., & Horvitz, E. (2023). *Capabilities of gpt-4 on medical challenge problems.* arXiv preprint arXiv:2303.13375

Obot, C. (2024). https://m.facebook.com/story.php?story_fbid=pfbid0rgMV4Pw417oQpHgZYzkYVFeK8oxUFJcQVcs7XgZkbzLdYY7h8pYRZCfUu2qQgStfl&id=100000852529949&mibextid=Nif5oz

O'Connor, S. (2022). Open artificial intelligence platforms in nursing education: Tools for academic progress or abuse? *Nurse Education in Practice, 66,* 103537–103537.

Ollivier, M., Pareek, A., Dahmen, J., Kayaalp, M. E., Winkler, P. W., Hirschmann, M. T., & Karlsson, J. (2023). A deeper dive into ChatGPT: History, use and future perspectives for orthopaedic research. *Knee Surgery, Sports Traumatology, Arthroscopy, 31*(4), 1190–1192.

OpenAI. (2023). Introducing ChatGPT OpenAI; 2022. https://openai.com/blog/chatgpt

Pichai S. (2023). An important next step on our AI journey: Google. https://blog.google/technology/ai/bard-google-ai-search-updates/

Rakha, E. A., Toss, M., Shiino, S., et al. (2021). Current and future applications of artificial intelligence in pathology: A clinical perspective. *Journal of Clinical Pathology, 74*(7), 409–414. https://doi.org/10.1136/jclinpath-2020-206908pmid:32763920

Ravi, A., Neinstein, A., & Murray, S. G. (2023). Large Language Models and medical education: Preparing for a rapid transformation in how trainees will learn to be doctors. *ATS Scholar, 4*(3), 282–292.

Sample, I. (2023, January 26). Science journals ban listing of ChatGPT as co-author on papers. *Guardian*.

Singhal, K., Azizi, S., Tu, T., et al. (2023). Large language models encode clinical knowledge. *Nature, 620*, 172–180. https://doi.org/10.1038/s41586-023-06291-2

Stokel-Walker, C. (2022). AI bot ChatGPT writes smart essays-should academics worry? *Nature*.

Stokel-Walker, C. (2023). ChatGPT listed as author on research papers: Many scientists disapprove. *Nature, 613*(7945), 620–621.

Tamny, T. (2024). Americans don't gain knowledge in school, they create it out of school. *Forbes*. https://www.forbes.com/sites/johntamny/2024/02/10/americans-dont-gain-knowledge-in-school-they-create-it-out-of-school/?sh=5cd6791a6544

Thorp, H. H. (2023). ChatGPT is fun, but not an author. *Science, 379*(6630), 313–313.

CHAPTER 2

How Symbiotic Is the Union Between Artificial Intelligence and Educational Broadcasting?

Beshel Cletus Ushie

Introduction

For some years now, there has been a wide array of discussion among scholars on the contributions, handicaps and prospects of artificial intelligence and educational practice. There seems to have divergent views among scholars and the end seems not in view in the nearest future. This chapter attempts to take an objective survey of the union between these two important and complementary partners in the affairs of the sustenance of viable and productive human communities. The basic concepts of artificial intelligence and educational broadcasting are x-rayed with a brief summary of the introduction of technologies into education. An attempt is made to highlight the benefits, opportunities and risks encountered with a postulation into the future.

B. C. Ushie (✉)
University of Calabar, Calabar, Nigeria
e-mail: beshelushie@unical.edu.ng

U. S. Akpan (ed.), *Educational Broadcasting in Nigeria in the Age of Artificial Intelligence*,
https://doi.org/10.1007/978-3-031-68530-9_2

Concept of Artificial Intelligence (AI)

Artificial Intelligence refers to the theory and development of computer systems able to perform tasks normally requiring human intelligence such as virtual perception, speech recognition, decision-making and translation between languages. It has also been described as the simulation of human intelligence processes by machines, especially computer systems. Specific applications of AI include expert systems, natural language processes, speech recognition and machine vision.

The four main types of AI are negative, machines which have no memory and are task specific, implying that an input delivers the same output. The second type of AI is the limited memory that imitates the way our brain and nervous work together. The third and fourth types that are still evolving are theory of mind and self-awareness.

Concept of Educational Broadcasting

Educational broadcasting may be said to be a process by which educators and learners stimulate meanings in their minds naturally, using verbal and non-verbal messages, transmitted by radio and television to impact the learning environment in order to facilitate learning. Educational broadcasting can exist either in formal, non-formal or informal modes. The main purposes of educational broadcasting are: To help in the delivery of high quality educational programs/content to the audience, assist learners to have the opportunity to listen and view relevant educational content which indirectly enhance their understanding and stimulate their interest toward learning. Educational broadcasting also helps to increase access and equalization of educational opportunities.

The Union Between Artificial Intelligence and Educational Broadcasting

From the aforementioned brief explanation of the two concepts, it can be deduced that they are intricately interwoven as both are geared toward ensuring that the greater population of human beings in any community/nation have the best of education. It is worthy to note that technology has been and will remain the vehicle through which education would continue to thrive. A summary of the evolution of technology in education becomes imperative here. As submitted by Malekos (2023, p. 33) "every technology that disrupted the social narrative was viewed as a game changer in education, from the radio to the television and even artificial intelligence 70 years ago." Modern classroom approaches have evolved from the roots of technologies of the 1800s without really changing the educational process.

Short History of Modern Technologies in the Classroom

- 1985: The wireless telegraph was invented by Guglielmo Marconi (radio)
- 1920s: Radio entered the classroom and on-air classes caused an uproar
- 1927: Electronic television debuts in San Francisco
- 1950s:
  - Artificial intelligence was just a theoretical concept for scientific papers and moves;
  - The first educational television programs were created for open broadcast
- 1954; "The Logic Theorist," the first AI program is ever written
- 1960s: Programmed Logic for Automatic Teaching Operations (PLATO) was created by the University of Illinois to offer coursework to students and the community.
- 1980s:
  - A scientific journal dedicated to Artificial intelligence in education was circulating for a few years and was discontinued.
  - Intelligent Computer-Assisted Instruction (ICAI) systems were developed and distributed to schools
- 1990s:
  - Intelligent tutoring systems (ITS) were implemented trying to replicate the role of the teacher in the schools
  - Early Learning management systems (LMS) were created and popularized on the Internet
- 2002: The next generation of LMS including the first iteration of Moodle was created

- 2008: The term MOOCs (Massive Open Online Courses) was coined for the first time
- 2014: Learn Worlds, a modern cloud-based LMS was founded in 2014
- 2022: ChatGPT was released for public use in late 2022 and has re-inspired the world of education
- 2023: The year of AI? (Malekos, 2023)

Integrating AI in Education: Benefits, Opportunities, and Risks

As it has previously been mentioned, the impact of the emergence of any technology is variously viewed by scholars. Presented here are the postulations of two leading scholars specialized in the influence of technology use in education (1) Malekos (2023 holds that the use of AI. in education has the potential to transform the way we learn, making it more personalized, engaging and accessible for everyone. However, we need to be mindful of its potential drawbacks, such as content overload, fake news, and lack of critical thinking skills. We have seen both success stories and cautionary tales about the use of AI. in education, which underscores the importance of implementing it responsibly. This means being transparent about how algorithms are used, protecting students' privacy, and using AI. in a way that fosters creativity and innovation. The educational revolution that AI promises is an exciting prospect, but we need to be aware of its challenges and address them head-on.

Advantages of Using AI in the Classroom

Digital education has boomed in recent years, and with so many advantages for modern learners, and it is not hard to see why. Students able to access learning materials and interact and collaborate with their tutors and peers online, can enjoy flexible, engaging and motivating courses of study. Digital education can expand the reach of learning to communities who could otherwise be excluded and provides scope for rewarding, personalized and self-directed study in ways such as:

1. **Personalized Learning**—Personalized learning tailors tuition according to the needs of each individual. This can be in terms of pace, content and delivery. It recognizes that one size rarely fits all when it comes to education. After all, students will learn in different ways and at different speeds. They will have varying needs and will respond in individual ways to visual, written and spoken information.

   A virtual learning environment is ideally placed to provide personal learning experiences. According to a Bill and Melinda Gates Foundation study, "vast majorities" of educators believe data and digital tools are "improving teaching through differentiation and personalization."

   A modern learning platform creates a space for learning, where each student follows their own learning pathway. For example, if students are struggling with a topic, additional resources can be triggered to help them backfill their knowledge. Another student, already competent in that area, wouldn't need additional content; sh/he might need to devote more time on another part of the course instead. By personalized learning, educators can aim to meet each student's particular needs for the best results.

   Radboud University in the Netherlands brings law to life by using release conditions in a role-playing fictional case assignment. Students can experience all the different perspectives on a fictional case by taking on the roles of defense counsel, prosecutor and judge. Information is released to students only when they meet appropriate criteria, so the "prosecutors" see different material to the "defense counsel," for example. This gives the scenario the dynamic feel of a real case: information builds up over time, and this interactivity is central to students' ability to progress.
2. **Gamification**—Gamification taps into models familiar to users of technology to deliver enhanced and engaging learning experiences for more successful outcomes. Easy-to-use digital tools, which many students will be familiar with from gaming, can be incorporated into course design to motivate them through rewards and real-time feedback.

   By drawing on the principles of the gaming model, education can make use of a range of techniques. These include the awarding of points and badges. After all, students will make regular achievements—recognizing and rewarding them motivates them to continue. Students have something to aim for when they can see a clear roadmap through their learning journal and when they are acknowledged for teaching key milestones.

Games-based learning need not reward just successful test scores either, it can also give recognition for desirable learning behaviors such as participating in discussions and carrying out independent research.

3. **Self-directed Learning**—As students progress through their education, they will need to become competent in self-directed learning. This refers to students' capabilities to manage their own time, do their own research and take ownership of their learning.

   Along the way, they will discover more about how and when they learn best. This will help them develop strategies for maximizing study time to ensure they get the most out of it. For some, that might mean learning first thing in the morning; for others, later in the day.

   Knowing how to take ownership of an activity, organize time to deliver it and get the best results are important career and life skills. Insights into how to plan and organize their time will stand students in good stead in the world of work.

   A digital learning platform provides an ideal framework for each student's learning journey. There, students can access their course schedules, see the range of their commitments over time and plan their course of action.
4. **Easier to Access**—Online learning provides students, who might otherwise struggle to access education, with a way to learn. In rural communities, where travel infrastructure may be limited, being able to study remotely is ideal. Likewise, students with additional responsibilities, such as work, childcare and other caring duties, will appreciate options that enable them to fit studying into their busy lives.

   Education must be for all; not everyone will be able to learn at set hours or from the same location. Through digital education, students and tutors can connect, regardless of where they are located. Materials in the learning platform provide students with all the content they need, even when they cannot go to the college, university or other sites of learning.

Whether learning is fully online, or a blend of in-person and digital, levels of interactivity and collaboration can still be high with the online learning environment providing the means for discussion forums, tutorials, and feedback.

5. **Students can Learn at their Own Pace**—As well as being able to access learning anytime, from anywhere, digital education also enables students to learn at their own pace. They can re-read materials to gain a deeper grounding in a topic or even revisit earlier modules.

   The learning platform gives students 24/7 access to a range of materials, including recorded lectures which they may wish to view again. Content is preserved, not lost, when a lecture ends.

   Self-directed learning, undertaken at students' own pace, gives learners ownership of their own experience, which is important to maximize successful learning outcomes, keep students motivated and engaged and avoid an "edutech reality gap."

6. **Digital Assessment Tracks Progress**—As students progress through their studies, they are likely to be assessed a number of times. Digital assessment need not be confined to the marking of written work—it can include live online or pre-recorded presentations.

   Students can demonstrate modern foreign language pronunciation through audio files, or video themselves completing a practical task. This is something West Bridgford School (WBS) in Nottingham, England did to great effect. WBS used the Video Assignments tool in the Brightspace for students to video themselves cooking whilst describing what they were doing in the language they were learning.

   For tutors, digital assessment provides the opportunity to precisely pinpoint feedback to a specific part of an assignment. This can be test-based, but can also be time-stamped on video submissions. Tags to content covered within the course can also form part of feedback so that students can link straight to topics they may need to revisit.

   Digital assessment includes timesaving features that make grading and giving feedback simpler and more effective to free up tutors from repetitive marking. That way, tutors can focus time on addressing learning points instead. Quizzes with correct and incorrect answers can be automatically marked, saving tutors a huge amount of time.

Students benefit from simple access to their grades and feedback over time through the online learning platform. That way, they can clearly see their progress and are able to revisit feedback whenever they need to.

7. **Blended Learning**—Blended learning combines some face-to-face tutoring with online learning. It is an approach that can work very successfully because it combines the convenience and flexibility of online, with the personal touch of in-class tuition.

   Each institution and educator will have their own approach to blended learning, according to the course type and needs of students. For many, blended learning enables a "flipped" classroom approach, in which students access content through the learning platform to prepare for in-person lessons. In this way, knowledge acquisition occurs outside the classroom, perhaps from recorded lectures, documents, videos and other resources, and knowledge application occurs in class.
8. **Competency-based Learning**—Competency-based learning recognizes that, within a specified period of study, learners will progress at different rates. Students will need to spend more time on some topics than others. They might also need to supplement main course material with other information to plug knowledge gaps.

   Digital education enables a competency-based approach to learning because it is flexible, with the capability for personalized learning journeys within a framework designed around achieving set outcomes. Built-in logic in the learning platform facilitates learners moving from one topic to the next, only when they have mastered the topic and met pre-defined criteria for progressing to the next stage.
9. **Collaborative Learning**—Many of today's learners are already familiar with sharing content online. As users of social media platforms, they are used to online spaces being collaborative.

   Digital education need not be solely two-way—tutor to student and student to tutor. Students can share their work with each other as well as the tutor so that they learn from each other. They can also work on group projects using document sharing tools, video conferencing and chat forums. This type of collaboration builds team working and social skills. Online, everyone is only a click away, so students can connect with their peers all over the world, broadening horizons and building diverse connections.

10. **Improves Digital Literacy**—We all need to be digitally literate in today's technology age. Digital literacy means being able to use technology to find and share information. It's an essential life skill, as well as a prerequisite for many jobs. Even the act of applying for a job is likely to include technology.

    According to Ofcom, nearly all UK children aged 5–15 years (97 per cent) went online in 2020; over half said they posted or shared content on video-sharing platforms. However, children's earliest experiences with technology now re-date school: the same report reveals that 82 per cent of children aged 3–4 went online in 2020 and nearly half (48 per cent) already owned a tablet themselves.

    Digital education helps learners build the skills they need to navigate technology and to get the best out of it. Students of digital education become comfortable with finding, accessing, consuming and sharing content online. They become discerning in the content they see, making judgments on what's legitimate, safe and fact-based.

Digital education provides a range of advantages whether learning is fully online or as part of a blended teaching model. The broad scope that digital provides for a range of content types help keep students engaged. All the while, they are building valuable digital skills that will serve them in their personal and professional lives. For educators and institutions, the digital learning platform helps connect students.

Unpacking the Challenges of AI in Education

On the other hand, we should recognize the dangers artificial intelligence comes with. There are several potential risks and challenges associated with using AI in education, even as a powerful assistant. Let us explore the most vital ones.

Content Saturation—An overwhelming amount of content given by AI may lead to content fatigue and demotivation. Too much educational content may end up having the exact opposite effects, and decrease academic performance.

Developing Lazy Minds—Critical thinking is becoming increasingly important, and in an age where misinformation spreads rapidly, the danger of developing lazy minds and non-critical thinkers is a danger to society in general.

Bias and Misinformation in Algorithms—AI algorithms can be biased if they are trained on data that is not representative of the student population. This can result in inaccurate assessments, also known as hallucinations or recommendations that may disadvantage certain groups of learners.

Data Privacy and Security—AI relies on collecting and analyzing large amounts of data, including sensitive information. The use of AI in education may pose a risk to students' privacy and personal information if not managed properly.

Lack of Human Interaction—While AI can provide personalized feedback and support, it cannot replace human interaction and the social and emotional learning that comes with it. Over-reliance on AI may result in students feeling isolated or disconnected from their peers and teachers.

Ethical and Legal Concerns—The use of AI in education raises ethical and legal questions around issues such as algorithmic bias, data privacy, content ownership, and transparency. Educational institutions and training providers must consider these issues when implementing AI tools.

Overall, while AI has the potential to be a powerful assistant in education, it is important to address these risks and challenges to ensure that its use is responsible, equitable, and effective for all students.

Preparing for the AI Powered Classroom of the Future

The rapid development of artificial intelligence (AI) technology is expected to revolutionize the education industry, transforming the classroom into an AI powered learning environment. This shift will have a significant impact on the role of educators and how they approach teaching.

Let's explore some scenarios:

Creating Curriculum Outlines and Prototyping Content (creating drafts, outlines, etc.) can be technology-assisted to draft and prepare the lesson material.

Developing Educational Content—will not be the same anymore. Creating assignments, lecture contents, handouts, and even videos, will be done with AI to speed up the process.

Eliminate Creative Blocks—Do you have times when the blank page is your worst nightmare? An autocomplete function or an AI writing tool can help push back and continue your work.

Developing Critical Thinking—Will become the most important skill to teach across all levels of education.

Grading the Assignments—A dreaded task for every educator is a pile of papers to read and evaluate objectively. This task may be partially automated or AI assisted soon.

AI will assist in every level of the teaching process, from how to write a question in the exams to correcting the papers, and even give options on how to respond to the students.

It will take the mundane tasks away from the teacher and the time-consuming work of the students, to be replaced with more valuable in-depth knowledge.

The AI powered classroom of the future will require educators to embrace new ways of teaching and learning, as well as to develop new skills and competencies. While the role of educators may change significantly, their ultimate goal of fostering student learning and growth remains the same.

AI Tools in the Service of Education

Let us explore the various tools that educators and students may soon have access to in the classroom, perhaps sooner than anticipated.

- Intelligent tutoring systems
- Adaptive learning
- Image recognition
- Chatbots
- Voice synthesizers
- AI impersonators (e.g. of historical figures or top scientists)

These and many more tools including specialized applications for learning will be more common, as creating web and mobile applications becomes easier and powered by artificial intelligence.

Already, Duolingo uses GPT4 for its language learning Chatbot, explaining key grammatical concepts and role plays as different personas to practice.

Education Entrepreneurs: Reinventing Themselves for the Future

Educators and course creators alike will be challenged and have to re-invent their identities to stay competitive and relevant.

As more tech-savvy creator-entertainers join the educational market, creating courses with AI assisted tools, the e-learning market will change. Then, a big question arises:

How Can We Stay Relevant as Educators?

As the AI revolution continues to reshape the education landscape, educators must adapt in order to remain competitive. Here are three strategies you can employ:

- Focus on developing your expertise
- Explore new ways to engage learners, e.g. build a community, entertain your audience
- Incorporate AI-powered tools and platforms in your teaching practice

With the emergency of AI technology, you must keep up with the latest advancements in your field to remain competitive. It's essential to develop expertise in your area of teaching to provide your students with the best possible learning experience. This can be done by taking part in professional development opportunities, attending conferences, networking with peers, and staying up to date with research and publications. By doing so, you will be able to offer your learners valuable insights and perspectives.

Then, remember, AI technology offers new and exciting opportunities to engage learners and create a more personalized learning experience.

You can explore new teaching strategies that leverage AI-powered tools to better understand and adapt to individual student needs.

Learning is a social process, we learn from each other and through interactions. While artificial intelligence can replace parts of the learning process, it cannot fully replace social interactions. By offering a community of learning and expert instructor guidance, you are positioning yourself above the masses.

AI-powered tools and platforms can help you streamline your teaching process, automate administrative tasks, and provide better insights into student performance. For example, learning management systems can track student progress and identify areas where students need additional support. Additionally, natural language processing tools can analyze student writing and provide feedback on grammar and style, helping students to improve their writing skills.

By incorporating AI-powered tools and platforms in your teaching practice, you can improve the overall learning experience for your students, while also making your job easier and more efficient.

A Legal View of AI Content: Copyright, Ownership, and the Legal Framework

Today, artificial intelligence is already vastly used to create and generate works in music, software, journalism, marketing, literature, etc. The produced work could be perceived as free to use because it has not been created by a human, thus not covered under the protection described below.

From a commercial perspective, this is terrible news for any company that could potentially spend vast amounts of money for the creation of a specific work of authorship by an A.I. Traditionally, the use of computers to generate literary, artistic, or any other work of authorship did not create any issue regarding the ownership of copyright as the computers were used as mere tools in the creation process.

In the same direction as the above, the position of the majority of European Union (EU) jurisdictions is that only works created by a human can be protected by copyright. There is ample room for legislators to tackle this issue of who will own the copyright to a work of authorship, if this is generated by an AI. There have been arguments that the ownership should be bestowed to the developer that has created the specific parameters for the said creative outcome. However, this could be perceived as granting ownership rights to the creator of the tool.

Already there are rulings from EU and United States (US) courts deciding that work products by an AI should not be copyrighted. But there is a silver lining there. If the artist or author can prove to exert creative control over the outcome of the AI then this particular work should be protected and ownership should be granted.

My opinion is that when a creator can exert creative control and prove that the vision and the idea belong to him/her, then the work product should be clearly protected and copyrights should be granted. The real issue emerges when the AI has created something entirely on its own without any creative control or direction. This is the field, where the legislator needs to step in and regulate in a way that does not hinder creativity and innovation.

Adapting to the AI Challenge for the Future of Educational Broadcasting

As technology continues to advance, AI is changing the way we learn. While this brings exciting new opportunities for education, it also brings challenges. In the future, teachers will need to find the right balance between using AI and interacting with students. They should focus on their expertise, build strong learning communities, and create engaging educational experiences for students.

New technologies tend to disrupt the status quo. The rise of AI in education has the potential to significantly transform the eLearning landscape and change how we work, learn, and search for information, along with a myriad of other social and economic processes.

In the AI-powered classroom of the future, educators will need to adapt their roles, focusing on critical thinking and learning to use the tools at their disposal. To stay relevant, educators must emphasize their expertise, foster learning communities, and provide engaging educational experiences.

As AI continues to develop, striking the right balance between AI and human interaction will be crucial for the future of educational broadcasting.

Buckingham (2022) holds that, the use of AI is already widespread in many arenas; image recognition software, search engines, file-sharing platforms and retailers' "recommender" systems all depend upon it. However, what we're talking about here is something more specific: that is, generative AI. This refers to software that (Like the algorithms developed by Google, YouTube, Spotify or Amazon, for example) is capable of gathering, processing, and analyzing and synthesizing user data. In this case, however, the outputs that ensue are not just a few more-or-less useful recommendations or suggestions, but extensive texts that users can subsequently refine or edit.

The debate has significantly gathered pace since the launch last November of the latest (fourth) iteration of Chat GPT, created by the US Company Open AI. Like some other Silicon Valley startups, Open AI began life in 2015 as a not-for-profit venture, but it has quickly become a hot commercial enterprise; it partners with Microsoft, and is currently (some might say conservatively) projecting annual revenues of $1 billion by 2024. Within two months of its launch, ChatGPT-4 apparently became the fastest selling application of all time, reaching 100 million users by the start of this year. However, some commentators may have fantasies about "banning" such products, they are very much here to stay.

ChatGPT has attracted the most attention, but it is only one of many such applications. Notable rivals in the field of verbal text (or "large-language-model") generation include Google's BARD and Microsoft's BING-AL. Others—such as OpenAI's own DALL-E, along with packages like Open Diffusion and Midjourney—are capable of producing high quality images based on fairly simple verbal prompts. This issue hit the headlines most recently, when the creative photo category in the Sony World Photography Awards was won by an image that turned out to be generated in DALL-E. (The winner, Boris Eldagsen, had entered precisely in order to draw attention to the issue, and turned down the prize).

Contrary to Open AI's rhetoric of "deep learning," when it comes to education, the fear is that this technology is actually about the very opposite: cheating. In the UK, the debate about AI has been dominated by an overwhelming anxiety about *assessment*—a phenomenon that reflects the absolutely determining role of high-stakes assessment in our current system. This takes on a particular force in higher education, where institutions are massively (and precariously) dependent on high-paying international students, and where language requirements have been progressively reduced.

Of course, plagiarism is by no means a new phenomenon—nor indeed are “essay farms” that will sell sufficiently competent and seemingly original work. Like most academics, I could tell some amusing and depressing tales about this that go back several decades. Yet while packages like *Turnitin* are now routinely used to detect cut-and-paste plagiarism, the threat with ChatGPT is that plagiarism is now becoming impossible to detect. While some maintain that new services (like gptzero.me) can already perform this task, others are less convinced.

Judging from results I have seen, packages like ChatGPT are pretty good at mimicking the “on the one hand this, on the other hand that” style of conventional essay writing. The essays that emerge are typically dutiful and mechanical: they are rarely personal or passionate or humorous or inspired, and of course they cannot include first-hand research. In the face of what seems like undetectable plagiarism, some institutions are already desperately turning back to sit-down written examinations; yet if the advent of AI encourages educators to develop more creative and challenging approaches to assessment than the predictable essay format, that may be no bad thing.

At my conference, I was asked how I thought the advent of AI would affect the media themselves, and how media educators might respond. Of course, the technology is changing so quickly that it may be too early to say very much about this. As with earlier technologies, we need to be wary of both excitable hype and of doom-saying: AI is unlikely to transport us to a creative utopia any more than it will take us all to hell. This was easy to say; yet as I listened to the hucksters enthusiastically promoting all that “cool stuff,” I felt the need to go further. What follows are some early thoughts on these two questions—from the position of one who is evidently far from an expert.

Media themselves might seem easier to identify that the use of AI represents a form of automation that seems bound to lead to job losses, or at least to a significant restructuring of working practices. Of course, this is an ongoing process in the media industries in any case; and it may be that the kinds of work that will be replaced will be fairly low-level. Applications like CharGPT are good at generating generic or descriptive content, and the kind of bland “space filling” reports that journalists routinely have to produce; they are much less good at being innovative or creative, and they don’t do original research. Yet if routine entry-level jobs disappear, where will creative careers begin?

This kind of software initially "trains" itself by scraping or gathering existing online data, and it does so largely without the consent or knowledge of those who originally created it. It does not require permission; nor indeed is it currently possible to prevent this from happening. Inevitably, this has massive implications for copyright and beyond that, for workers' livelihoods. Once again, this is not a new issue; but the potential for appropriating (or stealing) existing content from multiple sources and then reworking it is vastly increased when it is possible to do so invisibly.

Meanwhile, packages like ChatGPT—like Google in its early days—do not outwardly appear to depend upon advertising. They appear to talk to you, to be your friend, to help you, all for free. Yet, as the saying goes, if the service seems to be free, then you are the product. The profitability of such packages depends upon the recording and gathering—and eventually selling—of personal data. The more "interactive" they seem, the greater the potential for surveillance.

Critics gleefully report on the basic factual mistakes that can be made by applications like ChatGPT (which some refer to as "hallucinations")—although, as I've argued before, factual errors are generally easier to spot (and correct) than more complex and subtle forms of misinformation and bias. We might well ask whether misinformation is likely to be a much greater hazard than it is with existing forms of journalism. Likewise, visual AI applications are capable of producing convincing "deepfakes"; although the potential for this has also been available for several years.

Somewhat less obvious to most critics—but arguably much more concerning—are the environmental implications of such technologies. Some reports have suggested that a single CharGPT dialogue with 20–50 questions consumes half a liter of clean drinking water, and with 100 million global subscribers already, the environmental impact is potentially vast. It has been estimated that "training" the earlier interaction of ChatGPT (version 3) may have required as much as 700,000 liters to generate and cool the vast data centers that the industry euphemistically refers to as the "cloud."

To some extent, all these problems might be seen merely as extrapolations of existing trends, rather than entirely new developments; all that AI does is to automate (and thus accelerate) processes that have already been under way for some time. Nevertheless, they do undoubtedly reinforce the need for regulation. When Sam Altman, the CEO of Open AI, recently appeared before Congress, he appeared to accept the need for government regulation, and even called for a moratorium on new developments until this could be achieved.

While it might seem extraordinary for technology companies to be asking for their own products to be regulated in this way, Altman's performance recalled that of Mark Zuckerberg making similar requests to Congress in the wake of the Cambridge Analytical scandal—as the *New Yorker* correspondent pointed out. With this new market still in its infancy, companies like OpenAI are trying very hard to maneuver themselves into the key position of being early brand leaders, and to steal a march on the opposition. They may be keen to manicure their public image, but they surely recognize the likelihood that meaningful regulation will be lost in the miasma of bureaucracy.

So to the second question: *how might media educators respond to these developments?* On one level, the advent of AI Provides us with yet more new curriculum content. The crucial thing here, in my view, is to build on the critical frameworks and classroom approaches that we have developed over time. Just as with social media, it's both possible and productive to extend media education "key concepts" to this new medium. My observations above suggest a series of questions to do with the *political economy* of AI that might well be explored by students: basic questions about business, work and regulation are all familiar from the approaches we have developed with students relating to "older" media. Likewise, well-established questions about representation, reliability and trust, and about the wider social implications of AI, will be familiar, and can usefully be explored and debated by students.

However, there are other questions about how we might actively use AI in our teaching. Here, I begin with a paraphrase of a quotation adapted from the semiologist Umberto Eco's arguments about television, from almost fifty years ago: if you want to use media (or technology) to teach somebody, you first have to teach them how to understand media. Media education is not primarily about teaching *with or through* media, but teaching *about* media: it is not to be confused with educational media, or educational technology. This takes us well beyond the use of technology as an instrumental tool for learning—an approach that seems to be taken for granted in debates about AI, just as it has been in relation to earlier educational technologies. Arguably, the more effective and seamless the technology becomes, the harder (and yet more necessary) it is to take a critical distance from it: we need to slow it down, to de-familiarize it, and to consider how it might be otherwise.

There are numerous resources that explain the basic principles of how AI works, at least on a technical level. At my conference, I was impressed by some very straightforward materials produced by BSD Education, which are quite usable at primary school level; and from there, it would not be difficult to move on to more critical questions about algorithmic bias. (There are numerous others, notably Day of AI, which comes out of MIT; and a large collection here.)

However, "teaching the algorithm" should entail more than just showing how it works. One longstanding approach in media education is the practical simulation, where students experiment systematically to create different versions of a media text, in line with a defined brief, and then analyze and compare them. Thus, different groups within a class might be given slightly different parameters (different audiences, for example), or be encouraged to create different "prompts" for the software, and then assess the resulting outcomes. At least in the case of ChatGPT, it should be possible to show the sources from which the application has been drawn, which should allow some further interrogation (although it's not clear if this is still possible). Ideally, it should be interesting to compare outputs from different applications as well.

This could lead on to a more open-ended creative approach, provided it is handled thoughtfully. The most interesting insights on this at my conference came in a presentation by Glenn Malcolm, which can be accessed as a blog here. Glenn's overall approach is refreshingly critical; but he also offers some engaging and productive ways to use the technology to create media such as comics and animation. Of course, this by no means precludes the need to teach the "languages" of media (codes and conventions, as we used to call them); and there is always a danger of being seduced by the gloss and professionalism of the finished products, and forgetting the need for critical reflection. The work Glenn presents arises from the context of an elite international school: I'm not sure it is within the reach of most of us yet, although it surely won't be long before we have the simple AI equivalents of iMovie or Garageband.

Teaching almost always uses media and technology in some form. The book is a medium; the chalkboard is a technology. If a particular technology can accomplish certain mechanical tasks, freeing us up to think more deeply, that is surely a good thing; although we also need to weigh up the downsides. If we learn to collaborate with technology, then it is unlikely to replace us. As ever, the question is whether teachers can learn to use technology.

References

Buckingham, D. (2022). Artificial intelligence in education: A media education approach.

Georgarakou, R. (2023). Exploring the pros and cons of integrating AI in education: Benefits, opportunities and risks.

Malekos, N. (2023). The modern history of technology in education (Highlights). Routledge.

Montes, E. (2022). The advantages of digital education. Sage.

Palegeorgiou, G. (2022). Education entrepreneurs: Reinventing themselves for the future. Palgrave Macmillan.

Vassia, P. (2023). A legal view of AI content: Copyright, ownership and the legal framework. Learn the world. Routledge.

CHAPTER 3

Artificial Intelligence and the Transformation of Broadcasting: Implications for Nigerian Broadcast Professionals

Osakpolor Emwinromwankhoe

Introduction

First, let us consider these direct assertions: "The world around us is going to be transformed by AI over the next few years. The news media is no exception. AI is the latest wave of technological change and it pays to work with others to see what it can do for you" (International Media Support, 2021, p. 3), "If the Nigerian [broadcast] media does not embrace AI soon, it will be at a serious disadvantage" (Abiola, 2023, para. 1). The above assertions provide a foundation from which this article takes a leap. The human ecosphere has, from time immemorial, never been static. It has at various points been subject to changes occasioned by technological advancements, twinned with the proliferation of digital devices. Since the evolution of the Internet in the twentieth century

O. Emwinromwankhoe (✉)
Ambrose Alli University, Ekpoma, Edo State, Nigeria
e-mail: osakpolorgregory@yahoo.com

U. S. Akpan (ed.), *Educational Broadcasting in Nigeria in the Age of Artificial Intelligence*,
https://doi.org/10.1007/978-3-031-68530-9_3

culminating in a major global information revolution, other technological breakthroughs have swiftly followed suit and today, such concepts as Internet of Things, Knowledge Economy and Digitization are gaining grounds across various parts of the world, profoundly affecting and shaping disciplines such as the sciences, engineering, arts and humanities, amongst others. One striking development stemming from the threshold of technological transformations pervading our modern world is Artificial Intelligence (AI). Loosely defined to mean the sort of intelligence that is non-human and tied to the use of machines to solve human and societal needs, AI has crept into several aspects of human life, influencing, transforming, revolutionizing and even disrupting the order of things.

Within the global media terrain particularly the broadcasting sphere, AI holds sway as the major force driving significant changes in information gathering, content production, packaging, distribution, and consumption. This lends credence to Associated Press' (2022, p. 3) assertion that AI "has found a home" in the global broadcast industry "over the past decade." In a broadcast ecology that is increasingly hypercompetitive and where the desire to be the first to break the news is ingrained in the mind of many a broadcast practitioner (Emwinromwankhoe & Akpan, 2022b), AI provides a bedrock upon which peerless speed, spontaneity, credibility and versatility are enjoyed by broadcasters. To buttress this, a noteworthy occurrence in the US on 17 March, 2014 would suffice. A light earthquake had hit the city of Los Angeles and in a jiffy, Ken Schwencke, a reporter with the *Los Angeles Times* broke the story, much to the chagrin of other journalists. How could Schwencke report the event almost as immediately as it occurred? As Schwencke later revealed, the story was actually written by Quakebot, an AI-enabled app which regularly generated data from the US Geological Survey website. Thus, on getting wind of the newsworthy occurrence, Schwencke ran to his computer and noticed that the story was already written. All he practically did was revise and publish it.

AI has armed broadcast professionals with the capabilities of disseminating timely and enthralling stories to diverse audiences at the right time, the right place, and via the right channel(s). AI has pushed the limits of traditional broadcasting and expanded the frontiers of information gathering and dissemination so much so that stations that have refused to key into its vast potentials are already under the risk of folding up or losing listenership and/or viewership (Emwinromwankhoe & Akpan, 2022a; Kuyucu, 2019). Today, there are AI-enabled virtual newscasters and presenters who cannot only mimic the voices of their human counterparts but can also assist with other rigorous aspects of the broadcast profession. Oyedokun (2023) affirms that AI has terribly permeated the broadcast landscape that some Nigerians are already at home with AI presenters, stressing that AI has enabled a much more diverse, enriching, and enchanting broadcasting both locally and globally.

AI has simplified the process of scouring information by broadcast journalists through its provision of a large database (also called big data) from which vital, relevant, and specific stories can be sourced. Realism in broadcast news reportage has been achieved through the use of robots, drones, and creation of shots that appear incredibly natural to the audience. The quality of outside broadcast (OB) has been improved just as video-to-audio conversion and video (or audio)-to-text transcription can be carried out effortlessly and creditably. Corollary to the above is the ease of achieving multimediality (the use of texts, audio, video, pictures, charts and graphs) in the packaging of broadcast contents. AI-enabled facial detection software facilitates the generation of the names of discussants during interviews and discussion programs just as the personalization of broadcast contents to suit the specific needs of each audience member has been made possible. In fact, AI has become so useful to broadcasting that a broadcast station can become so useless without it.

It cannot be gainsaid that in the era of AI, the issue of digital or technological divide which has long been the bane of most developing economies has again been brought to the forefront of global conversation. In a survey carried out by the Associated Press (2022) to ascertain the readiness of local newsrooms in the US toward utilizing AI for news dissemination purposes, it was found that there was a palpable disparity between the larger news houses and smaller ones as the latter were disadvantaged by lack of finance and dearth of technical skills occasioned by a high turnover. If that could be the case with some newsrooms in a country as technologically advanced as the US, then the plight of many broadcast stations in Africa, a continent that keeps ebbing with regard to technology adoption can, at best, be imagined. Nigeria is no exception to this technological divide and in this ineluctable age of AI, the country's broadcast practitioners certainly have a whole lot to grapple with. The transformations AI has brought to broadcasting are conspicuous and ubiquitous, and Nigerian broadcast practitioners cannot turn a blind eye to them. Springing from this standpoint are some salient questions begging for immediate answers. How is AI transforming global broadcasting? How can Nigerian broadcast practitioners appropriate AI tools for mesmeric broadcasting? How can broadcasting ethics be entrenched in the era of AI where fake news constitutes a major challenge? What implications do AI-enabled transformations have for Nigerian broadcast professionals? These are the overarching questions that this article seeks to address.

AI and Broadcasting: Conceptual Clarifications

AI has unassailably become a central concept in contemporary broadcasting yet its definition has often been slippery. This is understandable because AI, aside from taking roots from the dual fields of computer engineering and information technology, is subject to different points of view from scholars and practitioners alike. International Media Support (2021, p. 9) describes AI as "a machine that can autonomously analyze its environment using a set of algorithms or pattern models to simulate human intelligence." The Associated Press (2022, p. 11), on its part, refers to AI as "a range of technologies that are human-designated to automate, accelerate or extend the human work required for specific tasks." The Associated Press further states that "AI helps to process data, does not have a mind of its own, depends on data that humans feed it, and produces results from human-fed information."

AI represents a major information technology breakthrough which deploys a set of enhanced and advanced technologies to copy and achieve cognitive and cerebral capabilities hitherto attributed to only humans. The key word in AI is *artificial* which conveys the idea of a simulation of something else—human intelligence in this case—with the use of computers. The implication of the aforesaid is that AI does not equate real human intelligence but rather a simulacrum of it. This explains the reason why AI is devoid of a mind of its own and cannot show such human emotions as love, affection or hatred. Whilst constructing this article, I typed in the words "Will you be my lover, please?" on my ChatGPT and the response I got, as expected, was "I am here to provide assistance as an AI, but I am not capable of being a romantic partner." AI cannot exist or thrive on its own without human input and though remarkably intelligent, its intelligible outputs are based on what humans constantly feed into it. With AI, it is garbage in; garbage out.

AI is a master at digging into big data archives both online and offline and gathering, analyzing, coding, interpreting, translating, and delivering results efficiently and within the shortest possible time. AI is not more intelligent than humans, but just a replica of a fraction of what the human brain can achieve. AI mostly uses algorithms and its technologies revolve around six interrelated areas which include machine learning, deep learning, natural language generation, speech recognition, robotics, and biometric identification (Lan & Zhou, 2023; Oyedokun, 2023). Examples of some AI software used in broadcast production include: RAMCOM which can be used to schedule adverts for airing, ChatGPT, Polly, Collaboratory, JavaScript, Adobe Premiere Pro, Transkriptor, Python, Data Wrapper, Listrak and PACER, amongst others (see Associated Press, 2021 for more).

The conceptualization of broadcasting by both Nigerian and Western scholars has often been stuck to the traditional line of information dissemination through radio or electromagnetic waves to a large, diverse and scattered audience simultaneously (Agbanu & Nwammuo, 2009; Hanson, 2005; Owuamalam, 2008 for such related definitions). Whilst such definitions are laudable, they are deficient in several areas, especially their failure to capture or outline contemporary trends within the field, one of which is the incorporation of AI into every aspect of broadcasting. As Emwinromwankhoe and Akpan (2022a) assert, information and communication technologies (ICTs) have made inroads into the global broadcast landscape such that broadcasting is now in dire need of reconceptualization as previous definitions have been rendered grossly obsolete, inadequate, and flawed.

As the Organisation for Economic Cooperation and Development (2007, p. 11) observes, "broadcasting services are continuously evolving" especially in this age of artificial intelligence and user-generated contents and by so doing, "it is no longer possible to provide a uniform, all-encompassing definition of 'broadcasting' that is adequate to capture all the particular features of the market for broadcasting services." Thus, as AI keeps impacting upon broadcasting, an updated and all-embracing definition is needed and this is why I have decided to settle for the definition proffered by the Organisation for Economic Cooperation and Development (2007) which states that broadcasting involves "the business of producing interactive information content and distributing it via telecommunication services." Unlike prior definitions which ascribed immense power and hegemony to broadcast stations, this definition factors in the transformations AI has brought into the world of broadcasting notable amongst which are interactivity and multimediality. Besides, by accentuating on interactivity, the definition acknowledges the supremacy of the broadcast audience who are now active rather than passive and whose tastes shape the nature of broadcast contents as well as the platforms through which they are relayed. To this end, the aforesaid definition is used operationally in my arguments, analyses, and discussion in this article.

Theoretical Pivot: The Technology Appropriation Paradigm

In the bid to properly and effectively discuss the transformations AI has brought to broadcasting vis-à-vis the implications for Nigerian broadcast professionals, I propose the technology appropriation paradigm (TAP) which I arrived at having considered and internalized the key tenets of the technological determinism theory, technology acceptance model, glocalization as well as homefrontism concepts. TAP states that if a technology must be put to optimal and best use, then its users must be able to adapt such a technology to meet the local and peculiar needs of those within their sociocultural milieu. I define appropriation as the suitable, acceptable, and correct use of technology (especially a new one) for the purpose of proffering solutions to local problems and enhancing the quality of life of people in localized communities. TAP entails the adaptation of global technologies to local communities the intention of which is to address or meet the local and peculiar needs of such communities.

Nigeria is localized and peculiar in diverse ways. First, it is an ethno-religious country unlike some other nations. Second, there is an insufferable gap between the country and a host of others in terms of technology adoption. Third, the majority of its broadcast professionals are underpaid, except those who manage to land jobs with federal government-owned stations, state-owned government stations, or private stations with national (and even international spread) like Channels Television and Arise Television. Fourth, owing to the third point, there is a high turnover rate of staff in private stations. Fifth, there are more private stations in the country compared to government-owned stations though this is an offshoot of the deregulation policy occasioned by the promulgation of Decree 38 of 1992. As of February 2023, statistics (the most recent) showed that there are a total of 740 broadcast stations in the country, most of which are owned by private individuals (Ayo-Olokun, 2023). Sixth, the Nigerian sociocultural space is different from those of other nations and this has largely shaped the country's media ethics and laws. Against the foregoing, I argue that TAP will best provide an impetus and drive for this discourse as it will help put Nigerian broadcast stations and broadcast practitioners properly into perspective.

Areas in Which AI Has Transformed Global Broadcasting

AI has left indelible marks on the global broadcasting sphere. Its stronghold is seen and felt in every aspect of the broadcast production chain, including program conceptualization, information gathering, broadcast writing, voicing, editing, packaging, and information dissemination. AI has deeply penetrated the global broadcasting space and chances are that it will, in years to come, completely overhaul, shape, and define what broadcasting is and what it is not. This is the exact point de-Lima-Santos and Mesquita (2021, p. 1416) underscore when they claim that "the future of journalism and its business models seem to be bound by the penetration of technological deployment" (as cited in Oyedokun, 2023, p. 3). With AI, broadcasting has been simplified, standardized, mutated, revolutionized, and glocalized. To begin with, AI has influenced program ideation and information gathering for broadcast professionals. With AI tools, broadcast professionals (especially presenters) can harvest a pool of program ideas which, when implemented, can help shoot their listenership/viewership rate to an unprecedented level. ChatGPT, Polly, or other related apps will provide a quantum of program ideas within the shortest possible time. The stress involved in broadcast research has also been significantly reduced. Emwinromwankhoe (2020, p. 9) notes that "for a broadcast station to remain on the top list of its audience, broadcast practitioners must regularly embark on research" geared toward conceptualizing programs that appeal to the demographic and psychographic tastes of the audience.

AI has also accelerated the process of news writing or broadcast scripting. With an AI-enabled application like Quakebot, for example, news stories are written within the shortest possible time. AI can scan through a large number of news and other websites, dig up a quantum of information, and write a timely story in an elegant, lapidary, or sophisticated style though such should be subject to revision(s) from the broadcast professional. AI can also travel through a collection of pictures and graphics and pick an image that can best be used to complement a story. AI is also used to verify or fact-check the contents of a broadcast write-up to ensure it is free from inaccuracy, illegalities, bias, or obscenity. Gone are the days when broadcast professionals expend much energy on fact-checking contents; with AI, fact-checking is achieved with the speed of lightning.

Moreover, AI has bettered the quality of broadcast audios and videos. With such AI tools as Adobe Premiere Pro, Wondershare, Filmora, and Runway, the quality of broadcast audios and videos can be swiftly enhanced to meet global standards. AI has equally improved audio or video editing. Gentile (2020) remarks that AI has relatively eased broadcast professionals' stress regarding the production and packaging of videos that are not only spellbinding, but can also stand the test of time. Furthermore, AI has given impetus to broadcast journalism, most especially electronic news gathering (ENG), live broadcast or outside broadcast (OB). With robotic and drone reporting, striking occurrences in crisis-ridden areas such as war zones and crime scenes are easily reported. Mountainous regions, hilly and undulated landscapes, rock tops, gullies, and remote places hitherto inaccessible to human journalists can be visited and clearly video graphed for news purposes. Realism in broadcasting is thus enhanced and in certain peculiar instances, AI can be used to simulate shots and videos that will enhance the believability of news stories.

In addition, AI has facilitated the conversion of broadcast contents from video to audio and vice-versa as well as translation from video (or audio) to text. Language translation for news and other programs is also seamlessly achieved. Riverside, Transcribe, Temi and Transkriptor, and Google Translate are some notable AI tools that can be used to achieve these. By so doing, AI has helped to enhance multimediality in broadcasting on the one hand and enhanced the experiences of those with sight and/or sound impairment on the other hand. Another key area where AI has impacted broadcasting is through its facial and voice detection capabilities. AI enables the easy detection of the faces and voices of people during interviews, discussion programs, and vox pops especially in countries maintaining a viable citizens' database. This lightens the burdens of broadcast professionals as they can easily focus on human intelligence-based aspects of broadcasting.

Perhaps the most remarkable development with AI is its ability to create virtual anchors, on-air-personalities, and presenters who can copy the voices of broadcast stations' renowned presenters and even carve a niche for themselves with their own dynamic voices. Though the creative abilities of such virtual anchors are limited because of their lack of a mind of their own (Lan & Zhou, 2023), they greatly help in reducing the everyday pressures of broadcast professionals. Lastly, the machine learning and algorithm features of AI have led to the customization, personalization, and tailoring of contents to meet the specific tastes of each member of the broadcast audience. For instance, if I visit the British Broadcasting Corporation (BBC)'s website and read a report of the ongoing Russian-Ukraine War, it will not take seconds before other related reports on the war will pop up for my reading pleasure. Thus, with AI, the uses and gratification abilities of the broadcast audience have been further strengthened.

Appropriating AI Tools for Mesmeric Broadcasting in Nigeria

I did argue earlier that Nigeria is peculiar in more ways than one and it is within the ambits of such peculiarities that Nigerian broadcast professionals function. Since AI has triggered the spread of the tentacles of broadcasting within the Nigerian space, it behooves Nigerian broadcast practitioners to appropriate AI tools for mesmeric broadcasting (Emwinromwankhoe & Akpan, 2022b) or as Akpan and Senam (2012) coined it, "sticky" broadcasting. Mesmeric broadcasting encompasses the form of broadcasting whereby broadcast contents providers intentionally and strategically produce, package and dish out standard, engaging and captivating contents that will keep audiences on the edge of their seats and increase listenership/viewership amidst the tremendous competition that AI has triggered within the industry. As Emwinromwankhoe and Akpan (2022b, p. 36) assert, "it is only when contents are highly mesmeric and appeal greatly to the audience that listenership and viewership would be attracted and subsequently sustained." This is because there is no middle ground as far as broadcasting is concerned: it is either the contents are mesmeric or nauseating.

To appropriate AI tools for mesmeric broadcasting, Nigerian broadcast professionals must consider some key factors the first of which involves the automation of content creation. In this age of AI-driven broadcasting, Nigerian broadcast professionals should not belabor themselves with the task of creating contents through manual, traditional, or orthodox means. Imagine how ludicrous it would be for someone to walk in the sun, dehydrated, and looking for the nearest shop to get a bottle of water when there is actually a bottle of chilled water in the person's bag. According to Akudoh et al. (2022), we are already in a period where AI can aid the skills of Nigerian broadcast professionals to engender the achievement of key tasks. Thus, Nigerian broadcast professionals must not expend significant energy on content creation when there are AI tools that can achieve that in a click.

Secondly, Nigerian broadcast professionals should toe the path of content personalization through accessible and affordable AI tools. It is exciting to know that some of the big names in Nigerian broadcasting, like the Nigerian Television Authority, Channels Television, and Arise Television already have such features enabled in their websites. For smaller stations however, the onus is on them to urgently borrow a leaf from the older ones. Content personalization will not only guarantee the satisfaction of their audience members but will also open the door through which other contents from such stations can be accessed thereby increasing listenership/viewership to an enviable level. This is because there is a correlation between broadcast content exposure and content consumption (Agbanu & Nwammuo, 2009; Owuamalam, 2008). Nigerian broadcast professionals must as well give primacy to real-time audience interactivity and feedback. Interactivity and feedback are mutually inclusive and the more a broadcast station opens its doors of interactivity through the use of AI tools, the more robust will be the feedback from audiences which can in turn be analyzed (using AI tools also) for improved broadcasting.

In addition, Nigerian broadcast professionals must ensure that they take cognizance of such significant factors as the religion(s), ethnicity(ies), culture(s), norm(s), and tradition(s) of their audiences in their use of AI tools for mesmeric broadcasting. Since Nigerian broadcast stations like their counterparts across the world are operating within sociocultural landscapes, they must ensure that the contents produced through AI tools do not violate the sociocultural dictates of the people. This point is sacrosanct due to the fact that most of the popular AI tools are manufactured in the West. For instance, it will be considered an anathema to see a Nigerian broadcast station develop AI news anchors whose dressing, speech, and mannerisms are hugely Western rather than local or who unequivocally support the LGBTQ+ movement. Lastly, cost-effectiveness and efficiency gains should underline Nigerian broadcast professionals' bid to appropriate AI for mesmeric broadcasting. For instance, it becomes disadvantageous when smaller broadcast stations try to adopt the same AI tools used by larger stations when they know they cannot afford them. Such smaller stations can go for alternatives which will give them the same (or better results). When the desirable is not available to these smaller stations, then the available should become desirable.

AI and the Question of Nigerian Broadcasting Ethics

There has always been an intersection between Nigerian broadcasting and ethics and in the era of AI, the question of broadcasting ethics has again been raised within the field of Nigerian media scholarship. Not only do we have the Nigeria Broadcasting Code, a publication of the National Broadcasting Commission which provides fundamental guidelines regarding what Nigerian broadcast professionals can air, the government across all levels, traditional rulers as well as religious leaders also have a stake regarding broadcast contents. The NBC, for instance, can wield its big stick by slamming fines on broadcast stations whose contents contravene its basic stipulations. Such fines are usually to the tune of millions of naira and although the body has always been excoriated because majority of its victims are the owners of private stations, the fact remains that Nigerian broadcast professionals must tread cautiously in order not to get themselves engaged in a battle of any sort with the NBC or the Nigerian Government. Where such offenses regarding content are considered grievous and unpardonable, the NBC reserves the right to revoke the license of such a station (Agbanu & Nwammuo, 2009).

On the part of religious and traditional leaders, they will not shy away from raising eyebrows and engaging in public outcry should a broadcast content go against religious or traditional principles. The backlash that trailed Peak Milk's advertising campaign on last year's Easter Friday tagged *Bruised and Pierced for Us* wherein the company displayed a punctured and pressed tin of Peak Milk and alluded to it as Jesus Christ the Messiah is a case in point. With the criticisms the ad garnered within the Christian circle, the company was forced to tender an open apology to Christians (*The Punch*, 2023). In another instance, a former Oba of Benin once expressed discontent with a program relayed on NTA Benin, stressing that it was painting the revered Benin traditional practices in a bad light to viewers and the station had no other option but to stop airing the program.

Aside from the above, there is accuracy, fairness, balance, and objectivity which are the basic ethics of the broadcast profession and which Nigerian broadcast professionals should abide by in the course of performing their tasks. Since AI relies on online data to function, its outputs will certainly be prone to fake news, misinformation, and disinformation. This is because research (Apuke, 2016; Dare, 2011) has indicated that most online information lacks authenticity. Besides, AI, in its gathering, analysis, and interpretation of information for broadcast purpose, can come up with a piece of information that will be considered an affront to traditional rulers or certain religious adherents in the country. The gruesome murder of Deborah Samuel, a Year 2 Home Economics student of the Shehu Shagari College of Education is a strong reminder to Nigerian broadcast practitioners on the need to always put ethics forward in their business of content production and dissemination. An omission of any sort will neither be tolerated nor excused by the authorities involved and even though the broadcast station concerned is not eventually closed down, having its name smeared in a debacle of any kind because of information that runs afoul of acceptable ethics is enough to negatively affect listenership/viewership. In light of the above, I provide some significant insights as contained in the succeeding part of the article.

AI and Broadcast Transformation: Implications for Nigerian Broadcast Professionals

The point has been accentuated that AI has brought enormous transformations to the global broadcast ecology and broadcast professionals across the world are already tapping into its vast benefits for better broadcasting. In order to appropriate AI tools and raise the ante of Nigerian broadcasting in line with global best practices, the following are required from Nigerian broadcast professionals:

Acquisition and Regular Update of AI Skills

Nigerian broadcast professionals should make tenacious efforts toward acquiring AI skills for effective broadcast production. The owners of broadcast stations can greatly help in this regard by organizing staff training sessions within the organization and (where they can afford it) sponsoring their trips for training within and outside the shores of the country. Admittedly, it takes a colossal sum to daily and optimally run a broadcast station but stations' owners must remember that an investment in their staff is an investment in the station itself, and will unarguably enhance output and productivity. These training sessions should be regular in order to enable the staff to keep updating their skills in line with the unending demands of AI technologies. Technologies, by their nature, are never constant. They keep undergoing improvements, iterations, and developments. Thus, the acquisition of AI skills and regular updates of such are imperative for Nigerian broadcast professionals because, as the saying goes, only an enlightened fish can effectively navigate deep waters.

Acquisition of ICT Gadgets

All AI tools require ICT gadgets such as smart phones, iPhones, tablets, iPads, and laptops to function and for Nigerian broadcast professionals to appropriate such AI tools for mesmeric broadcasting, it is expedient that they have such ICT gadgets handy. Needless to say, in this age and time, any broadcast professional without a smartphone is as good as a square peg in a round hole and such a staff should be replaced without second thought. Our world keeps moving forward technologically minute by minute such that a gadget that is in vogue at this moment might be replaced by another in a short while if the manufacturers do not seek ways of sustaining audience satisfaction. To this end, possession of ICT gadgets in this era of AI by broadcast professionals is completely non-negotiable for Nigerian broadcast professionals.

Collaborations

If there is any time when the saying that "no man is an island" is most apt, then it is in this era of AI. Nigerian broadcast professionals, especially those working in small broadcast stations, should seek ways to collaborate or synergize with other broadcast professionals for the purposes of pooling resources together, gaining easy access to AI tools, and putting such tools to good use. Abiola (2023) contends that this is not a time for Nigerian broadcast journalists to strive to thrive independently as many moves will stunt the industry's progress regarding the appropriation of AI tools. This collaboration should be both internal (between and among staff within a broadcast station) and external (with broadcast practitioners in other stations). Two will always be better than one and the more the number of persons in the synergy, the better the results.

Thorough Verification of Information

Fake news, misinformation, and disinformation are some of the thorns which AI has brought into the broadcasting space. Since AI relies on a vast pool of online information to generate, analyze, code, and interpret data, it is possible for inaccuracies to underline some of the data produced. As a consequence, Nigerian broadcast professionals must rise on their oars by adopting reliable fact-checking AI tools and even going a step further to manually check, double-check, triple-check, and quadruple-check information supplied by AI for accuracy and credibility. Broadcast professionals should always remember how much havoc the dissemination of wrong information can wreak on the station's image and should make frantic efforts to guard against that. Broadcast gatekeepers (or editors) have a pivotal role to play in this regard.

Glocalization of Broadcast Contents

Nigerian broadcast professionals must ensure that their contents are glocal, that is, they should meet the taste of local audiences as much as they meet the taste of global audiences. Broadcast contents in this AI era should be packaged in a way that will appeal to the culture(s), religion(s), tradition(s), and other peculiarities of the Nigerian populace. Silverbird Television, for instance, has been criticized again and again for its westernization of contents in spite of the 70:30 ratio of local versus foreign contents spelled out by NBC. Thus, the age of AI necessitates the call for Nigerian broadcast professionals to always glocalize, rather than westernize their contents.

Partnership with Technology-Based Companies

Nigerian broadcast professionals should make efforts to partner with technology-based companies in order to efficiently appropriate AI tools for enhanced broadcasting. For example, NVIDIA, a major technology-based company in Nigeria, once organized an inception program for startups wherein it trained some interested Nigerians on the use of AI tools. The same NVIDIA is credited to be the company to develop Africa's first speech-to-text AI chat tool capable of understanding 200 African accents (Abiola, 2023). There is also the Data Science Nigeria and a host of other technology-based companies that Nigerian broadcast professionals can partner with for the purpose of acquiring AI skills and purchasing AI tools at lower rates. This argument is hinged on the premise that the monetary demands for acquiring such AI skills and tools will no doubt be discounted against the background of such partnerships.

Investment in AI-driven Advertising

Nigerian broadcast stations and broadcast professionals alike can make so much money if they decide to appropriate AI tools for advertising purposes. Abiola (2023) describes AI-driven advertising as a cash cow that is yet to be bought by Nigerian broadcast professionals. All that large broadcast stations in the country have enjoyed so far are the monetary returns from Facebook, Google, and YouTube Ads, but these are just a tip of the iceberg. Nigerian broadcast professionals should expand their horizons by leveraging and appropriating such AI-driven ad channels as Amazon Advertising, Adobe Advertising Cloud, The Trade Desk, MediaMath, and Criteo, to mention only a few. All they need to do after appropriating such AI-based ad tools is pitch the ideas to some of their top advertisers and other prospective clients and the ad returns will start rolling in.

Final Thoughts

It is no news that AI has permeated the global broadcasting terrain, and is heavily impacting on the generation, production, packaging, and relaying of broadcast contents. As an offshoot of global technological advancements, AI has arguably widened the technological gap that has long existed between Western nations and their African counterparts and within Nigeria, the major challenge has been how broadcast professionals will effectively adopt AI tools for seamless and mesmerized broadcasting. While it is an acknowledged fact that most Nigerian broadcast stations are not as financially and technologically equipped as their counterparts in the West, these stations can actually put what they have to best use and achieve the same (and even greater) results with stations in Western nations. This is where technology appropriation comes into play. Nigerian broadcast professionals must constantly appropriate AI tools to meet the sociocultural needs of Nigerian broadcast audiences who are diverse in terms of religion, ethnicity, culture, norms, and traditions and must acquire and update their AI skills, acquire ICT gadgets, engage in collaborations, thoroughly verify information, glocalize broadcast contents, partner with technology-based companies, and engage in AI-driven advertising. While some media scholars are worried that AI might in the near future culminate in the retrenchment of broadcast professionals, I object to this and rather argue that AI, at its best, gives us a picture of the inexplicable and inexhaustible potentials of the human brain. With AI, the table of Nigerian broadcasting is already shaking and albeit Nigerian broadcast professionals are already late to the AI party, they must immediately get on board and start appropriating AI tools. The owners of broadcast stations have so much to do in this regard, especially by committing themselves to the financial aspects through regular training, proper remuneration, and enhanced welfare packages. The Nigerian Government at various levels should also come in by providing a stable power supply and subsidizing the prices of AI tools and ICT gadgets so that broadcast professionals can easily afford them.

References

Abiola, R. (2023). *Once again, the Nigerian media is late to the artificial intelligence party, when is it our time?* http://www.technext24.com/2023/11/14/nigerian-media-artificial-intelligence/

Agbanu, V. N., & Nwammuo, A. N. (2009). *Broadcast media*. Rhyce Kerex Publishers.

Akpan, U., & Senam, N. (2012). Broadcasting in a sticky way: Revisiting creativity on the Airwaves. *Benin Mediacom Journal, 5*, 97–106.

Akudoh, U., Nsude, I., & Oyeleke, A. (2022). Awareness of artificial intelligence for news production among journalists in Ebonyi State Nigeria. *International Journal of Network and Communication Research, 7*(1), 33–45.

Apuke, O. D. (2016). Nigerian journalists' knowledge and perceptions of brown envelope syndrome on journalism practice: A study of journalists in the Jalingo metropolis. *International Journal of Humanities & Social Studies, 3*(2), 319–334.

Associated Press. (2022). *Artificial intelligence in local news: A survey of US newsrooms' AI readiness*. Associated Press.

Ayo-Olokun, A. (2023). *With 740 functional broadcast stations in Nigeria, Industry craves for reforms*. https://www.ndr.org.ng/with-740-functional-broadcast-stations-in-nigeria-industry-craves-for-reforms/

Dare, S. (2011). The rise of citizen journalism in Nigeria—The case of Sahara Reporters. http://www.reutersinstitute.politics.ex.ac.uk/about/articles/the-rise-of-citizen-journalism-in-Nigeria

de-Lima-Santos, MF., Mesquita, L. (2021). The strategic value of data journalism. In R. Salaverría, M. F. de-Lima-Santos (Eds.), *Journalism, Data and Technology in Latin America. Palgrave Studies in Journalism and the Global South*. Palgrave Macmillan. https://doi.org/10.1007/978-3-030-65860-1_4

Emwinromwankhoe, O. (2020). Transformed broadcasting, transformed audience: Implications for broadcast practitioners in Nigeria. *Uniuyo Journal of Communication Studies, 3*(1), 1–12.

Emwinromwankhoe, O., & Akpan, U. (2022a). Rethinking broadcasting in an age of user-generated content. In E. Asemah, D. Ekhareafo, & T. Santas (Eds.), *Discourses on Communication and Media Studies in Contemporary Society* (pp. 145–153). Jos University Press.

Emwinromwankhoe, O., & Akpan, U. (2022b). Listenership and viewership in a time of hypercompetitive broadcasting in relation to the dictum that content is king. In E. Asemah, D. Ekhareafo, & T. Santas (Eds.), *Discourses on Communication and Media Studies in Contemporary Society* (pp. 32–39). Jos University Press.

Gentile, A. (2020). *How AI is changing TV production for the better*. http://www.googlr.com/amp/www.smpte.org/blog/how-ai-changing--tv-production-better%3fhs_amp=true

Hanson, R. (2005). *Mass communication: Living in a media world*. McGraw Hill Inc.

International Media Support. (2021). *The next wave of disruption: Emerging market media use of artificial intelligence and machine learning*. International Media Support.

Kuyucu, M. (2019, April 25–26). *Artificial intelligence in media: Radio automation systems as the first artificial intelligence application in media in terms of threats and opportunities*. A Paper Presented at the 4th International New Media Conference.

Lan, C., & Zhou, R. (2023). Artificial intelligence technology in the field of broadcasting and hosting. In G. Gigoras & P. Lorenz (Eds.), *Advances in artificial intelligence, big data and algorithms* (pp. 41–47). IOS Press.

Organisation for Economic Cooperation and Development. (2007). *Participative web: User-created content*. OECD Publishing.

Owuamalam, E. (2008). *Elements of broadcasting*. Top Class Agencies Ltd.

Oyedokun, I. (2023). *Effects of adopting artificial intelligence presenters in broadcasting on audience perception and gratification of broadcast content*. http://wwww.researcggate.net/

Punch. (2023). *Peak Milk apologizes to Christians over 'offensive' Easter advert*. http://www.punchng.com/just-in-peak-milk-apologises-to-can-over-offensive-easter-advert/

CHAPTER 4

Artificial Intelligence and Automated Educational Broadcasting in Nigeria: A Futuristic Technesis for Today's Consideration

Ubong Andem Obong

Introduction

Artificial intelligence (AI) is an emerging technological force that is technically transforming industrial practices and operations. In virtually every human-dominated sector, profession, and endeavour, there is a corresponding artificial intelligence striving to augment human intelligence, functions, and efforts (Bharadiya et al., 2023). Perhaps, AI's instrumentality and epistemic value in augmenting and threatening to replace human intelligence in mitigating complex, complicated, and myriads of dynamic challenges in splits of seconds is making human physical effort

U. A. Obong (✉)
Taraba State University, Jalingo, Nigeria
e-mail: ubong.obong@tsuniversity.edu.ng

U. S. Akpan (ed.), *Educational Broadcasting in Nigeria in the Age of Artificial Intelligence*,
https://doi.org/10.1007/978-3-031-68530-9_4

appear like a shadow of itself. This justifies why its applicability and relevance in solving real-time issues and problems within industrial contexts have become far-reaching, compelling, robust, and irreconcilable.

Quite uncompromising and boundless are AI's affordances in addressing specific, specialized, and assigned tasks in practical terms. Its high utility value lies in its relentlessness, consistency, spontaneity, and speed in performing dedicated and contextual functions with clinical precision without fatigue, stress, or complaint. The sophistication, perceived ease of use, expected performance, effort expectancy, social influence, and facilitating conditions associated with AI are the yardsticks that are presumably influencing and encouraging its wide adoption, acceptance, and use across industrial, organizational, and cultural contexts.

However, within the broadcasting industry, AI's influence has been disruptive, profound, and very instrumental in revolutionizing age-long industrial practices and systems that were exclusively subjected to human intelligence and efforts. AI's adoption in the broadcast industry specifically enhances and improves the efficiency and productivity of broadcast professionalism. Especially, in broadcast-related areas, environments, or contexts not particularly suitable or conducive for human professionals (Singh et al., 2013).

Before the proliferation of AI within the broadcasting domain, the broadcast industry historically relied on human creativity, effort, and intelligence in producing and presenting broadcast programs for members of audience in the public (Khan, 2023). The objectionable errors, shortcomings, flaws, mistakes, inadequacies, or setbacks in broadcast operationalization orchestrated by the vulnerability of human nature could only be imagined. Thus, making it quite obvious that human experts in the field of broadcasting were not infallible to errors due to their lack of immunity to fatigue-related negligence and stress-related blunders that often come with handling their retinues of routine broadcast operations. Most especially when working under pressure and tight schedules.

This development, more than anything else, must have opened the vistas of techno-savvy stakeholders in the broadcast sector on the need for smart and intelligent expert systems or machines to serve as auxiliaries to human functions and performances. With this renewed thinking, a sort of technological renaissance must have been inspired and heralded by the craze, trend, and demand for smart, soft, programmatic, and intelligent working tools to accomplish highly-specialized broadcast processes. This situation must have availed broadcast automation a sense of occasion, adventure, opportunity, or necessity to thrive. As Khan (2023) notes, broadcast operations are experiencing a seismic upheaval as a result of the adoption, utilization, or integration of AI innovations in mainstream practice.

AI is often touted as possessing multi-tasking features and profundities. Such features and profundities enable it to handle or perform variegated and dedicated broadcast-related tasks with (logical) consistency and clinical precision compared to human efforts. Hence, broadcast stations that leverage automation processes seem to have been relieved of the burden of putting undue quality control pressure on human experts which often amounts to nothing.

Moreover, with automated protocols and resources being integrated into the broadcast process, the level of inconsistencies, errors, shortcomings, and limitations in broadcast operations which, on many occasions, 'creep' into the professional practice by virtue of the infallibility of human nature are eliminated. This is because AI's programmatic protocols and resources ensure a high level of task efficiency (Yelwa et al., 2020). The possibility of its affordances being leveraged to perform more sophisticated and specialized broadcast-related tasks such as educational broadcasting abound in the future.

From the foregoing perspectives, notwithstanding the snail-speed associated with the adoption and application of AI in mainstream broadcast operations in Nigeria, automated educational broadcasting when implemented in the country will be the game changer. This chapter offers a forward-looking technological discourse for today's consideration on the need for automation of educational broadcasting in Nigeria.

Theoretical Framework

The theoretical frameworks that underpin this futuristic technesis are provided for by two techno-deterministic theoretical traditions: the Unified Theory of Acceptance and Use of Technology (UTAUT) and Media Ecology theory. Media ecology theory is a technological deterministic theory that seeks to explain how novel technological innovations (tech-novations) such as AI and automated protocols are extending, disrupting, or augmenting human functions and intelligence within social and industrial contexts. It specifically expounds on the ecological relevance of AI and automation processes as dominant tech-novations of the time, especially, on how they affect human work environments (West & Turner, 2014).

The theoretical concepts that laid the groundwork for the development of the theory was proposed by Marshall McLuhan in 1964. But the theory got its description from Neil Postman who in 1968 was noted to have first popularized the concept 'Media Ecology' (Gencarelli, 2006). 'Ecology', understood within the context of this theory, presupposes the physical environment, milieu, setting, or context in which the media tech-novations of the time are applied or are used as it pertains to their disruptive impacts on how society organizes itself. From the perspectives of McLuhan (1964) and Postman (2006), Media Ecology theory is a framework for providing analysis on the matter of how tech-novations affect, enhance, or augment human intelligent functions in ways that interaction, adoption, or experimentation with the tech-novations either facilitates or impedes man's chances of survival.

The theory strongly advocates that the tech-novations that dominate a given period of time act as the extensions of man (McLuhan, 1964). This includes how man's senses are organized so that perception, feeling, tastes, experiences, attitudes, behaviors, reactions, opinions, and thinking are imposed or influenced in certain ways.

Going by the overwhelming impact that AI exerts on virtually all human disciplines including broadcasting, it makes it very interesting to expound its likely impact in attempting to disrupt the crust upon which professional educational broadcasting is founded. The core tenets of the theory provide lucid explanations on the felt and expected impacts of AI in driving automated educational broadcasting in Nigeria. But beyond explanations on AI's proposed impacts in mainstream educational broadcasting in Nigeria, it is also of essence to establish the conditions that AI must meet before it is adopted and utilized for impact to be cultivated. This is the intersecting point where a discourse on Unified Theory of Acceptance and Use of Technology (UTAUT) becomes necessary.

The *UTAUT* is a well-articulated theoretical underpinning that explicates users' perception, intention, and behavior associated with the adoption of tech-innovations such as AI and broadcast automation across social, cultural, and industrial settings. As propounded by Viswanath Venkatesh, Michael Morris, Gordon Davis, and Fred Davis in 2003, the theory suggests that AI and automated protocols must have performance expectancy (PE), effort expectancy (EE), social influence (SI), and facilitating conditions (FC) before they can be accepted, adopted, and utilized by stakeholders in the Nigerian broadcasting industry.

Performance Expectancy (PE) implies that AI and automated protocols can only be accepted and used when stakeholders' expectations of their potentials in performing specialized broadcast-related tasks optimally are met. If AI and automated protocols perform as expected, they will be accepted and utilized in resolving subsequent issues. If not, they are rejected or discarded forthwith.

Effort Expectancy (EE) implies that beyond AI and automated protocols meeting performance expectations, they must be relatively easy to use by concerned stakeholders. This implies that their users' interface must be made with relative ease and should not be overtly technical and complicated.

Social Influence (SI) implies that before AI and automated protocols are accepted, they must have social relevance and applicability. They should have a reputation for resolving issues pertaining to educational broadcasting of concerned stakeholders in society. It is on the strength of this, that their perception of efficacy and efficiency is based.

Facilitating Conditions (FC) implies AI and automated protocols to serve as extensions of human functions, efforts, and intelligence in educational broadcast operations. They should be able to facilitate and augment broadcast professionalism and practices that could be done by human experts and intelligence.

AI and Broadcast Automation: A Conceptual Clarification

A plethora of definitions on AI abound. Some of those definitions consider AI as a programmatic intelligence demonstrated by machines in performing specific activities (Mohammed, 2019); or the study of computer systems that attempts to model and apply the intelligence of the human mind (Baum, 2023). Other definitions stress that it is a computer-controlled robot, or a software that thinks intelligently, in a similar manner the intelligent humans think (Nnamdi & Nwanyanwu, 2021; TutorialsPoint, 2015); or an innovative system that display intelligent behaviour by analyzing their environment and taking action with some degree of autonomy to achieve specific goals (European Commission, 2018). Manning (2020) sees AI as a clever machine that can learn and assimilate task-related queries, at least somewhat like human beings do. Boucher (2020) avers that AI is an all-encompassing concept that entails a wide range of smart technologies and programs that have no outstanding feature other than their clever display of intelligence which is highly contextual and controversial in interpretation.

From the above pool of definitions, it can simply be said that AI entails expert systems, softwares, or protocols programmed to carry out specialized, dedicated, smart, or intelligent functions, queries, tasks, or behaviors in contexts that would have otherwise been subjected to human intelligence, efforts, and expertise. As an expert system, AI 'is a machine system in which useful human knowledge is added to machine memory in order to give intelligent advice and offer explanations and justifications of its decisions or demands' (Singh et al., 2013, p. 1). It relies on a large database of well-defined and specialized knowledge about a particular area used by human experts in contrast to knowledge gathered from textbooks (Singh et al., 2013).

Within the context of broadcasting, the autonomy of human experts in the field of broadcasting grant AI to augment some specialized broadcast functions, queries, tasks or behaviours is the idea that connotes broadcast automation. Thus, broadcast automation specifies the designation and delegation of some or all of broadcast operational practices, functions, performances, tasks, responsibilities, or duties to intelligent machines or smart/expert systems to handle or control in place of human experts. It is the deployment of AI expert systems to serve as extensions of human functions or efforts in broadcasting.

Broadcast automated processes, functions, and services are all-encompassing, starting from the newsroom and terminating at the final on-air transmission (Hussein, 2015). Broadcast automation systems are deployed in the broadcast industry to help achieve tasks that would not have been possible using physical or manual labor (Cockett, 2024). With the innovation, stakeholders in the broadcast industry have to do more professional activities with less physical effort. Broadcast automation allows broadcasters to change or schedule their broadcast operations and systems on a predetermined basis that serve stakeholders' interests.

AI, Broadcast Automation, Educational Broadcasting, and Nigeria in Context

The level of AI's adoption and utilization in Nigeria's broadcasting is still a mirage. Practical knowledge and evidence are lacking concerning the number of broadcast stations that have fully adopted or integrated AI affordances in their operations. Thus, there is paucity of verifiable statistics on broadcast stations and operations in the country that have been automated. AI's adoption and utilization among broadcast stakeholders in the country is sparse, increasingly low, and inconsequential in mainstream broadcast professionalism. This sad reality is set against the backdrop of Nigeria's front-lining position in establishing a national centre for artificial intelligence dubbed the National Centre for Artificial Intelligence and Robotics (NCAIR) in 2020 (Effoduh, 2021).

So many factors are responsible for this trend. Some are rooted in the fact that there is a growing fear and paranoia among concerned stakeholders in the Nigerian broadcast industry that once AI affordances are fully engaged to drive broadcast automation, human experts would be redundant, retrenched, and eliminated. This is consequent on the fact that AI poses significant risk in replacing human jobs (Abuselidze & Mamaladze, 2021; Menghan, 2022; Yue, 2023). From this perspective is the unfounded speculation that AI's automated processes would render their human counterparts jobless and irrelevant in the process, practice, and art of broadcasting. To remain relevant and in-charge, these crop of myopic stakeholders supposedly exercised caution and restraint on wanton adoption and utilization of AI and automated processes in broadcasting so as to avoid shooting themselves in the leg.

Other factors necessitating the poor adoption and utilization of AI and automated broadcasting in Nigeria are epileptic and insufficient electricity to effectively power the AI applications; paucity of requisite infrastructure; low purchasing power parity to acquire and maintain AI tools; rising cost and instability of Internet connection; lack of training and workshops for AI handlers (Nnamdi & Nwanyanwu, 2021); poor attitude towards AI innovations; lack of technological skill sets to operate AI automated tools, resources, and protocols; and lack of technical and technological frameworks to integrate AI tools, resources, and protocols in mainstream broadcasting.

The foregoing implies that factors militating against robust adoption and utilization of AI and broadcast automation in Nigeria are multi-dimensional. Hence, this further affirms that broadcast journalists and other industry stakeholders are yet to fully embrace AI in their broadcast professionalism, and talk less of engaging robust broadcast automation (Nnamdi & Nwanyanwu, 2021).

This situation, however, leaves the fate of educational broadcasting in Nigeria hanging on the gallows of its sordid state. Educational broadcasting in the country, for obvious technological and technical reasons, has failed to meet its full objectives. This is owing to the lack of a functional policy on educational broadcasting; audience's declining interest in educational contents; the abysmal level of electricity power supply; lack of collaboration among broadcasters and educationists (Ijeh & Ojebode, 2015; Oyinloye & Adeleye, 2010); inefficient educator - learner interactivity, engagement, exchange, and feedback (Chandar & Sharma, 2003); lack of interpersonal discussions necessary for formative evaluations (Mann, 2010); flaws in the instructional design and strategies (Cemca, 2011); production issues; technical and technological glitches; wrong educational programming and scheduling; educator-induced constraints; and abstractual educational contents that distant learners find difficult to assimilate.

With these challenges besetting educational broadcasting in Nigeria, much is desired on how it can be harnessed and optimized to reach its full potential. Perhaps, automation of all its processes by AI resources can help it meet its core tripartite learning objectives: educator-learners' robust engagement and interface; exploratory and collaborative learning experiences and ambiance for learners; as well as predictive and simulated learning and problem-solving interfaces where lessons are matched with augmented exemplifications, analogies, and learning aids to create imagery. As automation of educational broadcasting is yet to be fully entrenched in Nigeria, the affordances of AI-assisted learning resources that would have been the game changer are yet to materialize. The parlous state of AI adoption and utilization in the country in this regard is robbing educational broadcasting of the advantage to engage target-driven, programmatic, algorithmic, and niche-based learning.

The Multi-layered Effects of AI and Automated Educational Broadcasting in Nigeria

The need for automated broadcasting in Nigeria is anchored on the premises that it would enhance human interactions in the learning environments (Oyeleye & Ademosu, 2021); improve on the processes of educational data production; engender substitution of human error-prone tutors in carrying out certain journalistic activities that concerns education; and amplifying learning interaction with the audience (Noain-Sánchez, 2022).

As the application of AI in broadcast journalism practice enhances human efforts and intelligence (Obong & Banigo, 2023), and improve media efficiency and effectiveness (Fayoyin, 2021), it is expected that it will bring monumental breakthroughs when it is applied in advancing the frontiers of educational broadcasting in Nigeria. It will, nevertheless, alter and disrupt the mediated learning processes, contexts, and landscape. The alternating and disruptive impacts of automated broadcasting are likely to be multi-dimensional but producing six inter-linked layers of effects as discussed with an illustration in Fig. 4.1.

Context Effect: This will be felt in the learning context, encounter, and environment. AI and automated protocols will significantly impact the learning encounter to the extent that the traditional tutor-learner roles and boundaries will be blurred and seamless. Learners will be confined to mediated platforms against physical classroom settings. They will be limited in interacting interpersonally as they will have to interact with simulated learning tools, aids, and interfaces in place of human tutors. Context-specific issues often occasioned by the peculiarities of the active participants in the learning encounter and process will be eroded and replaced with technology-based contexts with significant psychological toil and impedance on the learners.

Technological/Technical Effects: With the widening gap in technology acquisition and use among the elites and the poor masses, there is likely to be a kind of technological decimation effect heralded by AI and automated tech-innovations in the learning encounter. Indigent learners will be technologically denied access to educational resources in the automated broadcasting arrangement while the elites will be overly saturated with AI learning resources. In addition to the sociological disequilibrium that AI and automated broadcasting will herald in the Nigerian society, it

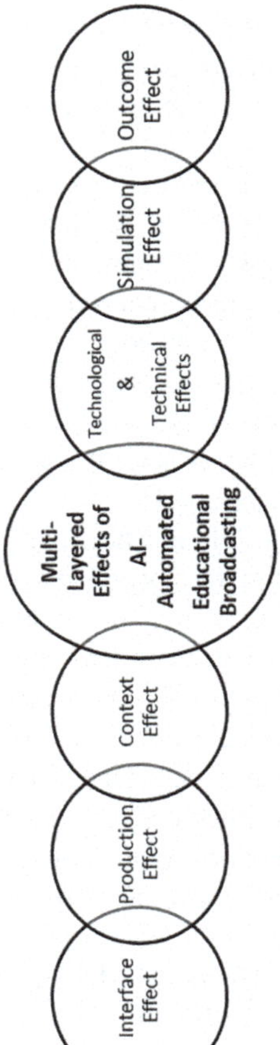

Fig. 4.1 Multi-layered effects of AI and automated educational broadcasting in Nigeria

is expected that over-reliance on AI will usher in a culture of technological addiction to its affordances. Addiction to AI resources will orchestrate a culture among techno-addicts to boycott mainstream academic settings and physical/manifest learning resources, processes, and materials.

Production Effect: The production of requisite artificial educational data needed to impart knowledge will orchestrate a significant effect in the simulated learning process. As learning resources are programmed ab initio, their delivery is likely to be fixated leaving limited room for context-specific adjustments. Having the vast learning data and resources gleaned from data centres and repositories for learners of all categories, the programmers will have a duty to manage and integrate these data to meet the target learners' unique and evolving learning concerns and outcomes. This frequent data management and integration to meet evolving learning concerns and outcomes of composite learners will exert considerable level of effects on the programmers to over-rely on algorithmic engagements (instead of interactions with the learners) to gain insights for educational data production.

Simulation Effect: AI-driven educational broadcasting aims to substitute human experts with automated protocols in carrying out certain educational broadcast activities. Human efforts will be augmented with simulated interfaces powered by AI. The tutors' physical presence which, in some 'traditional' sense, often invokes a sense of seriousness, discipline, and dedication among the learners within the Nigerian learning context will be blurred and obscured. As AI moderates the learning process, an overlapping field of experience that is often bound by shared emotions; empathy; homophily; and perceptible senses of touch, sight, hearing, smell, taste, and proximity between participants in the learning encounter cannot be guaranteed. AI and automated protocols are likely to herald an impersonal learning culture and context where human tutors have no business in the learning process.

Interface Effect: The simulation that comes with AI and automated learning experience via the smart broadcast mediated interface will engender interface effect. The interface for AI and automated educational broadcasting will be contextually programmed using programmatic tutors for mediated learners to interact and engage. This simulated interface will be one-way traffic, that is, programmed for learners to engage. Hence, robbing the mediated learners of the opportunity to discuss and dialogue with human teachers as characteristic of physical learning context.

Outcome Effect: The lack of measuring systems to analyze and evaluate the outcome of automated educational broadcasting in tandem with the learning outcomes and objectives of mediated learners present some outcome effects for consideration. As AI's performance in educational broadcasting is yet to be evaluated with precision using approved tools, the notion of whether it can or cannot meet the varied learning objectives and outcomes of mediated learners remains uncertain.

The Proposed Benefits of Automated Educational Broadcasting in Nigeria

Automated educational broadcasting is expected to be the game changer when fully implemented, integrated, or adopted in mainstream broadcast operations. It is expected to yield positive results in the following ways:

i. **Audio-visual exemplification of abstract learning concepts**: Understanding is likely to be profound as AI would model abstract concepts and learning aids in order to create imagery and mental spark among the learners. This entails that every explanation and analogy engaged in the learning process would be backed up with simulated visual representations, pictorials, infographics, and actions so as to concretize abstract phenomena that may breed misunderstanding and confusion. This will be a big win for Science, Technology, Engineering, and Mathematics (STEM) subject matters that are often riddled with rocket-science terminologies without visual or pictorial clarifications that the learners can relate with. Hence, any concept that the learners cannot easily relate with in their immediate environment will be substituted using AI simulated interface and visualization tools.

ii. **Targeted and niched-driven learning**: With advances in AI's remote sensing; geotagging; data mining; social listening; data mapping; cataloging and metadata detection; content and service personalization; audience analysis; content indexing and search; forecasting; and automated content creation, learning via the automated interface will be more niched-driven, personalized, and targeted at the right demographics. This will drastically eliminate trial and error and the culture of propagating unstructured instructional data to 'whom it may concern' using human intelligence.

iii. **Automated educational data production**: Educational data needed to build requisite knowledge will be subjected to programmatic processes and approved computer-scientific methodologies that are free from human errors, moribund curricula, outdated syllabi or second guessing approaches. As instructional materials will be tapped from globally-rated data centers and repositories of knowledge, the mediated learner will be given the opportunity to enjoy the current state of knowledge in their respective academic fields as well as gaining advantaged exposure to reservoirs of knowledge that are of global standard.

iv. **Consistency in logical reasoning and delivery pattern**: Contradictions, fallacies, trials and errors, second guessing, discrepancies, and inconsistencies in presentation, argumentation, and delivery of educational data which are often associated with human tutors (especially when subjected under undue pressure) are likely to be a thing of the past. With automated learning resources being programmed to follow certain protocols, conventions, and patterns, there is likely to be some sort of logical consistency and precision in the way those resources will be presented or delivered to learners. Hence, uniformity and objectivity in learning approaches are guaranteed with automated educational broadcasting.

v. **Precision**: As AI is involved in automated broadcasting, precision is likely to be achieved from all engagement ends. From the time set for educational broadcast to start; the duration of the lessons to be delivered; time slot for each of the segments to be treated; the learning aids to be used, infographics, statistics, information sources, and authorities; the language of instruction; mode of presentations; teaching methods and styles to be adopted; to the time set for educational broadcast to end, precision will be engaged optimally. Digression, time wastage, over-concentration on frivolities, poor time management, etc., will be totally eliminated.

vi. **Efficiency in educational programming and scheduling**: Broadcast automation will help broadcast stations in Nigeria to improve on the level of educational broadcast productivity by assisting them in real-time and efficient educational broadcast programming, planning, and scheduling. Huge burdens will be taken off the shoulders of station managers, heads of station operations, and directors of programming in enforcing strict adherence to the stations' running order. Once the stations are fully automated, educational program schedules can be done at predetermined occasions to cover specific periods of time/duration while the human experts that used to man those functions can go to rest with enough time on their hands.

vii. **Big data analysis, management, integration, and on-the-spot data insights**: The challenges educational broadcasters on traditional broadcast media used to go through in making references to existing data, statistics, extant literature, and relevant sources of information to buttress ideas will be drastically reduced. By leveraging AI's metadata detection, indexing, and search protocols and resources, vast arrays of informational and educational data can be retrieved from global internet-based data centers and repositories of knowledge and made available to learners in refined and meaningful patterns within a split of seconds. Hence, learners will be given insights from the massive pool of data available for learning in such a way that the stress, rigor, and fatigue of having to comb or wade through printed materials in search of limited information on a subject is eliminated. The massive pool of related data sought and retrieved will be integrated into the learners' learning experience for seamless understanding of subject matter of discourse.

viii. **Seamless problem-solving**: The hallmark of automated educational broadcasting will be solving diverse subject-related problems in the learning encounter without batting the eyelids. The seamless interaction between automated interfaces and data centers or repositories of knowledge powered by AI will enable relevant data to be retrieved in nano-seconds to solve context-specific problems in the learning process/encounter.

The Dangers Ahead

The proposed benefits of automated educational broadcast processes notwithstanding, there will also be some counterbalancing effects. The dangers ambushing educational broadcasting in the future are as follows:

i. **Information overload**: The massive volume of data that programmatic educational expert systems will make available for automated educational broadcasting to thrive are likely going to be too much for the learners to assimilate in each given context of learning. This will lead to information overload and the consequence being confusion as to what to do with too much information.

ii. **Lack of spontaneous learning contexts**: In a typical interpersonal learning encounter, there are often frequent occurrences of on-the-spot-contexts that either tend to enrich the learning encounter or threaten its outcome as a result of change or fluctuation in the tutor-learner behaviors, attitudes, emotions, or mannerisms. Such spontaneous contexts would demand spontaneous interventions between/among the participants for the learning objectives to be achieved. For example, a learner dozing off or a tutor showing signs of tiredness during the learning process needs the intervention of one another to improve the learning outcomes. Hence, the tutor has a duty to wake the dosing learner by either tapping or asking that the learner stand up and the learners too have a duty to politely ask the tutor to take a break. At whatever end, each of the participants aims at making an attempt to impact the learning encounter on the spur of the moment. This can hardly be established in the case of automated broadcasting. This is because it is programmed with protocols and conventions that are tasked to perform specific learning objectives with little or no consideration for context-specific issues that may arise in the course of learning.

iii. **The rise of the robotic learner**: Over-reliance on AI and automated protocols for educational purposes will give rise to learners that are robotic or 'mechanical' in learning orientation. Infrequent contact or interaction with human tutors over-time has the potency of making the learner become passive and emotionless in the learning encounter.

iv. **Decline in reading culture**: Reading culture, as it concerns printed materials, will drastically decline as learners get more inclined and attached to automated learning interfaces. There will be a rise in techno-dependency and decline in physical learning activities like reading printed materials and writing with the pen or pencil on books and other printed surfaces/materials.

Conclusion and Recommendations for Stakeholders

This technesis has attempted a robust discussion on the need for artificial intelligence and automated processes to be implemented in mainstream educational broadcasting in Nigeria. The discourse is situated within the framework of understanding that acceptance and use of AI and automated processes will yield beneficial dividends for broad spectrum of stakeholders concerned. Beneficially, it is proposed that AI and automated educational broadcasting will advance audio-visual exemplification of abstract learning concepts; engender targeted and niched-driven learning; enable consistency in logical reasoning and delivery pattern; and herald efficiency in educational programming and scheduling; among others. These proposed benefits will orchestrate multi-layered effects with severe consequences on the outcome of automated learning context.

For automated broadcasting to deliver optimally in Nigeria across contexts, it is recommended that its implementation, integration, adoption, and utilization in the country's broadcasting landscape should meet three basic objectives: operational-resourcefulness; technicity and technological-integrativeness; and solution-orientedness. These three conditions are codified into what the author termed as the OTS framework. The diagrammatic representation of the **OTS Framework** is presented in Fig. 4.2.

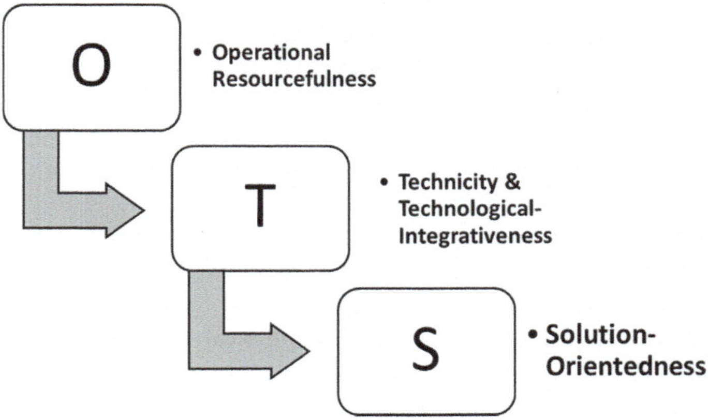

Fig. 4.2 The OTS framework

Operational-resourcefulness: This specifies that programmatic protocols and interfaces of automated educational broadcasting should be resourceful and useful when engaged by concerned stakeholders. The affordances of automated educational broadcasting should have operational value and relevance across cultural, economic, political, professional, and social contexts. Its value and relevance should be tangible in solving specific educational issues and challenges that analogue, traditional, and pseudo-digital broadcast interfaces, technologies, techniques, and processes could not.

Technicity and technological-integrativeness: This specifies that the programmatic protocols and interfaces of automated educational broadcasting should have a technological force that is flexible, easily adaptable or adjustable in addressing specialized problems without undergoing structural alteration or physical re-modification. It should have a multiplexing capacity in creating or implementing multi-layered solutions that integrate existing and emerging issues in educational broadcasting.

Solution-orientedness: This speaks to automated educational broadcast interfaces having the profundity to solve existing educationally-related problems. The solutions rendered should be such which can be qualified or quantified. This implies delivering a service-end benefit when learners engage with its affordances or explore its resources. It should have a reputation for yielding or delivering tangible results or values when used.

References

Abuselidze, G., & Mamaladze, L. (2021). The impact of artificial intelligence on employment before and during pandemic: A comparative analysis. *Journal of Physics: Conference Series, 1840*, 012040. https://doi.org/10.1088/1742-6596/1840/1/012040

Baum, H. (2023). *An introduction to artificial intelligence*. https://www.uc.edu/content/dam/uc/ce/docs/OLLi/page%20conetnt/artificial

Bharadiya, J. P., Thomas, R. K., & Ahmed, F. (2023). Rise of artificial intelligence in business and industry. *Journal of Engineering Research and Reports, 25*(3), 85–103.

Boucher, P. (2020). *Artificial intelligence: How does it work, why does it matter, and what can we do about it?* European Union. https://doi.org/10.2861/44572

Cemca. (2011). *Research in educational broadcasting*. http://www.cemca.org/books/Chapter%201.pdf

Chandar, U., & Sharma, R. (2003). Bridges to effective learning through radio. *International Review of Research in Open and Distance Learning, 4*(1), 1–14.

Cockett, I. (2024). *Broadcast automation without boundaries*. Pebble Beach Systems White Paper, pp. 1–8.

Effoduh, J. O. (2021). Factsheet on artificial intelligence in Nigeria: Artificial Intelligence project, Nigeria. *Paradigm Initiative*, pp. 1–3.

European Commission. (2018). Communication on artificial intelligence for Europe. *COM, 2018*, 237.

Fayoyin, A. (2021). Understanding the knowledge society, artificial intelligence and media nexus. In A. Fayoyin & A. Ifedolapo (Eds.), *Knowledge societies: Artificial intelligence and the media*. UNESCO/ACSPN.

Gencarelli, T. F. (2006). *Perspectives on culture, technology, and Communication: The media ecology tradition*. Hampton.

Hussein, N. (2015). *Broadcast automation system: Newsroom production* [A Thesis submitted to the Department of Media Engineering, Helsinki Metropolia University of Applied Sciences, Helsinki].

Ijeh, N. P., & Ojebode, A. (2015). Managing educational broadcasting in Nigeria: Reflectionson concept, prospects and challenges. *Delsu Journal of Educational Research and Development (special Edition), 2*(1), 169–178.

Khan, M. H. (2023). The impact of AI on the media industry. *A Master's Dissertation in Department of Informatics and Media*. Uppsala University.

Mann, D. (2010). Instructional Communication in CMC. http://www.slideshare.net/D.J.Mann/instructional-communication-in-cmc-damian-mann-presentation

Manning, C. (2020). *Artificial intelligence definitions*. https://hai.standford.edu/sites/default/files/2020-09/Ai-Definitions-HAI.pdf

McLuhan, M. (1964). *Understanding media: The extension of man*. Mentor.

Menghan, X. (2022). Research on the impact of artificial intelligence on employment: A bibliometric review based on Citespace. *Shandong Trade Union Forum, 28*(05), 10–20.

Mohammed, Z. (2019). Artificial Intelligence: Definition, ethics and standards. *Electronics and Communication: Law, Standard and Practice*, 1–4.

Nnamdi, C. N., & Nwanyanwu, M. (2021). Utilization of artificial intelligence in journalism in Nigeria. *KIU Journal of Social Sciences, 7*(2), 205–212.

Noain-Sánchez, A. (2022). Addressing the impact of artificial intelligence on journalism: The perception of experts, journalists and academics. *Communication & Society, 35*(3), 105–121.

Obong, U. A., & Banigo, E. (2023). Emerging digital media technologies and news agency journalism: A critical technesis. *Makurdi Journal of Communication Research, 10*(2), 82–99.

Oyeleye, S., & Ademosu, I. (2021). Communication made aasy? Patterns of AI-voice activated virtual assistants usage on mobile devices among young people.

In A. Fayoyin & I. Ademosu (Eds.), *Knowledge societies: Artificial intelligence and the media*. UNESCO.

Oyinloye, G. O., & Adeleye, I. (2010). Impact of the media on the senior secondary school students performance in speech work in English Language. *Academic Leadership: The Online Journal, 8*(4), Article 32. https://scholars.fhsu.edu/alj/vol8/iss4/32

Postman, N. (2006). Media ecology education. *Explorations in Media Ecology, 5*(1), 5–14.

Singh, G., Misha, A., & Sagar, G. (2013). An overview of artificial intelligence. *SBIT Journal of Science and Technology, 2*(1), 1–4.

TutorialsPoint. (2015). *Artificial intelligence: Intelligent systems* [e-book]. https://www.tutorialspoint.com

West, R., & Turner, L. H. (2014). *Introducing communication theory*. McGraw-Hill.

Yelwa, M. M., Abdulhameed, S., & Maigari, M. (2020). Artificial intelligence and the future of work in Nigeria: A shift from educational requirements to skills possession. *Social Science Research, 6*(1), 22–38.

Yue, Q. (2023). Study on the impact of Artificial Intelligence on employment and income inequality, based on technological determinism theory. In Y. Jiang et al. (Eds.), *ICFIED 2023, AEBMR, 237*, 329–338. https://doi.org/10.2991/978-94-6463-142-5_37

CHAPTER 5

Enhancing the Teaching and Learning of Educational Broadcasting Through Artificial Intelligence

Iniobong Courage Nda, Unwana Samuel Akpan, Ubong Andem Obong, and James John Adebayo

I. C. Nda (✉)
University of Uyo, Uyo, Akwa Ibom State, Nigeria
e-mail: iniobongcouragenda@gmail.com

U. S. Akpan
Department of Mass Communication, University of Lagos, Lagos, Nigeria

U. A. Obong
Department of Mass Communication, Taraba State University, Jalingo, Nigeria

J. J. Adebayo
Department of Mass Communication, Federal University Oye-Ekiti, Ekiti, Nigeria
e-mail: adebayo.james@fuoye.edu.ng

U. S. Akpan (ed.), *Educational Broadcasting in Nigeria in the Age of Artificial Intelligence*,
https://doi.org/10.1007/978-3-031-68530-9_5

Introduction

The objectives of this article are to identify the benefits AI brings into the teaching and learning of broadcasting, from available and current literature; ascertain the level of preparedness of students and teachers of broadcasting to embrace AI; and at the end identify key likely factors that could encourage or repel the use of AI in the teaching and learning of educational broadcasting in Nigeria. Artificial intelligence (AI), as Järvelä et al. (2023) aver, has generated a plethora of new opportunities, potential and challenges for understanding and supporting learning. Educational broadcasting is one field of learning that can simply be taught through the introduction of a digital approach to teaching and learning. In other cases, teaching and learning educational broadcasting become a herculean, disinteresting task that makes internalizing near impossible without the aid of AI. Today, artificial intelligence is becoming a more integral part of the classroom experience for both teachers and students alike. While the teachers will become better equipped to offer a more individualized learning experience for every student, the students on the other hand will have varied options to make learning engaging and sustaining. It has the ability to help teachers tailor their teachings. One of the significant contributions of AI to the educational process is the ability to personalize learning experiences. AI technology, as Kumar et al. (2023) maintain, streamlines administrative tasks, freeing up educators' time for more meaningful interactions with students. Automated processes such as scheduling, attendance tracking and data analysis can enhance operational efficiency and enable teachers to focus on instructional activities (Kumar et al., 2023). Artificial Intelligence, as Escotet (2023) opined, is a fast-evolving technology with enormous potential for education, higher education, and learning. AI can also negatively impact how societies and their citizens engage ethically with these generated, still-unexplored tools. These technological breakthroughs present both opportunity and potential peril (Escotet, 2023).

With 'AI,' vast amounts of data can be processed by the teacher and student alike, learning becomes more interactive. Also, with the advantage sight has over sound, the learning process is strengthened as the students do not only hear what is offered by the teacher but get involved and through the ability to internalize what is offered. AI has brought about a shift from digitization to a more advanced and wide range of technology leading to robotics, internet of things, machine learning, and expert systems, among others. According to Virtual Service Network (VSN) (2020) as quoted in Ukwela (2021), AI has opened the door for new possibilities. AI has revolutionized the broadcast media and by extension, its teaching and learning. This is witnessed in novel content creation, distribution, presentation and editing. The use of digital technologies is one of the most important trends in the global educational system today. Digital technologies make it possible to aid the educational growth process, make it mobile and adapted to realities of modern times (Malynovska & Smyrnova, 2023).

Theoretical Framework

This article is hinged on the Technology Determinism and the Uses and Diffusion theories. Propounded by Marshall McLuhan in 1962, the Technology Determinism Theory states that media technology models out how individuals act, feel, think and operate as it transits one technological era after another. With these advancements in media technology, human beings are influenced by the nature of the messages advanced by these modern technologies. Our society is transiting one technology into another, and another, and another; this is unending. Just when an individual is trying to gain conversance with one technology, another surfaces and the chain continues. Society changes as the medium of communication changes; it is evolving. In its bid to try to measure a link between the nature of the society and the prevailing media of communication, technology drives the society and defines the way it operates. However, some critics believe that technology never forces itself on anyone as these technologies were and are still being created by humans who possess the virtue of choice. Consequently, with the penetration of AI into the teaching and learning of Mass Communication, a new digital reality has emerged with the specific purpose to improve upon what we already have. Today, the teaching and learning of Mass Communication has been more interesting, engaging, interactive, attention-catching and the likes. The Technology Determinism theory therefore charts a course for a high level of knowledge dissemination at both the teachers and the students' end.

The Diffusion and Innovation Theory on the other hand, developed by E. M. Rogers in 1962, explains how an idea or innovation develops overtime and spreads to different locations and is adopted by people. This influences them to act differently in ways propagated by innovation. In other words, while some people adopt the innovation early, some have delayed adoption, typically waiting to see evidence of the workability of the innovation before keying into it. They are yet another set who want to be doubly sure before embracing any technology, and yet another very conservative set that are sceptical to change. In relation to this study, AI as one of the recent transformations in the information and media sector has received sufficient diffusion among teachers and students of Mass Communication. However, the extent to which it has been embraced cannot be ascertained despite its numerous benefits.

Historical Perspectives of Artificial Intelligence

Artificial Intelligence (AI) as a subfield of Information Technology (IT) is 'an artificial system designed to think or act like a human, including cognitive architectures and neural networks; a set of techniques, including machine learning that is designed to approximate a cognitive task' (CRS Report, 2020, p. 20, as cited in Nsude, 2022). According to Punchihewa (2018), as cited in Oyedokun (2023), the history of AI can be dated back to the last seven decades. In the 1950s, AI was officially born. In the 1960s, AI started getting attention and funding. The 1970s witnessed the first AI Winter with a cut in funding. In the 1980s. Japanese and UK Governments invested in AI; Second AI Winter, in the 1990s, AI started being deployed in the tech industry; IBM's Deep Blue beat the world chess champion. From 2000s onwards IBM's Watson beats human participants in the quiz show jeopardy; Internet revolution made more data available and AI reached funding peak in 2016 (Source; IABM). With its ability to engage in logical perception, reasoning, communication, learning, planning as well as readiness to achieve assigned tasks, it mimics and models human intelligence by acting and trying to reason the way a man would. With the data provided, AI competes with human intelligence and can make decisions based on the algorithms working in it.

Concerns with AI

Artificial Intelligence (AI) and machine learning technologies have become increasingly prevalent in the academic world. This growing trend has led to debates about the impact of these technologies on academia (Livberber & Ayvaz, 2023). The digital age, as Mambu et al. (2023) maintain, has rapidly changed the educational landscape, affecting the roles and tasks of teachers. Teachers are faced with new challenges, such as managing an abundance of information, adapting teaching styles to individual needs, and providing effective feedback to students. In the face of these challenges, AI technology offers significant potential. With the outstanding breakthroughs witnessed in the broadcast industry as well as the teaching and learning of broadcasting, AI has been adopted in the operations of institutions, media organizations, industries as well as organizations in advancing its numerous tasks more efficiently. The classroom experience is becoming more interesting, more engaging, more participatory and more memorable. Students and teachers alike can have a fulfilling encounter when they do not only theorize but engage in the practical aspects of learning.

The integration of AI in education has sparked a paradigm shift in teaching and learning, presenting both unparalleled opportunities and complex challenges (Alasadi & Baiz, 2023). As practical as the teaching and learning of broadcasting must be, the heartburning concern is however the level of preparedness of our educational sectors to embrace and sustain AI, its teaching and learning of broadcasting coupled with its attendance challenges like power, accessibility, availability, sustainability and technical-know-how, among others, at both the teacher and student levels.

Broadcast Media: Yesterday, Today and Tomorrow

The broadcast industry has witnessed several transformations which have led to its present state. There has been a move from analogue techniques to digital procedures which has been witnessed through all the stages of broadcast production. Ukwela (2021) maintains that 'for all the arms of broadcasting, from programmes/programming, engineering, marketing, administration, editing, to presentation; change has been a recurring decimal'. Today, several digital tools and software such as digital cameras, teleprompter, transmitter and wirecast amongst other studio equipment geared at improving the quality and quantity of information output, are commonplace in any station that has embraced digitization. This however is not the last bus stop as there are still some innovations in the broadcast sector; while some countries are already on it, others have left there for yet another level of digitization. As others are attempting to get there, a lot others are still coping with the analogue technology and lagging behind in the embrace of digitization. This is indeed a case of different strokes for different folks. With the emergence of Artificial Intelligence and all its components, there has been a marked difference in journalism practice, broadcasting, and broadcast education. In other words, AI has come to stay; in fact, it is around us and its presence is felt in virtually all sectors of our economy.

Preparedness of Students and Teachers of Broadcasting to Embrace Artificial Intelligence

Utilization of AI for broadcast educational purposes among students and teachers comes with mixed feelings and reactions. The mixed feelings and reactions are as a result of the perceived disruptive impact of AI in the broadcast learning process amidst inherent systemic, ideological, contextual, and cultural inhibitors that tend to threaten its robust entrenchment. Adding to this controversy is the perceived individualized and divisive functions that AI learning resources and teaching tools would likely bring to the learning encounter especially in terms of its influence in swapping role specification, assignment and description between the learners and the tutors. As both learners and the tutors explore and exploit AI learning resources and tools towards educational ends, the role of the tutor in the broadcast learning process would tend to diminish traditionally as both of them (learners and tutors), by virtue of AI, have become learners. The learners, to some extent, would even exert more influence in the broadcast learning process as they tend to ignore or disregard the input of tutors but turning their attention/focus to the source of the tutors' knowledge and pedagogy—AI. AI, in this context, tends to create a more divisive and highly individualized educational learning context for tutors and learners of educational broadcasting.

Against this background, the tone of the perceived level of preparedness of teachers and students of broadcasting to embrace AI in pedagogy and learning is set. The tone is not disjointed from the tendency for teachers and students of broadcasting to have a varying degree of preparedness to adopt and integrate AI in their learning and pedagogical pursuits. Especially when such may be defined and shaped by individualized intents, purposes, aspirations and expectations. This further makes the issue porous and fluid.

This porous situation, though can inspire wild thoughts, should not push one into the temptation of making assumptions that the students'/teachers' level of preparedness to adopt AI in broadcast education is parlous or hopeless. At the least, certain degrees of certainty may be established on the fact that the issue may be tilting towards the ambivalent and contextual domains with no watertight compartmentalization. Especially, when teachers or students of educational broadcasting are uncertain on the particularity of engaging AI in their teaching or learning experiences (Rudolph et al., 2023).

Although a lot of studies have been conducted on the perceived influence, impact or perception of AI in supporting teaching and learning (Crompton et al., 2018; Jones et al., 2018; Jung et al., 2007; Park & Shin, 2017; Popenici & Kerr, 2017; Shin et al., 2007); teachers' level of preparedness and perception to leverage AI (Kaplan-Rakowski et al., 2023; Kim et al., 2017; Kohnke et al., 2023; Moorhouse, 2024; Starkey, 2020); and students' readiness for AI instruction (Yoon, 2019) on different specific subjects, there has been paucity of literature on the level of preparedness of students and teachers of educational broadcasting to embrace AI. This makes it very difficult to ascertain the current level of knowledge on the subject. But going by the direction of scholarly inputs in related literature, critical positions can be established on the subject. Insights from available extant literature reveal deep layers of evidence that point to and affirm the position that teachers are more apprehensive when it has to do with the adoption of AI into pedagogy (Moorhouse, 2024). This also includes their intents to expose their students to the wielding and expansive affordances of AI learning resources. Part of the apprehension has been premised on lack of knowledge on the potentials of AI (Moorhouse, 2024) and the erroneous or credulous notion held by some teachers that AI will replace their traditional functions (Holmes & Tuomi, 2022) and make obsolesce of their over-enduring influence in the learning encounter.

Teachers' apprehension towards technological innovations such as AI in their teaching practices (Moorhouse, 2021) suggests that they do not feel adequately prepared for such reality in the teaching contexts (Starkey, 2020) which further strengthens their lack of readiness and reluctance to adopt and utilize it for professional teaching purposes (Kaplan-Rakowski et al., 2023; Kohnke et al., 2023; Moorhouse, 2024). Such a level of unpreparedness to embrace AI has strong implications on their confidence in AI's efficacy and efficiency in delivering on the job.

These claims make it easily admissible that AI's teaching/learning resources, tools, affordances and protocols may specifically empower the students at the expense of the teachers. Studies conducted by Kong et al. (2021) and Xia et al. (2022) have shown that students have competencies in the use of AI more than some teachers. This tends to insinuate that students may be more ready and receptive to the adoption and utilization of AI in the learning process compared to their teaching counterparts. Empirical evidence in Yoon's (2019) study proved that though students show interest in AI by considering it useful and convenient, they perceive it to be particularly inappropriate as their teachers, counselors, and for skills involving language output and interaction. This, obviously, makes them show strong preferences for human teachers in their classrooms. In this perspective, students' readiness in adopting and utilizing AI does not seem to be as receptive as imagined.

Willy-nilly, AI is an 'acultural' and 'apolitical' expert systems designed and programmed for specific and specialized functions and tasks of which derivative meaning and benefit are defined by the users and not the creators. Hence, AI has no emotions and cannot yield to gainful exploration from students against the teachers. It is an entirely GIGO (garbage in, garbage out) and an input–output innovative interface. This makes it even more implicative to say that a teacher who has competency on the use of the expert system can manipulate it to support or extend his/her physical teaching efforts or functions. This is the same situation for the learners too. But in a situation where the learners explore and exploit the AI affordances across/beyond learning contexts and outcomes, certain levels of threats in alternating the learning-teaching roles may be inevitable. In such contexts, AI should be absolved of the blame for equipping the students more than the teachers. Teachers should take the blame for lack of competency and for failing to integrate, adopt, utilize, and leverage AI to gain advantage. It follows from the above submissions that teachers who are not receptive to new technologies are likely to show a sceptical (Kim & Kim, 2017; Yoon, 2019), nonchalant, indifferent, repulsive, and withdrawal attitude towards AI and its affordances in augmenting their efforts. Most especially, when appraising the possibility of AI's 'augmenting' role as a groundwork to replace their physical efforts and intelligence (Jones et al., 2018). For this crop of teachers, the level of preparedness to welcome AI in the teaching of educational broadcasting will always be low, if not non-existence. The opposite is the case for techno-savvy teachers who are likely to see AI and its affordances as appendage, auxiliary, and extension of their physical labour, efforts, and intelligence (Bharadiya et al., 2023). For this crop of teachers, AI's adoption, utilization, and integration into their mainstream professional teaching practices in educational broadcasting would be highly welcomed. This made it possible to hypothesize that the level of preparedness of teachers and students to embrace AI in mainstream professional teaching practices in educational broadcasting is a consequence of teachers' and students' mindset. By this, we mean that the level of preparedness to embrace AI is more of emotional and attitudinal predispositions than it is rational and logical.

The current and available literature reviewed shows that AI has had a significant impact on teaching, learning, and other operational procedures in schools (Alasadi & Baiz, 2023; Escotet, 2023; Livberber & Ayvaz, 2023). AI is used more and more in the classroom to augment and support learning experience. AI is the subfield of computer science that deals with theory and practice of creating smart devices aping human reasoning and behaviour (Voskoglou, 2023). As with many industries, TV and video production is likely to be transformed by artificial intelligence (AI) and machine learning (ML), with software and algorithms assisting production tasks that could only be carried out by people (Wright et al., 2020). A new broadcast technology known as AI-Smart Driven Production is being developed. AI-smart driven production conveys information to the viewers using artificial intelligence quickly, accurately, and automatically (Yamanouchi et al., 2018). Al-Driven Smart Production, as Yamanouchi et al. (2018) opine, consists of two technical components. The first component uses programme production assistance technologies to automatically extract useful information from big data and present it to the programme producers (Yamanouchi et al., 2018). The technologies are social networking service (SNS) data analysis for prompt news gathering, speech recognition for generating closed captions, and image analysis for generating metadata of video footage. The other component, as Yamanouchi et al. (2018) maintain, uses a technology for automatically converting broadcast data into forms that can be easily understood by all viewers, i.e., sign language computer graphics animation for the hearing impaired and automatic audio description generation for the visually impaired. The use of video broadcasting platforms as well as competition for developing platforms for the broadcasting and sharing of movies and television series is on the rise daily (Çakar et al., 2021). Film and

TV series platforms use artificial intelligence algorithms for these shares (Çakar et al., 2021).

Microcomputers, the Internet, and the World Wide Web and artificial intelligence are shaping the current generation of teaching and learning (Kerka, 1996). Artificial Intelligence (AI) is likely to become increasingly present in the entertainment, educational, and technology industries (Patchunka, 2019). The migration of audiences to the digital environment has empowered the media to evolve a content distribution strategy that has a presence in the new digital spaces.

Factors That Encourage the Use of AI in the Teaching and Learning of Educational Broadcasting

As Artificial Intelligence (AI) technologies advance, their potential for disrupting and transforming educational practices becomes increasingly evident (Reyna, 2023). AI has been applied in many spheres of national life, chief of which is education. Some AI immediate applications, as Escotet (2023) avers, include student support, tutoring personalization, automated qualitative and quantitative grading and assessment, education data analytics, course programmes, content development and educational planning, administration, and academic performance. AI is used in classrooms to tailor lessons and improve communication between teachers and the students. AI, as Chhatwal et al. (2023) maintains, enables the teachers to gauge the strengths and weaknesses of individual students. The use of AI allows thorough evaluation of both instructors' and students' progress in the classrooms (Chhatwal et al., 2023). AI may be used to build virtual tutoring systems, provide students with instant feedback, and design engaging and interactive classroom experience (Chhatwal et al., 2023). Administrative operations such as grading, taking attendance, and registration of students, as Chhatwal et al. (2023) note, could also be automated with the help of AI. The use of AI techniques in educational broadcasting has brought significant benefits to teaching and learning, to student and teacher assessment and training, and to several other educational processes (Voskoglou, 2023). Despite some limits, artificial intelligence has assumed many dimensions with regard to applications (Kirn et al., 2022). Artificial Intelligence (AI) applies now in all areas of mankind activity, including creation of new films, music, and modern technologies (Kalyatin, 2021). As artificial intelligence (AI) gains space in the media, public broadcasters are testing and experimenting with these technologies to raise their services to the new standards of the audiovisual ecosystem (Fieiras-Ceide et al., 2023).

The AI-assisted radio and television dissemination mode has the advantages of improving the effectiveness of information communication, promoting optimization and integration of news sources, and enhancing audience stickiness (Jia, 2022). The application of AI in education worldwide has increased dramatically with its importance growing at an increasing rate (Sanabria-Navarro et al., 2023). The development of artificial intelligence (AI) technology and the planning and dissemination of radio and television must not only learn to quickly and deeply process a large amount of content and extract structured information such as classification, themes, tags, and styles from information sources, but also learn to use audience behaviours to explore and discover potential content, jump out of the editor's subjective vision, and realize personalized content presentation. AI technology, as Jia (2022) notes, can be used for smart lyrics, smart writing, smart broadcasting, smart translation, smart recommendation, smart stripping, and smart retrieval, and so on. The AI-assisted radio and television planning, as Jia (2022) maintains, gives audiences the right to choose news, provides them with more targeted news content by means of data capture and resource integration, and caters to audiences' all-round and in-depth information needs.

Furthermore, some other factors account for the motivation to accept and utilize AI in the teaching and learning of broadcasting. Though the factors are diverse in nature, they are interrelated in the sense that they are influenced by the users' (teachers and students) perception of AI resources within the context of applicability and usefulness. Hence, the perception of users regarding AI's ease of use, the expected performance it is to serve, its effort expectancy, social influence, and facilitating conditions (Venkatesh et al., 2003) go a long way in influencing acceptance and use of AI. It is from the broad perspectives discussed above that the following can be enlisted as motivating factors for the acceptance, adoption, and use of AI in the teaching and learning of educational broadcasting:

i. **Users' perception**: At the crux of AI's acceptance, adoption, and use among teachers and students for specialized purposes such as educational broadcasting lies the issue of perception. As Kohnke et al. (2023) note, teachers and students have multi-layered perceptions, worldviews, and concerns relating to AI adoption. This makes perception fundamental and critical to the decisions these stakeholders make regarding whether or not to adopt or use AI to accomplish or augment specialized learning/teaching tasks/outcomes. Critical decisions to or not to adopt and use AI can only be made when users' perception of AI in terms of its utility, resourcefulness, innovativeness, result-orientedness, and troubleshooting value are clearly satisfied. It is unlikely for users to adopt and use AI when their perception of the innovation is skewed, shaky, and negative and its utility value is uncertain.

ii. **Users' expectation**: Closely related to users' perception is the issue of users' expectations for AI to serve designated teaching/learning purposes and functions. The users of AI have certain levels of expectations for engaging and integrating AI affordances in their mainstream teaching and learning processes. These expectations could entail the strong desire by [intended] users for AI to perform in a concerted fashion and yield the intended value for utilization. It could also encompass AI's expected contextual applicability to solving specialized and specific teaching/learning problems or performing tasks within specific teaching/learning contexts of engagements. In addition to these perspectives, the issue of users' expectation of AI interfaces to be relatively easy and simple to use and access in accomplishing specific tasks across contexts cannot be relinquished to the backdrop. Especially, in specific unconducive contexts where AI affordances could be considered critical to facilitating human conditions, extending human functions, and augmenting physical efforts, labour, and intelligence (Bharadiya et al., 2023). It is only when these expectations are met that acceptance and use of AI become inevitable. This implies that AI can be embraced with full arms by teachers and students of educational broadcasting when it has a reputation for meeting their teaching and learning expectations when utilized.

iii. **Users' experience**: The experiences users encounter in the course of engaging AI learning/teaching resources determine whether or not they can be relied upon and used in subsequent learning/teaching encounters/situations. Hence, if teachers and students of educational broadcasting derive satisfying experiences from their utilization of AI for learning/teaching purposes, a culture of dependence will be foisted on AI's usage for similar purposes in subsequent encounters. Experience is a significant motivator for adoption and use of AI for academic purposes among teachers (Moorhouse, 2024).

iv. **AI's performance value**: AI's social influence among the users (teachers/students) can only be achieved if it is efficient in solving specific teaching/learning challenges; efficacious in troubleshooting assigned teaching/learning queries and tasks; relevant in meeting teachers/students' need with exact or near precision; insubmersible to objectionable errors in the learning encounter; optimal in teaching/learning task performance; and a sense of real-time application to existing problems pertaining to educational broadcasting. The performance value of AI speaks to its ability and proficiency in meeting the varied offline or mainstream operational teaching/learning demands, needs, and goals that are eminent in the educational broadcasting learning encounter.

v. **Users' accessibility**: This entails the condition of AI's affordances, protocols, or resources being at the reach of teachers/students from an economic, technical, practical, and cultural point of view. Economically, if AI's learning resources and tools must be adopted and used within educational broadcasting context, they should be affordable to acquire and subscribed to by teachers/students. The premium cost associated with access to some AI tools poses a great challenge for most users (Nyaaba & Zhai, 2024). Technically, if AI's learning resources and tools pose certain technological difficulty to teachers/students when attempting to operate or interact with their interfaces, the possibility of adopting and using them would amount to zero. Practically, AI's learning resources and tools should avail teachers/students the opportunity and platform to apply their affordances and processes in solving specific and specialized learning or teaching problems in practical terms. Culturally speaking, the linguistics, language of engagement, and interactive codes should be such that suit the nuanced learning and teaching peculiarities of teachers/students. The language of interaction between AI interfaces and the users (teachers/students) must overlap in order for the users' experience in the learning encounter to be intensified and clarified. In essence, providing teachers/learners with the wherewithal to access AI resources from the point of views raised above can facilitate its adoption (Zhang & Aslan, 2021).

vi. **[End users'] learning outcome**: The particular and specific outcome envisaged about AI has a way of affecting its adoption and utilization within the learning context. This is to say that if AI can guarantee seamless delivery and organization of learning experience to the extent that certain predictable learning outcomes are influenced in certain ways with consistent degree of precision, there is a great possibility that it would be adopted and used towards such ends. So, contextual applicability of AI to educational broadcasting learning objectives and the certainty of achieving predictable learning outcomes determine to a great extent why AI should be adopted or used by teachers/students of educational broadcasting.

Repelling Dynamics to the Use of AI in the Teaching and Learning of Educational Broadcasting

Artificial intelligence (AI) can transform education by improving teaching and learning outcomes. However, as with any new technology, there are also risks associated with its use (Ayala-Pazmiño, 2023). It is important to consider that AI technology cannot completely replace the role of teachers, but only serves as a powerful tool (Mambu et al., 2023). The economic cost of adapting these systems to each corporation and the difficulties in hiring experts to develop AI solutions prevent a complete deployment of these tools in public broadcasters (Fieiras-Ceide et al., 2023). With the perceived benefits of the affordances of AI in the teaching and learning of educational broadcasting notwithstanding, certain militating factors serve as repellants to the wide adoption and utilization of the innovation. These repelling forces are classified into seven major categories which encompass the psychological, professional, economic, environmental, ethical, legal, and knowledge and competency dynamics. Some of the problems or repellants of AI, as Chhatwal et al. (2023) opine, are:

i. **Psychological dynamics**: These constitute a whole lot of factors compelled by AI users' cognitive, affective, and cognitive responses to the idea of accepting and using AI learning resources and tools. Psychological dynamics such as perception, belief, knowledge, thinking, emotions, feelings, attitudes, and behaviours constitute some levels of impediments and hindrances to teachers/students' intentions to (or not) adopt and use AI within learning contexts. Teachers/students' cognitive responses/products such as belief, knowledge, and thinking of AI as constituting negative influences have a way of disconnecting their mental readiness and intentions to adopt and use AI for contextual teaching/learning purposes. This often engenders cognitive unattachment to AI and its attendant resources and tools. From the affective domain, teachers/students' emotional releases and responses such as expression of feelings of apprehension and fears of uncertainties about the impending negative consequences of AI can trigger negative emotions and dissonance towards adoption and utilization of AI for teaching/learning purposes. This may snowball into severe cognitive implications and consequences as negative emotions tend to trigger negative attitude and behaviour towards AI thereby making acceptance, adoption, utilization, integration, or engagement of AI for teaching and learning outcomes difficult to come by.

ii. **Lack of AI experts/professional dynamics**: AI requires expertise in both technology and education, but there is a dearth of AI professionals, especially in developing countries of Africa and Asia. The prognostications expressed by technological enthusiasts and determinists on the possibilities of AI replacing human functions and intelligence of which the presumption of human job loss and displacement are strongly anchored, have made it difficult for AI to be accepted across organizational and cultural contexts. Human professionals and industry experts in the fields of education and broadcasting are sceptical of adopting innovations such as AI which pose significant threats to their jobs (Du & Gao, 2023), level of professionalism, careers, professional relevance, and general expertise. With these threats becoming more profound, human experts in the field of educational broadcasting tend to develop apathy towards AI's adoption in order to prevent a situation whereby their adoption of AI within pedagogical context would lead to their own redundancy. From a professional perspective, impending threats expressed by pundits on AI disruptive influence within pedagogical and learning contexts where teaching jobs, roles, specifications, descriptions, performances, evaluation, and quality would be greatly impacted by the affordances of AI have engendered a cancel and reluctance culture on AI's adoption among techno-sceptics and non-techie human experts.

iii. **Economic dynamics**: Introducing AI into the educational system is expensive and requires a significant amount of time to develop and maintain. The econometrics surrounding the utilization and application trends of AI resources and tools indicate that such service ends do not come without some profound economic consequences and implications for the users. The fact that AI resources and tools would be bought, acquired, or subscribed is to suggest that it impose certain levels of economic inconveniences on users. Whether from a micro or macro-economic perspective, AI utilization and application are capital intensive and economically draining for economically disadvantaged users. Hence, when the economics of AI utilization and application overwhelmingly become a burden on indigent teachers/students, outright refusal to integrate it in their mainstream teaching/learning processes may be inevitable (Nyaaba et al., 2024). Going by the economic principle of comparative cost advantage, teachers/students may hold on to traditional teaching and learning methods if they are considered economically affordable compared to novel AI innovative interventions and initiatives. Considering the worsening economic situations, unpredictable economic disasters, rising spate of inflations, economic recession, and the decline in purchasing power parity witnessed by major economies of the world, subscribing to AI-related merchandising could be considered as an economic luxury: a waste that a lot of teachers/students cannot afford.

iv. **Environmental dynamics**: This encompasses a whole range of issues that tend to disrupt the general ambiance in which robust utilization and application of AI resources and tools can find practical expression and the needed motivation to thrive. It is from this perspective that a critical factor such as the nature of a nation's political system and climate where the issues of political economy, political culture, and the political will to enforce the right legislation on big data governance can be questioned and challenged. Including making regulatory frameworks that directly and impliedly safeguard the rights of individuals to data privacy and terms of references for the diverse use of AI within a national boundary (Effoduh, 2021). The political environment of AI is a motivating factor that can either encourage or discourage AI utilization across contexts. In addition to this is the infrastructural environment which speaks to whether or not relevant infrastructures such as electricity, internet connectivity and penetration, accessible funds, availability of composite AI applications and hardwares, availability and functionality of big data centers, availability of research and development hubs, etc., are on ground to drive AI teaching and learning initiatives. Adoption of AI can be greatly hindered by paucity and of the abovementioned basic infrastructure (Nyaaba et al., 2024; Popenici & Kerr, 2017; Sharma et al., 2022). Also worth considering is the cultural environment which is concerned with users' sociological characteristics such as worldviews, social ties, social connections, and cultural variations and how these characteristics tend to affect their readiness to accept and engage AI's novel innovation in tackling age-long 'traditional' practices such as teaching and learning. In summation, the political, infrastructural, and cultural environments exert considerable level of influence on the intents and purposes to utilize AI for specific traditional practices such as teaching and learning. As these environments are relatively marred with varying degrees of uncertainties, adoption and utilization of AI for the teaching and learning of broadcasting among teachers/students hang in the balance.

v. **Ethical dynamics**: AI can be used to make decisions that could have a major impact on students' lives, such as admissions and grading. Consequently, it is important to consider the ethical implications of using AI. The wanton utilization of AI, especially its generative counterparts, within academia has always raised ethical concerns on plagiarism, copyright infringement, intellectual impropriety, data breaches, data theft, impersonation, transparency, etc. As teachers are concerned about the ethical implications of AI (Nyaaba et al., 2024), these ethical concerns are still standing in the way of robust engagement of AI resources and generative interfaces/protocols for an ethically sound pedagogy and learning of educational broadcasting.

vi. **Legal dynamics**: As unguided and unguarded use of AI learning resources, generative interfaces, protocols, and tool kits may avail teachers and learners with solicited but unattributed learning data that may land teachers/students in an ethical quagmire when applied in specific context, they also have the propensity to attract legal consequences like lawsuits and litigations. To avoid legal actions against copyright owners, patent creators, etc., most users have approached the utilization of AI with caution while others have totally declined from leveraging its affordances for serious academic exercise and activities.

vii. **Knowledge and competency dynamics**: Paucity of technical and technological knowledge and competencies on AI can cause the users to avoid its utilization within learning context. As Kohnke and et al. (2023, p. 2) have noted, some 'teachers may not possess the technical or pedagogical knowledge and expertise to integrate AI-driven tools into the classroom, leading to apprehension and reluctance.'

viii. **Lack of data**: AI requires a large amount of data to make accurate decisions and predictions. However, most schools do not have enough resources to train their AI systems.

While the benefits of AI in education are substantial, there are challenges associated with its integration. Ethical considerations, privacy concerns, and the need for effective human-AI collaboration, as Kumar et al. (2023) maintain, are some of the challenges of AI, especially in the developing nations of the world. Despite these advantages inherent in the application of AI, academics all over the world also have ethical concerns, such as plagiarism and misinformation (Livberber & Ayvaz, 2023).

Benefits of AI in Education

1. Artificial Intelligence makes for a more personalized learning. This is so because a single source (teacher) will not be able to reach at all the students in a class except the students who have access to this technology that can give to them a one-on-one interaction as well as understand their varied needs, strengths, and weaknesses.
2. AI has the ability to determine the student's learning styles, knowledge acquired over time and can tutor, support, and instruct the student in line with his or her proposal.

3. AI is advantageous in grading students, compiling data, setting examination questions, and simplifying abstract subjects to the understanding of the students. It can also assist teachers in analyzing copious data at ease.
4. AI allows for feedback on the quality of learning and areas of improvements either in the materials or methods used.
5. AI makes learning possible for the physically challenged students like blind students. With the aid of AIs, a physically impaired person can read passages while the deaf can actually see what he or she could not hear through AI.
6. AI can help in the management of facilities by alerting the people to any problem or issue that requires urgent attention. Safety and security is achievable through the use of AI.
7. The teachers' teaching packages are improved through AI. Also, the students' writing skills are given a face-lift through AI.
8. Plagiarism is easily detected through AI
9. Cyber security
10. It makes for efficient communication without and outside the classroom setting. Student–teacher relationship is enhanced, teacher-parent relationship is made possible, student-task interaction is achievable.

In terms of AI-infused specific technologies, University of San Diego identifies a list of AI now used in education; the list grows longer every day. Here are just a few:

- Thinkster Math: Described by its creators as a math tutoring programme leverages human interaction and groundbreaking artificial intelligence to create personalized learning programmes
- Jill Watson: An AI-enabled virtual teaching assistant introduced by the Georgia Institute of Technology in 2016
- Brainly: A social media site for classroom questions
- Nuance: Speech recognition software used by students and faculty; capable of transcribing up to 160 words per minute; especially helpful for students who struggle with writing or have accessibility needs

- Cognii: AI-based products, including a virtual learning assistant, for K-12 and higher education institutions, as well as corporate training organizations
- KidSense: AI educational solutions designed for children, including a voice-to-text tool with algorithms built to recognize the sometimes harder-to-translate speech of young learners
- Content Technologies: Instructional design and content application solutions fuelled by artificial intelligence research engines.

Conclusion

AI, being utilized in the teaching and learning of educational broadcasting, makes for a more personalized learning interface. Such a personalized learning interface creates an overlapping, intensifying, and clarifying field of experience between the teacher and the learner which tends to enhance the outcomes of the learning encounter. This is consequent upon the fact that AI has the ability to determine the student's learning styles, knowledge acquired over time, and can among others, tutor, support, and instruct the student. It also allows for feedback on the quality of learning and areas of improvements either in the materials or methods used.

These, among other benefits, are the strong point for strengthening the argument on the necessity to apply its affordances, resources, protocols, and tools to the teaching and learning of educational broadcasts. In the argument sustained in the corpus of this work as supported by extant literature, those benefits are likely to hang in a balance as the level of preparedness of tutors and learners are uncertain and shaky. This gave us the strength to hypothesize that the level of preparedness of tutors and learners to embrace AI in the teaching and learning of educational broadcasting is a consequence of the stakeholders' mindset. By that, we mean that their level of preparedness to embrace AI is more of emotional and attitudinal predispositions than it is rational and logical.

Hence, factors such as perception, expectation, accessibility, learning outcomes, and performance value of AI are likely to influence users' intents to embrace and use AI for the teaching and learning of educational broadcasting. These factors notwithstanding, to give a balanced perspective to both sides of the issue, we also weigh that psychological, professional, economic, environmental, ethical, and legal dynamics exert some repelling forces on the utilization and engagement of AI towards the accomplishment of educational broadcasting across diverse contexts.

From the foregoing, Artificial Intelligence has come to stay. With focus on the teaching and learning of Mass Communication, AI has the ability to make the teaching experience of Mass Communication more rewarding and should be encouraged. However, the Nigerian climate may threaten the survival of AI in the teaching and learning of Mass Communication.

Recommendations

From our explanative pontifications and narrative discourse on the need for entrenchment of AI resources, protocols, and tools in the teaching and learning of educational broadcasting, we thus recommend that:

1. Artificial Intelligence should be encouraged in the teaching and learning of Mass Communication.
2. Heavy reliance on AI will deaden students' and teachers' insight hence it should be cautiously used.
3. Adequate preparations should be put in place to sustain the use of AI in the teaching of Mass Communication and not just a once off thing.
4. The use of AI requires constant power and should be provided.
5. AI should be made accessible to teachers and learners of educational broadcasting both in language, nuance, content, technicity, and technological interface.
6. AI resources and tool kits for accessing educational data for the teaching and learning of educational broadcast should be made affordable to users of diverse economic background and stratification.
7. Sensitization campaigns should be launched and staged to allay the fears that most industry practitioners hold about AI relinquishing humans of their jobs, functions, and expertise. They should be pointed to the augmenting and supporting perspective of AI across contexts of application.
8. AI programmers should work towards implementing a robust and wholesome generative interface and data-centric interfaces for AI where sources of information, and data are dutifully acknowledged with cogent references, source attribution, and citations to address

the issue of plagiarism and copyright infringement on intellectual properties.

References

Alasadi, E. A., & Baiz, C. R. (2023). Generative AI in education and research: Opportunities, concerns, and solutions. *Journal of Chemical Education, 100*(8). https://doi.org/10.1021/acs.jchemed.3c00323

Ayala-Pazmiño, M. (2023). Artificial intelligence in education: Exploring the potential benefitsand risks. *593 Digital Publisher CEIT, 8*(3). https://doi.org/10.33386/593dp.2023.3.1827

Bharadiya, J. P., Thomas, R. K., & Ahmed, F. (2023). Rise of artificial intelligence in business and industry. *Journal of Engineering Research and Reports, 25*(3), 85–103.

Çakar, M., Yildiz, K., & Demir, Ö. (2021). Thumbnail selection with convolutional neural network based on emotion detection. *International Journal of Advances in Engineering and Pure Sciences, 33*. https://doi.org/10.7240/jeps.900561

Chhatwal, M., Garg, V., & Rajput, N. (2023). Role of AI in the education sector. *Lloyd BusinessReview*. https://doi.org/10.56595/lbr.v2i1.11

Crompton, H., Gregory, K., & Burke, D. (2018). Humanoid robots supporting children's learning in an early childhood setting. *British Journal of Educational Technology, 49*(5), 911–927.

Du, Y., & Gao, H. (2023). Determinants affecting teachers' adoption of AI-based applications in EFL context: An analysis of analytic hierarchy process. *Education and Information Technologies, 27*, 9357–9387. https://doi.org/10.1007/s10639-022-11001-y

Effoduh, J. O. (2021). Factsheet on artificial intelligence in Nigeria: Artificial intelligence project, Nigeria. *Paradigm Initiative*, 1–3.

Escotet, M. Á. (2023). The optimistic future of artificial intelligence in higher education. *Prospects*. https://doi.org/10.1007/s11125-023-09642-z

Fieiras-Ceide, C., Vaz-álvarez, M., & Túñez-López, M. (2023). Designing personalisation of European public service media (PSM): Trends on algorithms and artificial intelligence for content distribution. *Profesional de La Informacion, 32*(3). https://doi.org/10.3145/epi.2023.may.11

Holmes, W., & Tuomi, I. (2022). State of the art and practice in AI in education. *European Journal of Education: Research, Development and Policy, 57*(4), 542–570. https://doi.org/10.1111/ejed.12533

Järvelä, S., Nguyen, A., & Hadwin, A. (2023). Human and artificial intelligence collaboration for socially shared regulation in learning. *British Journal of Educational Technology, 54*(5). https://doi.org/10.1111/bjet.13325

Jia, Z. (2022). Analysis methods for the planning and dissemination mode of radio and television assisted by artificial intelligence technology. *Mathematical Problems in Engineering*. https://doi.org/10.1155/2022/7538692

Jones, S., Richards, A., Cho, Y., & Lee, Y. J. (2018). The effect of the fourth industrial revolution on general English education—A case study of native English instructors' perspections at a Korean University. *Korean Journal of General Education, 14*(2), 169–197.

Jung, J., Choi, J., & Han, J. (2007). Analysis on children's response depending on teaching assistant robots' styles. *Korean Association of Information Education, 11*(2), 195–203.

Kalyatin, V. (2021). Rights to intellectual works generated with artificial intelligence: A Russian view in the global context. *Legal Issues in the Digital Age, 1*(1). https://doi.org/10.17323/2713-2749.2021.1.42.63

Kaplan-Rakowski, R., Grotewold, K., Hartwick, P., & Papin, K. (2023). Generative AI and teachers' perspectives on its implementation in education. *Journal of Interactive Learning Research, 34*(2), 313–338.

Kerka, S. (1996). *Distance learning, the internet, and the world wide web* (Eric Digest, ED395214).

Kim, H. S., & Kim, H. (2017). A study of Korean English teachers' future readiness for the fourth industrial revolution. *Multimedia-Assisted Language Learning, 20*(3), 179–205.

Kirn, H., Anwar, M., Sadiq, A., Zeeshan, H. M., Mehmood, I., & Butt, R. A. (2022). Deepfake tweets detection using deep Learning algorithms †. *Engineering Proceedings, 20*(1). https://doi.org/10.3390/engproc2022020002

Kohnke, L., Moorhouse, B. L., & Zou, D. D. (2023). Exploring generative artificial intelligence preparedness among university language instructors: A case study. *Computers and Education: Artificial Intelligence, 5*, 100156. https://doi.org/10.1016/j.caeai.2023.100156

Kong, S. C., Cheung, W. M. Y., & Zhang, G. (2021). Evaluation of an artificial intelligence literacy course for university students with diverse study backgrounds. *Computers and Education: Artificial Intelligence, 2*, 100026. https://doi.org/10.1016/j.caeai.2021.100026

Kumar, D., Haque, A., Mishra, K., Islam, F., Kumar Mishra, B., & Ahmad, S. (2023). Exploring the transformative role of artificial intelligence and metaverse in education: A comprehensive review. *Metaverse Basic and Applied Research, 2*. https://doi.org/10.56294/mr202355

Livberber, T., & Ayvaz, S. (2023). The impact of artificial intelligence in academia: Views of Turkish academics on ChatGPT. *Heliyon, 9*(9). https://doi.org/10.1016/j.heliyon.2023.e19688

Malynovska, I., & Smyrnova, I. (2023). The key role of artificial intelligence in education 4.0. *Scientific Journal of Polonia University, 58*(3).https://doi.org/10.23856/5820

Mambu, J. G. Z., Pitra, D. H., Rizki, A., Ilmi, M., Nugroho, W., Leuwol, N. V, Muh, A., & Saputra, A. (2023). Pemanfaatan Teknologi Artificial Intelligence (AI) Dalam Menghadapi Tantangan Mengajar Guru di era digital. *Journal on Education, 6*(1).

Moorhouse, B. L. (2021). Beginning teaching during COVID-19: Newly qualified Hong Kong teachers' preparedness for teaching online. *Educational Studies*. https://doi.org/10.1080/02607476.2021.1952844

Moorhouse, B. L. (2024). Beginning and first-year language teachers' readiness for the generative AI age. *Computers and Education: Artificial Intelligence, 6*(100201), 1–8.

Nsude, I. (2022). *Artificial Intelligence (AI), the media and security challenges in Nigeria*. https://doi.org/10.4000/ctd.6788

Nyaaba, M., & Zhai, X. (2024). Generative AI professional development needs for teacher educators. *Journal of AI, 8*(1), 1–13. https://doi.org/10.61969/jai.1385915

Oyedokun, I. (2023). Effect of adopting Artificial Intelligence presenters in broadcasting on audience perception and gratification of broadcast contents. *ResearchGate*. https://doi.org/10.13140/RG.2.2.32818.99529

Park, J. H., & Shin, N. M. (2017). Students' perceptions of artificial intelligence technology and artificial intelligence teachers. *The Journal of Korean Teacher Education, 34*(2), 169–192.

Patchunka, C. (2019). Netflix killed the cable TV star: Cable TV is definitionally disadvantaged for use of artificial intelligence. *Federal Communications Law Journal, 71*(2).

Popenici, S. A. D., & Kerr, S. (2017). Exploring the impact of artificial intelligence on teaching and learning in higher education. *Research and Practice in Technology Enhanced Learning, 12*, 2. https://doi.org/10.1186/s41039-017-0062-8

Punchihewa, A. (2018). AI in Broadcasting and media. https://doi.org/10.13140/RG.2.2.18811.77607

Reyna, J. (2023). *AI in the classroom: A comprehensive framework for ChatGPT integration in teaching and learning in higher education*. www.Jorge-Reyna.com.

Rudolph, J., Tan, S., & Tan, S. (2023). ChatGPT: Bullshit spewer or the end of traditional assessments in higher education? *Journal of Applied Learning & Teaching, 6*(1). https://doi.org/10.37074/jalt.2023.6.1.9

Sanabria-Navarro, J. R., Silveira-Pérez, Y., Pérez-Bravo, D. D., & de-Jesús-Cortina-Núñez, M. (2023). Incidences of artificial intelligence in contemporary education. *Comunicar, 31*(77). https://doi.org/10.3916/C77-2023-08

Sharma, H., Soetan, T., Farinloye, T., Mogaji, E., & Noite, M. D. F. (2022). AI adoption in universities in emerging economies: Prospects, challenges and recommendations. In E. Mogaji, V. Jain, F. Maringe, & R. E. Hinson (Eds.), *Re-imagining educational futures in developing countries*. Palgrave Macmillan. https://doi.org/10.1007/978-3-030-88234-1_9

Shin, N., & Kim, S. (2007). What do robots have to do with student learning? *The Journal of Educational Information and Media, 13*(3), 79–99.

Starkey, L. (2020). A review of research exploring teacher preparation for the digital age. *Cambridge Journal of Education, 50*(1), 37–56. https://doi.org/10.1080/0305764X.2019.1625867

Ukwela, C. O. (2021). Artificial intelligence and broadcast media presentation in Nigeria: What does the future hold? In *Knowledge societies: Artificial intelligence and the media*. UNESCO/ACSPN

Venkatesh, V., Morris, M. G., Davis, G. B., & Davis, F. D. (2003). User acceptance of information technology: Toward a unified view. *MIS Quarterly, 27*(3), 425–478.

Voskoglou, M. (2023). *Artificial intelligence and digital technologies in the future of education*. Qeios.

Wright, C., Phillipson, G., Shotton, M., Allnutt, J., Campbell, R., Evans, M., Forman, R., Gibson, J., Jolly, S., Kerlin, L., & Lechelt, S. (2020). AI in production: Video analysis and machine learning for expanded live events coverage. *SMPTE Motion Imaging Journal, 129*(2). https://doi.org/10.5594/JMI.2020.2967204

Xia, Q., Chiu, T. K., Lee, M., Sanusi, I. T., Dai, Y., & Chai, C. S. (2022). A self-determination theory (SDT) design approach for inclusive and diverse artificial intelligence (AI) education. *Computers & Education, 189*, 104582. https://doi.org/10.1016/j.compedu.2022.104582

Yamanouchi, Y., Goto, J., Kawai, Y., Mochizuki, T., Sato, S., & Imai, A. (2018, September). AI-driven smart production. *ABU Technical Review, 2018*(275).

Yoon, S. Y. (2019). Student readiness for AI instruction: Perspectives on AI in university EFL classrooms. *Multimedia-Assisted Language Learning, 22*(4), 134–160.

Zhang, K., & Aslan, A. B. (2021). AI technologies for education: Recent research & future directions. *Computers and Education: Artificial Intelligence, 2*, 100025. https://doi.org/10.1016/j.caeai.2021.100025

CHAPTER 6

Prospects and Challenges of Artificial Intelligence in Children's Radio Programmes in Rivers State, Nigeria

Keziah Akuoma Achuonye and Emmanuel Nnabuchi Okwumabua

Introduction

The advent of Artificial Intelligence (AI) has ushered in a new era of innovation and transformation across various industries, and the field of broadcasting is no exception. In particular, the potential applications of AI in children's radio broadcasting are promising, as it can enable content that is more engaging, educational, and tailored to individual preferences. Children's radio programmes play a pivotal role in shaping the minds

K. A. Achuonye (✉)
Department of Curriculum Studies and Instructional Technology, Ignatius Ajuru University of Education, Rivers State, Port Harcourt, Nigeria
e-mail: Keziah.achuonye@iaue.edu.ng

E. N. Okwumabua
Virtues International Academy, Rivers State, Port Harcourt, Nigeria

U. S. Akpan (ed.), *Educational Broadcasting in Nigeria in the Age of Artificial Intelligence*,
https://doi.org/10.1007/978-3-031-68530-9_6

and values of the younger generation. In today's digital age, where technology is increasingly intertwined with everyday life, the prospects, and challenges of integrating artificial intelligence (AI) into children's radio programmes in developing countries like Nigeria and Rivers State specifically, are worth exploring. AI has the potential to revolutionize content creation, engagement, and education, but it also raises concerns related to privacy, ethics, and accessibility. This opinion paper delves into the opportunities and hurdles that AI presents in the context of children's radio programmes in Nigeria and River State specifically. However, when it comes to implementing AI in this context within the chosen domain area, a myriad of challenges arises. This paper explores these challenges, focusing on Nigeria as a case study, and offers insights into how they can be mitigated.

The Concept of Communication and Broadcasting

The concept of communication is as old as man and has remained an essential ingredient of human survival. Communication refers to a purposeful transfer of information from a sender to receiver(s). Depending on the nature of the mechanism and receiver, communication could be intra-communication (with oneself—soliloquy), inter-communication (between two or more persons), or mass-communication (through mass media covering a geographical area). This last format is also called broadcasting, which is the crux of this study.

Broadcasting is the heart of mass communication because it is the media that appeals the most to the audience. As a concept, broadcasting is a communication art which is concerned with the systematic dissemination of entertainment, information, educational programming, and other features for simultaneous reception by a scattered audience with appropriate receiving apparatus. It may be sound only, as in radio, or visual or a combination of both, as in television. Radio broadcasting is traced to have started about 1920, while television broadcasting began in the 1930s.

Radio Broadcasting for Children

Radio is a one-way audio communication, and so requires good listening skills to benefit from the broadcast. Listening skill is the ability to pay attention to and effectively interpret what other people are saying. Children have a very short attention span and can listen with focus for five to ten minutes only as their listening skills are still being refined. Based on the distinguishing traits, writing and/or producing children's radio shows require special considerations. It should be interesting, and fun filled. It should be short, properly segmented, and meaningfully embellished with exciting songs, rhymes, poems, playlets, and stories. Children's radio programmes are always better when they are interested, able to filter out distractions, engage and sustain attention to comprehend what they are supposed to be listening to. Interest is heightened when the child can connect with the content of the programme hence the need for local contents in such programmes. Suitably packaged kiddies' radio programmes make education and learning fun and exciting for children-listeners.

Children's radio has long been recognized as a valuable educational tool. It can teach children about language, culture, history, and moral values. Educational content delivered through radio programmes can complement formal education, especially in areas with limited access to schools or other educational resources. When children listen to other youngsters on radio, they pay rapt attention and follow through especially if the discourse is relatable to their current study or immediate environment. This is how children learn to know that they will dictate the leads for tomorrow. Children's radio programmes often encourage family participation, with parents and caregivers listening alongside children. This shared experience can strengthen family bonds and provide opportunities for parents to engage in discussions with their children. Radio allows children to exercise their imagination. Audio-only content encourages listeners to visualize stories and characters, fostering creativity and critical thinking. It provides an alternative to screen-based entertainment, which is increasingly prevalent in today's digital landscape. This is how children first learn to multitask, take responsibility, seek clarity, and hone imaginative and creative skills. Children's radio can help preserve and promote cultural heritage. Folktales, traditional music, chants, mimes, and storytelling are often featured in children's radio programmes, helping to pass down cultural knowledge and values to younger generations. This helps them to build requisite vocabulary, grammar structure on subject matters, and cultural aesthetics.

Finally, radio is a highly accessible medium, even in regions with limited access to electricity or the internet. Battery-powered radios and low-cost receivers make it possible for children in remote and underserved areas to access educational and entertaining content. Radio has the potential to reach marginalized and underserved populations, including those who speak minority languages or live in regions with limited infrastructure. It can contribute to social inclusion by providing content that caters to diverse communities.

Kiddies-Zone on Treasure FM 98.5

There are about 22 radio stations in Rivers State out of which the eight most popular are: Radio Rivers 99.1 FM (oldest), Rhythm 93.7 FM, Garden City Radio 89.9 FM, 91.7 Wave FM, Nigeria Info 92.3 FM, Cool FM 95.9, The Beat 99.9 FM, and Treasure FM 98.5.

Taking a closer look at Treasure FM 98.5, for example, this radio station was set up by the Federal Radio Corporation of Nigeria; and located at Mgbouba, Port Harcourt to bring the programmes of the Federal Government to the grassroots. In addition, the station features some educational and entertainment programmes including the children's programme known as Kiddies-Zone (K-Zone). It is a radio-show designed for children-listeners between 4 and 12 years old. K-Zone shows focus on topical issues concerning the family, school, and society simplified and presented in the language and perspective of children. What is worthy of note is that K-Zone features children as presenters, discussants, and participants in songs, poems, riddles/jokes, and playlets for the listening pleasure of mostly children.

Examples of Contents in K-Zone Radio Shows

Several topical issues are handled in Children's Radio programmes in Rivers State, some of which are as follows:

Child abuse: This is an intentional act of misuse of a child in any form, it is the situation where a child is not being provided the much-needed necessities of life, where a child is maltreated physically, sexually, or emotionally and this is detrimental to the future growth and development of such a child; the effects include anxiety, agitation, guilt feeling, neurotic disorder. These young derelicts graduate to armed robbery, kidnappers, and dare-devils criminals in the society. Kiddies' radio programmes help to enlighten children on the forms of abuse, discourage the practice of child abuse and labour, and educate the public on the social dangers of child abuse. These social miscreants become parents, and the circle continues unbroken unless government civil society groups, parents, schools, and religious institutions rise properly against it to curb the ugly act (Elizabeth, 2022) (http://www.projecttopics.org.ng)—Garden City Radio.

Good manners—Respect: This is good and required by everyone as it helps us to live a good and peaceful life with one another. It is one of the qualities of good boys and girls irrespective of religion, skin colour, or socio-economic background. Children are encouraged to avoid disrespectful behaviour because it breeds bad feelings, unfriendliness, anger, quarrel and even fighting. People love and praise a respectful child.

Poverty as one of the social problems around us: This helps children to know that we live in a society; and poverty is one of the problems bedeviling the society. Children are made to understand that poverty is not forever; they should not use poverty as an excuse to engage in criminality, rather they should work harder in their schoolwork and other good activities; and over time, would overcome poverty.

Other flash topics include Safety Tips, Climate Change, Personal Hygiene, and some academic topics such as Parts of Speech, Animals Around Us, National Symbols, Balanced Diet, etc.

Dearth of Children's Broadcasts

It is very unfortunate to note that Treasure FM is just one of the very few radio stations in Rivers State that has such weekly programmes solely devoted to children. Other radio stations have never had one or simply slot in children programmes only during festive periods. Even among the few that have children programmes are tendencies to abandon them, hence, the call for the reintroduction of children's educational programmes on TV and radio stations across Africa to enhance children's learning capacity. This is properly documented by Ubongo kids, Africa's leading producer of kids' edutainment, in their programme 'Storytelling for Change'. The team is a non-profit social enterprise that creates fun, localized and multi-platform educational content that helps kids learn, and leverage their learning to change their lives.

Olatayo observed that there is a dearth of educational content on television and radio stations in Nigeria; calling on educational sectors, and broadcasters and content developers to come up with edutainment content that will enhance the learning ability of the Nigerian child; to reach up to 60 million African children by 2025. Using the power of fun catchy songs and storylines, to create and deliver educational content in local languages to kids across Africa. Technology seems to offer a helping hand to reinstate, reinvigorate, and sustain children's broadcasts.

Artificial Intelligence (AI) in Broadcasting

As technology continues to advance at a rapid pace affecting every facet of human endeavour, broadcasting including radio is constantly witnessing transformations from traditional format to digital satellite and webcast broadcasting via the internet. Podcasting is a popular form of media distribution that involves creating and sharing audio or video content on the internet. It is like traditional radio or television broadcasting. The sporadic AI advancement is another technology that is transforming the broadcasting sphere. Intelligence is an integrated combination of many abilities such as thinking, reasoning, comprehension, learning, judgement, and inference (Cebeci, 2021). According to Techopodia (nd), AI asserts are aspects of computer science that lay emphasis on creating intelligent machines that work, act, and react like humans. It is a broad field of computer science that focuses on the development of intelligent machines and performing tasks that typically require human-like intelligence, such as perception, reasoning, learning, and decision-making. AI technology involves the development and implementation of algorithms, computer programmes, and models that enable machines to analyse and understand complex data, recognize patterns, and make decisions based on that data. AI Tech, as a concept, has existed since the 1950s, but it is only in recent times that technology has advanced to the point where it can be considered reliable enough to deploy for important business tasks. Artificial Intelligence (AI) has grown worldwide and is applied in different sectors to quicken production processes, increase productivity, ensure accuracy and ease in ways businesses are run. It is deployed to power industries, shipping, hotel services, home deliveries, and financial services. However, according to Okiyi and Nsude (2019), AI technology is yet to become commonly used and entrenched in different sectors across industries in most African countries.

Journalism has benefited from AI as robots engage in journalistic processes and produce results quickly in broadcast and print media types. Through AI, software stories are produced automatically by computers rather than human reporters (Okiyi & Nsude, 2019). These programmes interpret, organize, and present data in human readable forms. They each start with content creation or collection, move to processing and editing, and end with the distribution of such content. Immediately artificial intelligence gets the mechanics of one creative process, it can quickly be applied to another. Artificial intelligence is formulaic in nature and applies to stories which are based on statistics and numerical figures. It has innovated and changed how media work is carried out by learner staff. Journalism can draw on the relevance of AI in different sectors like education and entertainment that intertwine with its daily media cast.

Prospects of AI in Educational and Entertainment Programmes

In education, AI algorithms analyse students' learning behaviours and adapt educational content to their individual needs. This personalization can enhance engagement and improve learning outcomes. AI-powered virtual tutors provide students with real-time help and explanations, reducing the need for human intervention. They can answer questions, provide feedback, and track progress. AI can generate educational content, such as practice exercises, quizzes, and even essays. AI tools have transformed the way radio broadcasting is used to enthuse learning. When used in children's broadcasting, it can save time and provide students and broadcasters with additional resources, engage and get all lost in a world of the unimaginable. AI-driven language learning apps use speech recognition and natural language processing to help learners practice and improve their language skills. AI systems can quickly and consistently grade assignments, quizzes, and exams, reducing the burden on educators and radio hosts in providing prompt feedback to students. AI can identify students at risk of falling behind and alert educators, enabling early intervention to prevent academic struggles. AI-powered tools can assist students with disabilities, providing text-to-speech or speech-to-text capabilities and other accessibility features. AI analyses educational data to identify trends and insights, helping institutions make data-driven decisions to improve curriculum and teaching methods.

Streaming platforms like Netflix, radio and TV podcasts, and YouTube use AI to recommend content based on users' preferences and viewing history, enhancing user experience. AI-generated music, art, and even script contents for radio, movies, and TV shows (Gwari, 2023) it can assist artists and content creators in generating new ideas and producing content. It plays a vital role in video game development, creating realistic characters, generating in-game dialogues, and optimizing gameplay experiences. AI-driven chatbots provide customer support and entertainment experiences. Virtual assistants like Siri and Alexa offer interactive and entertaining responses to user queries. AI-driven interactive narratives allow users to shape the story's outcome through their choices, providing immersive and personalized entertainment. It enables voice-activated devices and services, making it possible to control entertainment systems and interact with technology through voice commands.

Case Studies of Successful AI Integration in Children's Media

IBM Watson's Content Discovery: IBM Watson's AI-powered Content Discovery platform helps broadcasters and media companies analyse large volumes of content, making it easier to find and curate relevant content. Content Discovery aids in the efficient and personalized curation of media content. It can be employed to curate educational content for children's media, ensuring that it remains relevant and engaging.

Minecraft Education Edition: Microsoft's Minecraft Education Edition incorporates AI to enhance learning experiences. The platform uses AI algorithms to provide personalized recommendations for educational content within the game. The integration of AI helps educators tailor lessons to individual students' needs, making learning more engaging and effective. Teachers can track student progress and receive insights to inform their teaching strategies.

Duolingo: Duolingo, a language-learning app, utilizes AI for personalized language instruction. The app adapts its lessons based on a user's proficiency and learning progress. Duolingo's AI-driven approach has made language learning accessible and engaging for millions of users worldwide, including children. It offers interactive lessons, immediate feedback, and gamification to motivate learners.

Woebot: Woebot is an AI-powered mental health chatbot designed for adolescents and young adults. It uses natural language processing and cognitive-behavioural techniques to provide emotional support. Woebot offers accessible and stigma-free mental health support for young users. It engages in conversations, provides coping strategies, and tracks users' moods, offering valuable assistance for emotional well-being.

StoryStream: StoryStream is an AI-driven content curation and storytelling platform. It helps media companies and brands create and curate user-generated content into engaging narratives. By leveraging AI to filter and arrange user-generated content, StoryStream enables the creation of interactive and engaging storytelling experiences. This approach can be adapted for children's media to encourage participation and creativity.

Netflix's Content Recommendation Algorithm: Netflix uses AI algorithms to personalize content recommendations for its users, including children. These algorithms analyse viewing history and preferences to suggest age-appropriate shows and movies. Netflix's AI-driven recommendation system enhances the viewing experience for children by offering a tailored selection of content. This encourages continued engagement with the platform.

Sphero's Educational Robots: Sphero's educational robots incorporate AI to engage children in programming and problem-solving. These robots provide a hands-on learning experience and adapt to user interactions. Sphero's robots foster an interactive and educational play environment for children. They encourage coding skills development, creativity, and critical thinking through engaging activities.

These case studies demonstrate how AI can be successfully integrated into children's media and educational platforms to enhance content, engagement, and personalization. The examples span various applications, from language learning to mental health support and content curation, showcasing the versatility and potential of AI in improving children's media experiences.

Challenges of Using AI in Children's Radio Programmes in Nigeria

Infrastructure Limitations: One of the primary challenges of implementing AI in children's radio broadcasting in Rivers State is the state of the existing infrastructure. AI systems require robust internet connectivity, high-quality hardware, and advanced software capabilities. Unfortunately, many parts of radio stations, especially in rural areas, lack access to reliable electricity and internet connections. Adeloye and Ogunbode (2019), reviewed the healthcare infrastructure in Nigeria and found significant disparities in access to basic services and infrastructure between urban and rural areas. The lack of infrastructure, such as stable electricity and internet connectivity, poses a significant challenge to implementing AI-powered systems in children's radio broadcasting. AI algorithms require constant data connectivity for updates and maintenance, which is often lacking in many regions of Nigeria. Addressing this challenge requires a concerted effort by both government and private sectors to improve infrastructure. Investment in reliable power generation and distribution, as well as the expansion of internet access to underserved areas, would pave the way for the successful deployment of AI in children's radio broadcasting.

Content Appropriateness and Cultural Sensitivity: Children's radio programming should be carefully curated to ensure that it is appropriate for the target audience in terms of content and cultural sensitivity. AI systems, while powerful, may lack the nuance and cultural understanding required to create content that resonates with Nigerian children. Awe (2019) conducted a historical analysis of children's broadcasting in Nigeria and highlighted the importance of culturally relevant content. Broadcasting content that is not culturally sensitive or that does not align with local values can lead to a lack of engagement among children and their families. To address this challenge, AI systems must be trained on culturally relevant datasets and fine-tuned to understand the nuances of Nigerian culture and values. Additionally, involving local content creators and experts in the development and oversight of AI-generated content can help ensure appropriateness and cultural sensitivity.

Access Disparities: Another significant challenge in Nigeria and Rivers State specifically, is the unequal access to technology and digital resources. While AI-powered content can provide tremendous benefits to children, it is essential to ensure that it reaches all segments of the population, including those in remote and underserved areas. UNESCO's Education for All Global Monitoring Report (2020) highlights the digital divide in education and access to information in developing countries. Many children in rural Nigeria lack access to smartphones, computers, or even basic radio receivers. Therefore, relying solely on AI-generated content could exacerbate existing inequalities. To tackle this challenge, a multi-pronged approach is necessary. Initiatives to provide affordable digital devices to underserved communities, along with educational programs that teach digital literacy, can help bridge the access gap. Simultaneously, traditional radio broadcasts, which are more accessible to a broader audience, should not be replaced entirely but complemented by AI-generated content.

Privacy and Data Security: The implementation of AI in children's radio broadcasting involves the collection and processing of vast amounts of data, including children's personal information and preferences. Ensuring the privacy and security of this data is paramount in Nigeria especially in Rivers State where data protection regulations may not be as robust as in developed nations. Privacy concerns and data security issues were raised by Goyal and Kant (2020) in their examination of AI in education. Children's data must be handled with extreme care, and stringent safeguards should be in place to protect against data breaches and misuse. To address this challenge, regulatory frameworks for data protection need to be developed and enforced. Moreover, organizations involved in children's radio broadcasting should adhere to best practices for data security and transparency, ensuring that parents and guardians are well-informed about data collection and usage.

Conclusion

Over the years, radio has become one of the important channels of entertainment and information dissemination in society. Radio broadcast is a one-way communication and generally conversational, making radio broadcast effective. It demands the use of short sentences, and directional language with not much complication bearing in mind that the spoken word of radio is often only heard once, people won't rewind it (Manvell & Camacho, 2023). The script should have personality and be engaging for the listener so that the listener feels that they are being spoken to. It should, therefore, be clear to create a picture in the mind of the listener. In addition, good quality radio producers/presenters need to be creative, able to conceptualize ideas quickly, and possess a clear and distinct voice with the ability to talk enthusiastically with others. Such presenters need to be good observers, possess interest in what they are talking about, and be able to conclude from experience.

The integration of Artificial Intelligence (AI) into children's radio broadcasting holds immense promise in terms of creating engaging and educational content tailored to individual preferences. However, implementing AI in this context in Rivers State presents numerous challenges, including infrastructure limitations, content appropriateness, access disparities, and data privacy concerns.

Addressing these challenges requires a collaborative effort involving governments, private sector organizations, and civil society. Investments in infrastructure development, cultural sensitivity, and digital inclusion are essential to ensuring that AI benefits all children, regardless of their geographic location or socioeconomic background. Additionally, robust data protection regulations and security measures must be in place to safeguard children's privacy and ensure responsible AI implementation.

As we continue to explore the possibilities of AI in children's radio broadcasting, it is crucial to remain mindful of the challenges and work collectively to overcome them. Only then can we fully harness the potential of AI to provide children in developing countries like Nigeria with high-quality, culturally relevant, and accessible radio programming that enriches their lives and enhances their learning experiences.

Recommendations

Implementing AI in children's radio broadcasting in Rivers State comes with its share of challenges. However, these challenges can be overcome with careful planning and strategic interventions. Here are some recommendations to address the challenges and facilitate the successful integration of AI in children's radio broadcasting in Rivers State, Nigeria:

Infrastructure Development: The government and private sector should collaborate to improve access to stable electricity and internet connectivity, particularly in rural areas. This will provide the necessary infrastructure for AI implementation. Given Nigeria's abundant sunlight, investing in solar-powered infrastructure can help ensure reliable power sources in remote areas where grid electricity is scarce. Promote initiatives that make mobile internet access more affordable and widely available, as many individuals in developing countries rely on smartphones for internet connectivity.

Cultural Sensitivity and Content Development: Collaborate with local artists, educators, and storytellers who understand Nigerian culture and values to create culturally sensitive and engaging content for children. Train AI systems on datasets that reflect Nigerian cultural nuances and preferences, allowing AI-generated content to be more contextually relevant.

Digital Inclusion and Access: Launch educational programs that teach digital literacy skills to children and their families, ensuring they can navigate and benefit from digital resources. Support initiatives to provide affordable digital devices, such as low-cost tablets or radios with digital capabilities, to underserved communities. Establish community access points with internet-connected devices, allowing children in remote areas to access AI-powered content.

Data Privacy and Security: Develop and enforce data protection regulations that prioritize the privacy and security of children's data, aligning with international best practices. Ensure that parents and guardians are well-informed about the data collection and usage practices of AI-powered systems and obtain their informed consent.

Collaboration and Partnerships: Encourage collaborations between government agencies, NGOs, and private sector organizations to pool resources and expertise in addressing infrastructure and content development challenges. Offer grants and incentives to encourage research and development in AI technologies tailored for children's broadcasting in developing countries.

Awareness and Education: Conduct public awareness campaigns to inform parents, caregivers, and communities about the benefits of AI in children's radio broadcasting and how to access it. Provide training to teachers on integrating AI-powered content into the classroom, enhancing the educational experience.

References

Adeloye, D., & Ogunbode, O. (2019). A review of healthcare infrastructure in Nigeria. *Journal of Public Health in Africa, 10*(1), 1231. https://doi.org/10.4081/jphia.2019.1231

Awe, J. O. (2019). Children's broadcasting in Nigeria: A historical analysis of its development and impact. *International Journal of Communication, 13*, 2323–2344.

Cebeci, H. I. (2021). Artificial intelligence applications in management information systems: A comprehensive systematic review with business analytics perspective. *Artificial Intelligence Theory and Applications, 1*, 25–56. www.aita.bakircay.edu.tr

Elizabeth, A. (2022). The role of societal institutions in curbing social vices. *Journal of Social Issues, 78*(3), 432–433.

Goyal, A., & Kant, K. (2020). Artificial intelligence in education: Current trends and future prospects. In S. R. H. Hoque, A. I. Manogaran, & A. K. Tiwari (Eds.), *Handbook of research on artificial intelligence techniques and algorithms* (pp. 134–153). IGI Global.

Gwari, C. (2023). *10 best AI audio tools in 2023 (for podcasts, music & more).* https://www.elegantthemes.com/blog/business/best-ai-audio-tools#what-is-an-ai-audio-tools

Manvell, R., & Camacho, J. A. (2023). Broadcasting. In *Encyclopaedia Britannica.* https://www.britannica.com/technology/broadcasting

Okiyi, G. O., & Nsude, I. (2019, June). Adopting artificial intelligence to journalistic practices in Nigeria: Challenges and way forward. *International Journal of Communication: An Interdisciplinary Journal of Communication Studies, 24.*

Techopodia. (nd). https://www.techopedia.com/definition

United Nations Educational, Scientific, and Cultural Organization (UNESCO). (2020). *Education for all global monitoring report 2020.* https://unesdoc.unesco.org/ark:/48223/pf0000374023

CHAPTER 7

Challenges of Educational Broadcasting in a Digitized Age of Artificial Intelligence (AI)

Oluwakemi Aweda-Akinuliola

Introduction

Digitization has been inputted into every sphere of human lives. With each passing day, there is an invention of a new application, software, or gadget that has brought about digitization to our lives thereby improving our daily living in one way or the other. Budhwar (2017) explains that technology and digitization plays a huge part in every field man is involved in, however one of such fields where the presence of digitization is powerfully felt, is in the education sector. Digitization is changing the education sector in Nigeria, and the world at large. People do not want to wait to be educated at the source's timing and desire. With digitization, education waits for the people to serve the people at their own timing. Digitization has changed how educational resources are accessed,

O. Aweda-Akinuliola (✉)
University of Lagos, Lagos, Nigeria
e-mail: oakinuliola@unilag.edu.ng

U. S. Akpan (ed.), *Educational Broadcasting in Nigeria in the Age of Artificial Intelligence*,
https://doi.org/10.1007/978-3-031-68530-9_7

how research is done, and how education is joyful, engaging, and easier. Education is no longer seen as a boring or cumbersome task, with the help of digitization, education is an everyday task that is interesting and cuts across physical and distance barriers.

Also, with the advent of social media infused in the educational sector, education is now made simpler than ever. Haleema et al. (2022), reveal that social media as learning tool in the educational sector has created an essential venue for exchange or information at any time of the day, the ability to communicate information from anywhere in the world, and the ability to form and build educational networks. Social media infused in the educational sector has also changed the face of education in our society today. With WhatSapp and Facebook educational group discussion, Twitter educational discussion, forum and meetings, Zoom meetings, the learning management system (LMS) used by university organizations, and the ever ending educational resources on YouTube, education has been fully digitized in our society.

Nigeria has been fully digitized especially in the education sector. We have digital classrooms for all age groups ranging from different subjects for younger and older children. In tertiary education, we have online LMS class rooms, zoom class rooms, Twitter forum, and YouTube classes. And with the advent of Artificial Intelligence (AI), we have different applications that are AI-infused. Indeed digitization has completely changed the face of education in Nigeria. Afolabi and Uhomoibhi (2017) opine that digital education and the use of AI in education has been well utilized in the past however, it became a thing of necessity especially in the era of the COVID-19 pandemic. However even in the post-COVID-19 era, digital education is here to stay for good. Because of the major benefits of digital education such as ease, access, participation, engagement, cost-effectiveness, etc., digital education remains a major necessity for all educational institutions in Nigeria.

The advantages of a digitized educational broadcasting have come to rival the traditional educational broadcasting we have in Nigeria. Gone are the days where people depend on just radio and television to educate them. Budhwar (2017), reveals that traditional education and digital education are both similar and also different at the same time. Budhwar noted that there would not be a digital or technological education without the foundation laid by traditional education. This goes further to state that traditional educational broadcasting was educating the Nigerian masses just fine, however digital educational broadcasting has brought more advantages over the traditional broadcasting methods and in great strides improved and advanced on the methods of the traditional educational broadcasting methods.

The world has moved beyond traditional educational broadcasting of waiting for their favourite programmes to be aired via radio or television at a particular time of the day, and sometimes having to struggle with a good network for some radio stations to digitize educational broadcasting, where educational contents can be easily accessed at the demand of the user. From going to television and radio stations' websites to look up any educational programmes of the user's choice, to listening to educational broadcasting podcasts, and going to YouTube to view past educational broadcasting programmes, etc. It is therefore against this background that this study was prompted to analyse the challenges and prospects of educational broadcasting in a digitized age among selected University students in Lagos, Nigeria.

Theoretical Framework

Social Responsibility Media Theory

One of the theories of the press propounded by Siebert, Peterson and Schramm, is the social responsibility theory of the press. It was propounded in 1963, and came about as a composite of ideas developed from the writings of W. E. Hocking, the works of the 1947 United States Press Freedom Commission (Hutchins Commission), the ideas of mass communication practitioners and media codes. According to Anaeto, G. S. et al. (2008), social responsibility theory is a theory that states that the media is obliged to the society for carrying out certain essential functions of mass communication. Below are some of the assumptions of the social responsibility theory by Mcquail (1987 as cited in Ojobor, 2002):

1. That the media should accept and fulfil certain obligations to society.
2. That, through professional standards of informativeness, truth, accuracy, objectivity, and balance, these obligations can be met.
3. That the media should regulate itself within the framework of law and established institutions to be able to carry out its responsibilities.

The relevance of the social responsibility theory of the press is based on the theory's assumption that the media is responsible to the society for ensuring they are presented with educational, accurate, and credible information. It is the media's obligation to educate the masses. The people depend on the media for certain functions and one of the major functions is educational broadcasting.

Technological Determinism Theory

The theory was believed to be propounded by Thorstein Veblen. Amobi (2010), explains that technological determinism theory posits that we are living in a new age of technology that has never been experienced in the history of mankind, and this technology is changing the way people think, act and feel about their environment. Chukwu (2014), opines that technological determinists interpret technology in general and communications technologies in particular as the sole basis of society in the past, present and even the future. The technological determinists hold that technologies such as writing or print or television or the computer "changed society." In its extreme form, the entire form of society is seen as being determined by technology; new technologies transform society at every level, including institutions, social interaction and individuals.

According to McLuhan (1969), one of the technologist determinists, argued that it is the medium itself that alters human perception and affects human consciousness, e.g. reading a description of a scene on the page of a newspaper has a different effect from seeing a picture of it or watching it on television or computers. The underlying concept of McLuhan's view of electronic technology is that it has become an extension of our senses, especially those of sight and sound. McLuhan summed it up as the medium is the message. Today people rely heavily on the new media technologies for their reference on what's happening and how to reach more people within a relatively short space of time.

The world has moved on from the initial wave of the electric age and is now able to understand more media. Computers and other interactive media have supplanted television and radio. They are no longer considered the major media in our society. We have really come a long way since McLuhan's pronouncement of the digital age. The world has evolved from radio and television as the medium that brings families together to living in a digital world where all individuals in the world are connected. From radio and television we have moved to a digital age of streaming content on the go, from books to electronic books, and unending videos and contents.

The relevance of the technological determinism theory to this study is based on the theory's assumption that the message is the medium. The world has moved from receiving educational content via radio and television to the digital era of educational broadcasting. Audiences now prefer educational content via online television, online radio, YouTube, Twitter, AI applications and the internet at large. People now get educated and get certification via YouTube content and the school's LMS, distance is no longer a barrier to one's education. Via the digitized way of educational broadcasting, learning is easier, faster, participatory and enjoyable, as learning is not local, but global. After all, with digital educational broadcasting, the world is a global village. Students now prefer to use AI technologies to get answers to their educational problems.

Contextual and Conceptual Clarifications

Education

There is a popular saying alluding to the fact that the day one stops learning is the day one dies. Education is a necessary commodity in Nigeria. Education in Nigeria is divided into three sections- Primary, Secondary and Tertiary Education. The primary section is usually for the age of five-ten years old. The secondary section is usually from the age of 10–16, while the tertiary education is from the ages of 16 or 18–20 or 25. The age range varies according to when the individual starts a particular section. Nwagwu (1976 in Nkwam-Uwaoma & Onu, 2017) defines education as a process where the society intentionally preserves and upgrades the continuous growing knowledge, skills and attitudes in its cultural setting and heritage in order to foster the well-being of mankind and guarantee its survival against unpredictable, hostile elements of man and nature. Education is really a process that is unending, and it majorly focuses on passing across knowledge, skills, and attitude from one generation to the next in order to preserve the cultural elements of education.

Olenor (1975 in Nkwam-Uwaoma & Onu, 2017), opines that there are five major aims of education.

- Education is to equip men and women with the barest skills possible so that they can take their place in the society as seek further knowledge

- Education is to equip men and women in the society with vocational skills so that they would be an asset in the society and not a liability
- Education is to awaken an unending interest in knowledge among individuals in a society
- Education is to enable individuals in a society to be critical in thinking about issues pertaining to them and their environs and
- Education is to ensure individuals in a society appreciate and ensure the preservation of their culture for mankind.

Education embodies the process of acquisition of knowledge and skills by individuals in a society that ensures that the individual becomes an asset and not a liability in the society. In reality, education ensures the progress, achievements and the preservation of mankind.

Broadcasting

Broadcasting can be defined as the process of producing, distributing and disseminating ideas, messages, and information through electronic technology, Onabajo (2000). Broadcasting entails the encoding and decoding of information, it starts right from the conception of ideas for programmes to the pre-production stage, production stage and the post-production stage before the messages will be decoded by the audience's receiving set. Onabajo (2004 in Nkwam-Uwaoma & Onu, 2017) explains that broadcasting passes across the ideas of:

- Dissemination of audio and video messages
- To a heterogeneous or dispersed audience
- Through an electronic mass communication medium
- The mass communication medium uses an electromagnetic spectrum
- In a one-to-many model.

Broadcasting is passing across vital and relevant information to a group of dispersed audience through electromagnetic medium in a one-to-many model. Before the advent of the digital world, broadcasting was limited to radio and television. Now with the internet and technology, broadcasting has been extended to online radio, online television, YouTube and a radio or television's website.

Educational Broadcasting

Educational broadcasting can be understood from the perspective of a channel of communication, which can carry information, facts and figures that are designed for instructional objectives. Educational broadcasting refers to programmes that are particularly enlightening, informative and intellectually stimulating. We have two major types of educational broadcasting.

We have extensive educational broadcasting which is using broadcasting medium to provide information and knowledge on general matters. Extensive educational broadcasting is also known as informal broadcasting. It focuses on teaching its audience about extensive general knowledge. We also have intensive educational broadcasting. This type of broadcasting focuses on formal educational subjects and matters. It is also called formal educational broadcasting.

History of Educational Broadcasting in Nigeria

Educational broadcasting in Nigeria started with the introduction of radio in Nigeria in 1932. The British Broadcasting Corporation (BBC) set up the first radio receiving set in Lagos. One of the main aims of setting up that radio station by the BBC was majorly for education. The British colonial masters wanted to make sure that Nigerians were learning the English language. Nkwam-Uwaoma and Onu (2017), revealed that the first educational radio programme were to teach English Language that was broadcasted once a week in the early 1940s.

In 1959, the Western region in Nigeria established the first television station in Nigeria called the Western Nigeria Television (WNTV). The sole aim of the establishment of the television was to educate the masses. It was believed that television will enhance learning more than radio medium because of the visual feature. In 1960 and 1961, other regions in Nigeria (eastern and northern region) also established television stations. Onabajo (2000 in Nkwam-Uwaoma & Onu, 2017), revealed that in the 1960s, the Ministry of Education directed that each regional television station begin their own educational broadcasting programmes which must include classes on elementary science, arts, crafts, English language, mathematics, and history. This class was broadcasted via television from Monday to Friday between the hours of 1am and 1 pm. Educational broadcasting programmes have now transitioned from only formal learning to informal and a combination of both. Almost all programmes produced by broadcasting stations have educational elements infused in them.

Digitization

Witten and David (2003 in Onyia, 2021) defines digitization as the process of converting traditional learning materials that are in book form and papers to electronic form where they can be stored, viewed and manipulated via the internet and computers. Also, Jagboro et al. (2012) explain that digitization is the process of making available historical and other materials online. It is simply converting all hardcopy to soft copy, it also means that all materials can now be accessed online with the navigation of the internet. According to Ding (2010), here are some of the advantages of digitization:

- Digitization means no new buildings are required; improvement in information sharing and redundancy of collections reduced.
- Digitization leads to the development of Internet in digitized based institutions
- Digital materials can be transmitted, sorted and retrieved easily and quickly.
- It is cheaper to access electronic information than its print counterpart when storing files in an electronic device with compatible facilities and equipment.
- Digital texts can be linked, made interactively; and improves the retrieval of more information.

The advantages of digitization can bring about major transformation in any sector of the society. For example, with digitization there is easy and universal access to information online, with digitization, materials and information can be uploaded and accessed on a low or no cost budget. Also with digitization, there is instant feedback and engagement on the contents uploaded online, and physical location is no more a necessity.

Artificial Intelligence (AI)

AI has taken over the digital space. Celik et al. (2022) explained that the term artificial intelligence was first used in 1956 by John McCarthy. AI are referred to as computers that are used to perform cognitive tasks (such as learning and solving problems) that are usually associated with a human mind. This method can be classified under diverse analytical methods. AI is therefore integrated into several instructional technologies such as Chabot, intelligent tutoring and automated grading systems. These technologies do the work of a human. It thinks, analyses and solves the intended problem that a human should solve. These AI technologies are now embedded into applications such as ChatGPT, Google Bard, Midjourney, Canvas magic, and a whole lot more. They can be downloaded via computers and smart mobile phones. These AI technologies are quickly transforming the society at large and especially the educational sector.

Digitization, Artificial Intelligence (AI) and Educational Broadcasting in Nigeria

Since the advent of the internet in the 80s and 90s, we are indeed living in a world of digitization as all sectors have gone digital, and we are currently experiencing an upward trajectory when it comes to technology disruption in our society. There seems to be daily new inventions with technology. This disruption in our society has transformed our education sector globally. Asogwa (2011) opines that whenever we have questions from the simplest of questions to the most complicated, we ask the internet. Technology has redefined the face of education.

AI software and applications have transformed our lives exponentially. In the area of education, AI has changed the game. For example a student is faced with an educational question, he types it into ChatGPT and ChatGPT analyses the question by analysing all the algorithms relating to that question on the World Wide Web. In return, ChatGPT relates the answer to the student, already solved, analysed and written in a well-presentational style. The usage of AI by students is numerous, some of which are; the student learn at their own personalized time 24/7, immediate feedback is provided for the students' problems, gamification and immersive learning experiences for the students, learning barriers are broken down for the students, we now have students from different countries and languages who can now collaborate on projects and learn from one another.

In Nigeria, Bashir (2022) revealed that over 100 million people are estimated to have a mobile device and more than half of them being smartphones. Most Nigerians are in the digital space, and most of them use these digital worlds for education and learning. Digital dependence and transformation was majorly seen during the COVID era, and even after the COVID era, digital space and learning in Nigeria has been widely accepted and recognized by a number of institutions and people. Bashir (2022) also revealed that in a bid to encourage digital learning, the National Information Technology Development Agency (NITDA) said that it will continue to foster investment in digital innovation which would indirectly boost the education sector and the economy as a whole. Salau (2019) disclosed that Lagos state governor Babajide Sanwo-olu distributed tablets to teachers in state's public schools to aid teaching and learning especially as the world has gone digital.

Challenges of Educational Broadcasting in the Digitized World of AI

Roll and Wylie (2016) quoting Henry Ford stated that if one had asked people what they wanted, they would say faster horses. In reality, we now have faster schools and faster learning processes. With the advanced technology of AI in our educational sector, the process of learning is omitted, people just move over to the result, thereby relying on AI for the whole cognitive process. Below are some of the challenges associated with AI and educational broadcasting:

- **Lack of cognitive skills by the students**
  When students rely on AI for information and solutions to their educational problems, they tend to leave the whole analytical solving technique to the technology application. In return, the students go through life without acquiring the; how to do it' skill, i.e. the analytical skill. They do not gain any analytical, problem solving or research skills since the AI technology does it all for them. In relating it to educational broadcasting, with AI, the process of getting to the problem isn't shown or taught to the students, rather the students

are just exposed to the solution. With AI, educational broadcasting is ditching out the shortcut to learning to the students.

- **Replacement of physical tutors with digital tutors**
  With AI and educational broadcasting, physical tutors/educational broadcasters are replaced with online tutors. The online tutors might be physical or might just be eliminated with text or pictorial representation. The human figure explaining the solutions to educational problems is eliminated.
- **Lack of credibility, accountability and trustworthiness**
  With AI, the information and resources gotten online cannot be trusted because it is unknown as to where the researcher got the materials from only if the researcher credits his source. Secondly, if the researcher gets a material from a particular source and states his source, you have to believe the researcher for his word as there is no other way to ascertain the truth. Unlike educational broadcasting, the broadcaster gives the information or educational resources and is accountable for whatever information he uses.
- **Plagiarism/ethical issues**
  With AI, plagiarism is very common. The students take materials or educational resources off the AI applications and pretend that the work is originally theirs, they just copy and paste the research and educational materials off the AI sites without acknowledging or referencing the source.

Conclusion and Recommendation

The paper concludes that AI and the digital world is changing the educational broadcasting world in our society today, and despite the numerous benefits of the digital world and AI in our educational broadcasting, the challenges AI poses are a serious threat to educational broadcasting. The paper therefore recommends that:

1. Training of usage of AI for students and teachers-students need to be trained on the use of the digital space and especially AI usage so as to avoid the abuse of the usage of AI, and to also learn how to optimize the usage of AI to give the maximum result for their educational search. Teachers should also be trained on the use of

AI, and especially to detect students who use AI word for word without inputting their originality.

2. Gadgets should be made available to all the stakeholders of education-electronic gadgets should be made available to the tutors and students for further access into the world of educational broadcasting using AI. So as to close the digital divide, electronic gadgets to foster more access for both students and teachers are needed.

References

Afolabi, O. O., & Uhomoibhi, J. (2017). *E-learning implementation in higher education: Aspects of infrastructure development challenges and students learning approaches*. https://pure.ulster.ac.uk/en/publications/e-learning-implementation-in-highereducation-aspects-of-infrastru-3

Amobi, I. (2010). New generation, new media and digital divide: Ownership, access and usage of social media among young people in Nigeria. *A Journal of the Department of Mass Communication of University of Lagos.*

Anaeto, G. S., Onabajo, S. O., & Osifeso, J. B. (2008). *Models and theories of mass communication*. African Renaissance Books Incorporated.

Asogwa, B. E. (2011). Digitization of archival collections in Africa for scholarship communication: issues, strategies, and challenges. *Library Philosophy and Practice*. http://www.webpages.uidaho.edu/~mbolin/asogwa.htm

Bashir, A. M. (2022, February 23). Digital learning and Nigeria's education sector. *Daily Trust Online Newspaper*. https://dailytrust.com/digital-learning0and-nigerias-education-sector/

Budhwar, K. (2017). The role of technology in education. *International Journal of Engineering Applied Sciences and Technology, 2*(8), 55–57.

Celik, I., Dindar, M., Muukkonen, H., & Arvela, S. (2022). The promises and challenges of artificial intelligence for teachers: A systematic review of research. *TechTrends, 66*(1), 616–630. https://doi.org/10.1007/s11528-022-00715-y

Chukwu, C. O. (2014). Online journalism and the changing nature of traditional media in Nigeria. *International Journal of African Society Cultures and Traditions, 2*(3), 1–9.

Haleema, A., Javaida, M., Qadri, M. A., & Suman, R. (2022). Understanding the role of digital technologies in education: A review. *Sustainable Operations and Computer Journal, 3*(1), 275–285. https://doi.org/10.1016/j.susoc.2022.05.004

Jagboro, K. O., Omotayo, B. O., & Aboyade, W. A. (2012). Digitization of library collection in developing countries. In *Library Philosophy and Practice* (pp. 1–11).

McLuhan, M. (1969). The medium is the message. *Understanding Media: The Extensions of Man*. Retrieved from https://web.mit.edu/allanmc/www/mcluhan.mediummessage.pdf

Nkwam-Uwaoma, O. A., & Onu, M. D. (2017). *Educational broadcasting in contemporary society*. Gabtony Prints Ltd. ISBN: 978-978-54833-7-6

Ojobor, I. J. (2002). Mass communication theories. In C. S. Okunna (Eds.), Teaching Mass Communication: *A multi-dimensional approach. Enugu: New Generation Books*.

Onyia, M. N. (2021). Digitization of education in Nigeria: A path to technological advancement. In *Association for digital education and communications technology conference proceedings*. https://open.library.okstate.edu/adect2021/chapter/digitization-of-education-in-nigeria-a-path-to-technological-advancement/

Roll, I., & Wylie, R. (2016). Evolution and revolution in artificial intelligence in education. *International Journal of Artificial Intelligence in Education, 26*(2), 582–599.

Salau, G. (2019, December 10). Sanwo-olu begins digitalisation of teaching and learning. *Guardian Online Newspaper*. https://guardian.ng/news/sanwo-olu-begins-digitalisation-of-teaching-learning/

CHAPTER 8

Potentials of Digitalized and AI Enhanced Educational Broadcasting

Adeline O. Nkwam-Uwaoma, Mishack Ndukwu, and Ucheyamere C. Nkwam-Uwaoma

Introduction

The process, method, the fastest, and most effective means of acquiring education in the twenty-first century has taken a totally different approach due to recent advancements in science and technology. The twentieth century restricted education to the classroom, physical contact with the instructor and formal enrollment with a recognized institution. All these have changed in recent times. Means of acquiring knowledge has migrated from the formal setting and traditional mass media to a more diversified and multidimensional level with digital technology. What was previously

A. O. Nkwam-Uwaoma (✉) · M. Ndukwu
Imo State University, Owerri, Nigeria
e-mail: nkwamuwaomaadline@yahoo.com

U. C. Nkwam-Uwaoma
Bournemouth University, Poole, UK

U. S. Akpan (ed.), *Educational Broadcasting in Nigeria in the Age of Artificial Intelligence*,
https://doi.org/10.1007/978-3-031-68530-9_8

known as educational broadcasting has assumed a new outlook with greater potential.

Contemporary educational broadcasting in a digital and artificial intelligence era has taken a new dimension as it is no longer left for radio and television channels alone. With the emergence of other social media and streaming platforms like Twitter, Instagram, Facebook, YouTube, etc., the mass audience of educational broadcasting at present has the opportunity to access any educational broadcast content that will meet their immediate educational need. With a diversified audience, objectives and method of delivery, the potential of a digitalized and AI-assisted educational broadcasting is becoming a go-to channel for quality and audience-specific contents for education and enlightenment. Many people today acquire skills and knowledge that earn them a living and improve their social life through several digital platforms with little or no guidance. This is a testament that digitalization and artificial intelligence are reinvigorating the potentials of educational broadcasting.

Definition of Educational Broadcasting

Many scholars have defined the concepts of broadcasting and educational broadcasting. Because of the seemingly inseparableness of the two concepts, it will be right to first define broadcasting before delving into the concept of educational broadcasting. According to Onabajo (2004), as cited in Nkwam-Uwaoma and Onu (2017, p. 54), "broadcasting is the transmission of information via radio waves from a radio or television station to the audience in far and near places through their receivers, which helps in decoding such information." This means that when a message intended to enlighten and educate a large audience is broadcast with the use of technology, it can be considered educational broadcasting. Radio (and television) educational programmes are broadcast works that are created with the goal of using them to impart certain knowledge or ideas to the audience (Schryer, 2014). The act of educating people in all facets of life through a variety of broadcast channels is referred to as educational broadcasting (Nkwam-Uwaoma, 2020). Agun and Imoggie (1988), who were referenced by Babalola (2012), claimed that broadcasting is referred to as educational broadcasting when it is initially packaged with the intention of educating a group of people or audience, whether in a formal or informal context. Ijeh (2022) opined that there are three different ways through which educational broadcasting might be integrated into the formal education system in Nigeria. It can be for a classroom reception supervised by a teacher who is physically present in the room with the students. The instructional programming would either have to be broadcast during school hours or the recorded version would have to be played back for the students to watch in their classrooms. Receiving official instructional broadcasts at public radio listening stations or television watching areas, with or without facilitators, is yet another level. If the target audience includes kids and children during the school day, official educational programmes would be transmitted or played back outside of school hours. This level of formal education delivery through broadcasting usually becomes necessary in societies where schools are non-functional or deficient as a result of crises, natural disasters, under-development, inadequate number of teachers, incompetent teachers, and subpar teaching facilities. Home consumption constitutes the third stage of official instructional broadcasting. Here, formal education is provided by radio and television broadcasts, which are meant to be listened to either privately at home or in small groups with family members and other acquaintances.

Conceptualizing educational broadcasting in the digital and artificial intelligence age will definitely factor other channels that are now very useful for educational broadcasting. This is because the task of packaging broadcast programmes or contents that aims to educate the various segments of the public is no longer the preserve of broadcast stations and media practitioners. Such channels like YouTube, Twitter Space, Zoom Microsoft teams, Google Meets, Podcast, etc., have revamped the method and approach to educational broadcasting. They offer the opportunity for participants to ask questions on the go, exchange ideas and even express their satisfaction or dissatisfaction towards the message. The audience of such programmes is also able to access the messages at their most convenient time. So many broadcast stations today are also taking advantage of some of these platforms to beat the traditional transient nature of broadcast messages. In essence, it is in order to declare that a digitized educational broadcasting will definitely unlock too many fortunes in the broadcast industry economically, socially, and otherwise.

Digitization of Educational Broadcasting

In the words of Lakshmi (2023, p. 56), Gone are the days when chalkboards and textbooks were the main teaching materials, and students were constrained to learning inside the four walls of their classrooms. However, the landscape of education has significantly transformed with the introduction of the newest technology. Numerous academics have embraced the idea of digitization and provided clear formulations that explain it in detail. The recent definitions of digitization are presenting a clear mental picture of the benefits of digitization to educational broadcasting in particular and the general broadcast industry. According to Idachaba (2018), digitization is the process of converting analogue data in any form, including text, images, audio, and more, to digital data using appropriate electronic devices, like a scanner or specialized computer chips, so that the data can be processed, stored, and transmitted via digital circuits, devices, and networks. There are so many digital platforms for educational content for personal enlightenment as well as formal education. Some are organized and managed by institutions, while others are owned by individuals who specialize in offering educational content in one particular field of their expertise. Lakshmi (2023), observed that educational video platforms have emerged as a popular alternative, providing learners access to quality content from anywhere. With so many options available, choosing the best video platform for education can be overwhelming.

Importance of Artificial Intelligence in Educational Broadcasting

The place of artificial intelligence in the broadcast industry cannot be neglected by contemporary broadcast journalism. This is the same for educational broadcast content producers who intend to reach a diverse audience. For the avoidance of doubt, the term artificial intelligence (AI) simply designates a field of computer science that focuses on creating computer programmes to carry out tasks that would otherwise require human intelligence. According to Saleh (2019), AI algorithms can deal with learning, perception, problem-solving, language understanding, and/or logical reasoning. Meihui Hu et al. (2021, p. 33) note that AI is popular in the broadcasting area because ôf its significance in contemporary culture. Effective usage of broadcast content is beneficial for the growth and mining of big data in this age of big data. In the age of big data, it also makes the broadcasting industry more convenient while enabling instant information access for everyone. Additionally, they argued that "the use of AI in broadcasting stations can effectively improve the efficiency and speed of broadcasting, and staff and technicians can receive regular training to improve the rational use of AI technology." According to Fieiras-Ceide et al. (2022, p. 16), "the media must choose how they approach the installation of intelligent systems in the application of AI tools." The first is to develop an internal algorithm, which entails not only a big financial investment but also significant challenges in locating suitable employees on the market with the ability to establish and oversee an AI infrastructure. The second choice is to look for third-party goods on the market, which may not be suitable, especially in the case of public service media (PSMs), due to their unique content and data processing requirements (Rojas-Torrijos, 2019). No doubt to the fact that AI is revolutionizing the broadcast industry in general and educational broadcasting in particular as it provides an easy method of information processing and production to the benefits of the mass audience of mass communication. "Broadcasters can leverage AI not only to automate repetitive and time-consuming tasks currently done by human operators, but also to support the operators in their activities, enhancing their experience, making the job easier, less repetitive leaving more room for creativity and cognitive resources" (Pietro et al., n.d.). WTi (2020), adumbrated ways Artificial intelligence can be employed by media and educational broadcasting agencies, which includes the following:

- Automated search capabilities
- Media File specific segment retrieval
- Automated editing
- Content moderation
- Content research and aggregations
- Content creation
- Fact checking
- Content Tailoring
- Consumer communications

All of these AI applications create unique opportunities for broadcast and other news agencies to enhance the productivity in the media industry, and in some cases, efficacy of their work (WTi, 2020). For instance, the fact checker tool played a significant role in the 2023 general election in Nigeria.

AI Tools for Educational Broadcasting

Ivo (2020), explains four (4) AI tools that are very useful in the production of broadcast programmes aimed at educating the wider public. They include the following.

- Facial Recognition
  One of the most exciting tools is facial recognition which allows an automatic arrangement of the clips depending on the faces of the persons in the photo. This option could significantly speed up the production process, especially if the post-production is based on a very large video and/or there are many candidates and there is a need to find a specific one, like in a close-up.
- Synthetic media
  AI-produced content is referred to as synthetic media. There are many apps available that can produce this specific media. One in particular, Synthesia, is a standout. Translation and customization are their two main areas of expertise. With Synthesia, one can capture a video and then translate it into any language you like. Of course, video marketing is the ideal game for this technology, but it might also work well in a production where the host takes the lead instead of the competitors or in a documentary.
- Speech To Text Transcription powered by AI
  It's a great tool to have. This instrument is quite helpful, and the market currently has excellent software available at a very appealing price per minute. Here is a comprehensive article on the subject. The tools that might work well for a television production are briefly listed below, but truly, the market today has pretty everything that businesses could possibly need, from television to video marketing.
- Video Classification
  With the help of the data received after the machine learning-based video process of video classification, one may analyse the movie's contents and endow them with a kind of superpower. Inappropriate content may be moderated, brands can be located in films, athletes can be tracked as they move throughout a game to identify

plays for post-game analysis, and much more can be done. A significant argument to experiment with is video categorization. Without a question, using this technology to set up a TV firm server is a winning technique today.

- Advantages of Digitization of Educational Broadcasting

  There are several advantages of a digitalized educational broadcast system. We will approach these advantages from the learners' perspective or as they benefit media consumers who are in need of educational broadcast contents. These benefits are as follows:

  a. **Unlimited and timeless access**: Media audiences are no longer mandated to be available at the airing time of the educational programme they are in need of. They are now able to go online and access such information for their benefit.
  b. **Affordability and less involvement**: Previously, you needed a power supply television set or radio to watch or listen to an educational programme. All those are not necessary under a digital system. You just need an internet-enabled phone to watch or listen to such programmes.
  c. **Availability of Multiple Content Source**: This means that audiences of educational broadcasting are not just depending on the few radio and TV stations for enlightening contents. Rather, a quick search online will offer varieties of options for digital broadcast platforms that can meet their educational needs.
  d. **Audience Specific Educational Broadcast**: In an analogue situation, the audience only listens to any educational content offered by a radio or television station. Under a digitalized setting, each person is driven by a specific educational need. For example, if you want to learn how to cook a particular meal or you want to know how to prevent a disease like cervical cancer. Once you search for any of these topics in a digital streaming platform like YouTube, you will get a specific broadcast on that topic.
  e. **Creation of Employment Opportunities**: Digitization of the broadcast industry is key to unlocking employment for unemployed youths full of creative talents in Nigeria. A lot of young Nigerians are already doing great things in content creation including educative and enlightening contents.

f. **Less Production Cost**:

Challenges to the Digitalization of Educational Broadcasting

There are numerous challenges that are frustrating the digitization efforts of the government of Nigeria. Because these challenges are more institutional, most government-owned broadcast organizations are still struggling to find their feet within the digital space. Meanwhile, their private counterparts are achieving digitalization with high speed. Regarding educational broadcasting, the challenges are similar and interconnected. As such, this section will discuss the challenges from a broader perspective.

i. **Government Attitude Towards the Project**: the overall attitude of government authorities has been quite discouraging on the issue of digitalization. There have been numerous deadlines set by succeeding governments, but nothing productive has come of them. Increasingly, it is focused more on politics than the potential economic gains.
ii. **Manpower**: the state of manpower in our media organizations today is highly inadequate and cannot care for the manpower needed to successfully carry out the migration from analogue to digital educational broadcasting. This is due to Uwaoma and Ihechu's (2012) observation that there is a need for corresponding staff as more sophisticated and delicate technology is introduced. A difficulty for the race is the task of retraining and training personnel to integrate into the digital process.
iii. **Capital**: Though digitalization will unlock the economic fortunes of the country, it is a very financially involved project. It will take money to acquire the needed equipment. It will also require money to train and retrain staff. Money is also needed to consistently produce educational programmes that will be used to run the 24/7 programme schedule of the various broadcast stations in the country.
iv. **Creative Talents**: This is another challenge that the educational broadcasting digitalization is facing. The job of broadcasting is not an all-comers affair. More so for educational broadcasting. It not only requires knowledgeable people, but also talented people who

can convey the messages appropriately. As such, getting round pegs in round holes for educational programmes can be and is very challenging.

v. **Poor Power Supply**: The problem of power supply is one that Nigerians are now permanently living with. It is no longer news that every sector in Nigeria today is facing the frustrating situation of epileptic power supply. This definitely will hamper productivity in a digitalized situation.

vi. **Unprofessional Interlopers**: Another serious challenge a digitized educational broadcasting is facing today is that of interlopers. There is so much unprofessionalism in the field. People for the sake of making money provide misleading content in the name of educating people in one subject area or the other. It will only take proper professional regulations to curb the excesses of interlopers who are there for money making, rather than enlightening the public.

Conclusion

This chapter discusses the potentials of a digitalized educational broadcasting. From the preceding sections, it is quite evident that a digitalized and AI-enabled educational broadcasting will not just unlock our economic fortunes as a country. It will also bring educational contents closer to the various underserved populations in our country thereby spreading literacy among Nigerian citizens. More so now that every aspect of learning is moving from physical to digital, a digitalized educational broadcasting is a sure route for Nigeria to join other leagues of nations that are doing great things today. With the COVID-19 lockdown experience and the emergence of platforms like U-lesson and more, there is no better time for Nigeria to invest in the digitalization of educational broadcasting as a means of educating her teaming population. As was the case during the lockdown, broadcasting was very resourceful in keeping our children engaged with educational programmes. Given that this is also the direction that the world is going, Nigeria will have to act fast to fast-track the digitization process as the benefits are numerous and cannot be ignored any further. We therefore recommend that:

1. Government of Nigeria should provide the necessary resources for digitalization and fast-track the process to ensure that it is achieved within the shortest possible time.
2. Broadcast manpower (both technical and non-technical) should be trained on how to effectively deploy AI tools to improve their production of educational programmes that will benefit the public.
3. Regulatory agencies should provide a strong regulatory framework that will deter interlopers from producing and broadcasting misleading or substandard educational contents in the country.

References

Automated Insights. (n.d.). https://automatedinsights.com/customer-stories/associated-press/

Artificial Intelligence. (n.d.). https://csrc.nist.gov/Topics/Technologies/artificial-intelligence

Babalola, B. K. (2012). Educational broadcasting in Nigeria: A historical development perspective. *Journal of Communication and Culture, 3*(2), 2141–2758.

Fieiras-Ceide, C., Vaz-Álvarez, M., & Túñez-López, M. (2022). Artificial intelligence strategies in European public broadcasters: Uses, forecasts and future challenges. *Profesional de la información, 31*(5), e310518.

Idachaba, A. I. (2018). *Digitization of broadcasting in Nigeria: Policy and implementation.*

Ijeh, N. P. (2022). The use of educational broadcasting in formal education delivery by delta state government, nigeria. *Joural of Media, Communication and Languages.*

Ivo, V. (2020). *Four AI tools that will accelerate your broadcast TV post production.* https://www.google.com/url?sa=t&source=web&rct=j&opi=89978449&url=https://medium.com/%40ivo.vacca/four-ai-tools-that-will-accelerate-your-broadcast-tv-post-production-f6763d19dd77&ved=2ahUKEwj9xLb_zYaBAxWtUUEAHXM3BX0QFnoECBQQAQ&usg=AOvVaw0B9epC3RDQAbdcz2W43Mw2

Lakshmi, B. (2023). *Comparing the 10 best online video education platforms 2023.* https://www.google.com/url?sa=t&source=web&rct=j&opi=89978449&url=https://www.contus.com/blog/best-video-platforms-for-education/&ved=2ahUKEwj93fji1oaBAxXVWUEAHQ1yCsAQFnoECCIQAQ&usg=AOvVaw0t5rmaPq9wiC8wgjg_Q6TP

Hu, M., Zhiwei, X., & Kai, L. (2021). Application of artificial intelligence voice technology in radio and television media. *Journal of Physics: Conference Series.* https://doi.org/10.1088/1742-6596/2031/1/012051

Nkwam-Uwaoma, A. O. (2020). Educational broadcasting. In C. S Okunna (Ed.), *Communication and media studies multiple perspectives* (pp. 337–362). New Generation Educate Ltd.

Nkwam-Uwaoma, A. O., & Onu, D. M. (2017). *Educational broadcasting in contemporary society*. Gabtony Prints Ltd.

Onabajo, O. (2004). *Introduction to broadcasting*. Gabi Concept Ltd.

Pietro, S., Adriano, M., & Claudia, L. (n.d.). *AI solutions in broadcasting companies: How broadcasting companies can benefit from AI technologies*. https://www.google.com/url?sa=t&source=web&rct=j&opi=89978449&url=https://www.nttdata.com/jp/ja/-/media/nttdatajapan/files/services/ai/ai-solutions-in-broadcasting-companies.pdf&ved=2ahUKEwje--WCzIaBAxUViVwKHeYhBxkQFnoECBYQAQ&usg=AOvVaw3Lr_haJxYLi0dcMVl3rxjZ

Rojas-Torrijos, J.-L. (2019). La automatización en las coberturas deportivas. Estudio de caso del bot creado por The Washington Post durante los JJ.OO. de Río 2016 y Pyeongchang, 2018. *Revista latina de comunicación social, 74*, 1729–1747.

Saleh, Z. M. (2019). *Artificial intelligence definition, ethics and standards*. BUE. https://www.google.com/url?sa=t&source=web&rct=j&opi=89978449&url=https://www.nttdata.com/jp/ja/-/media/nttdatajapan/files/services/ai/ai-solutions-in-broadcasting-companies.pdf&ved=2ahUKEwje--WCzIaBAxUViVwKHeYhBxkQFnoECBYQAQ&usg=AOvVaw3Lr_haJxYLi0dcMVl3rxjZ

Schryer, E. (2014). The influence of educational television programming on preschoolers emergent literacy: A review of the literature. *Canadian Journal for New Scholars in Education, 5*(2), 21–30.

Uwaoma, U., & Ihechu, I. P. (2012). The challenges of digitization of broadcasting in Nigeria. *New Media and Mass Communication, 5*. www.iiste.org ISSN 2224-3267 (Paper) ISSN 2224-3275 (Online).

WTi-solutions. (2020). *AI in media and news broadcasting*. https://www.google.com/url?sa=t&source=web&rct=j&opi=89978449&url=https://www.contus.com/blog/best-video-platforms-for-education/&ved=2ahUKEwj93fji1oaBAxXVWUEAHQ1yCsAQFnoECCIQAQ&usg=AOvVaw0t5rmaPq9wiC8wgjg_Q6TP

CHAPTER 9

Artificial Intelligence in Educational Broadcasting: Tool for Dissemination of Effective Pedagogy Across Scholastic Levels in Nigeria

Stella N. Nwosu

Introduction

Societal development and progress hinge on the citizenry's education, knowledge, and skills. The effective dissemination of knowledge is crucial in ensuring that individuals are equipped with the skills and information needed to thrive in their personal and professional lives. One powerful tool that has been instrumental in facilitating the dissemination of teaching and learning is educational broadcasting. Educational broadcasting has played a significant role in educational development at Nigeria's various levels and sectors, particularly in primary and secondary

S. N. Nwosu (✉)
Institute of Education and Professional Development, University of Uyo, Uyo, Akwa Ibom, Nigeria
e-mail: stellanwosu17@gmail.com

U. S. Akpan (ed.), *Educational Broadcasting in Nigeria in the Age of Artificial Intelligence*,
https://doi.org/10.1007/978-3-031-68530-9_9

education (Obot & Inwang, 2017; Olumorin et al., 2018). With the advent of the digital era, especially with the advancement in Artificial Intelligence (AI), broadcasting has undergone significant transformations, offering new opportunities and challenges for pedagogical effectiveness.

In Nigeria, traditional broadcasting platforms such as radio and television have been widely utilized to support educational initiatives. Radio programs have been developed to facilitate mathematics, English, and Science lessons, enabling students to learn and review key concepts. Television broadcasts have showcased educational content, documentaries, and school programs, providing students access to educational resources and information (Obot & Inwang, 2017). However, the recent digitalization of broadcasting has revolutionized the landscape of educational broadcasting (Olumorin et al., 2018). Digital technologies, especially with the advent of Artificial Intelligence (AI), internet-based platforms, streaming services, mobile applications, and social media, have opened up new avenues for disseminating educational content. These platforms offer greater flexibility, accessibility, and interactivity, transcending the limitations of traditional broadcasting methods. However, in recent times, Artificial Intelligence has become a vital technological tool for effective service delivery in all spheres of life, including educational broadcasting. Moreover, the outbreak of the COVID-19 pandemic also brought about societal changes that have significantly impacted the educational sector. This has further underscored the need for educationists to explore technologies, especially AI technology, to leverage the shortcomings of other digital means of disseminating educational content at all educational levels.

The term "artificial intelligence" (AI) was first introduced during a workshop at Dartmouth College in 1996. Since its inception, AI researchers have pursued approaches collectively recognized as machine learning (ML), according to Marcus (2020). Machine learning technology can learn and comprehend logic like humans, enabling it to automatically perform tasks akin to human cognitive functions based on programmed data and information. The overarching goal is to streamline complex aspects of human life. As a facet of machine learning, AI encompasses software with capabilities for pattern recognition, iterative processing, intelligent algorithms, predictive capabilities, and the ability to learn to discern new patterns or autonomously make decisions (Fitria, 2021a).

The introduction of AI has profoundly impacted the educational curriculum, particularly within technology, science, mathematics, engineering, and beyond. Al empowers educators to gain a deeper and more intuitive understanding of student's needs (Fitria, 2021b). Furthermore, students can tailor their learning experiences to match their specific requirements without encountering significant obstacles. The integration of AI into education encompasses a broad spectrum of learning, spanning from primary education through secondary and tertiary levels (Miao & Holmes, 2021).

Consequently, it is unsurprising that many AI-driven innovations and breakthroughs are currently being explored and will continue to be applied to augment the educational process, rendering it more pragmatic and efficient. AI is widely believed to have the potential to enhance human learning and facilitate the achievement of educational outcomes. In providing a theoretical framework for integrating AI into educational dissemination, this article examines emerging trends in utilizing AI technologies and their possible benefits to Nigerian learners across primary, secondary, and tertiary education levels. We also explored various possible applications of these technologies to disseminate effective pedagogy in the Nigerian context.

A Theoretical Framework for AI Era Educational Broadcasting in Nigeria

Uses and Gratification Media Theory (Katz et al., 1974)

We can examine the benefits of AI in educational broadcasting in Nigeria within the premise of a theoretical framework, the media uses, and gratification theory (Katz et al., 1995 as cited in Ijeh, 2011). The theory advocates that the consumers of mass media content are not passive but are actively selecting which mass media content to consume. Thus, the audience's consumption of mass media content is goal-oriented and is by predetermined needs that must be gratified through the media content. This assertion is consistent with the application of AI in educational broadcasting in Nigeria as instructors and learners are now self-aware of the areas of need in which they wish to employ AI in educational broadcasting and can communicate such to educational stakeholders, researchers, programmers for the development of AI tools that gratify these needs. Additionally, given the Nigerian educational terrain, AI tools for Nigeria should be practical in pedagogical dissemination across rural and urban, disadvantaged and advantaged, and accessible and inaccessible learners at all educational levels to fulfill national educational goals.

Concept of Artificial Intelligence, Educational Broadcasting and Pedagogy

The concept of educational broadcast recognizes the power of broadcast media in reaching a broad audience and its potential to impact educational outcomes. It recognizes that broadcast media can go beyond entertainment and informational content to actively contribute to the educational development of individuals and communities (Endong, 2015). The concept of educational broadcast is closely aligned with the principles of effective pedagogy. Pedagogy refers to the art and science of teaching, including instructional strategies, learning theories, and assessment methods (Ijeh & Ojebode, 2023). Also, according to Omosekejimi et al. (2019), pedagogy refers to the science and art of teaching and learning, encompassing the theories, methods, and practices employed in instruction. By broadcasting pedagogical practices, educators can evolve engaging and interactive learning environments that cater to learners' diverse needs and preferences. Broadcasting pedagogical practices in education is valuable for expanding access to education, particularly in regions with limited resources and infrastructure (Bukola, 2020). It allows learners to engage with educational content regardless of their geographic location or socioeconomic background. Utilizing radio, television, and digital platforms via AI educational broadcasts can provide better-quality learning experiences that transcend physical barriers and reach individuals who may not have access to traditional educational institutions.

The integration of AI into educational dissemination has the potential to revolutionize pedagogy in numerous ways. In its early stages, AI in education primarily focused on several aspects of educational dissemination tools, such as virtual courses, automated assessment tools, gamification of digital learning, voice assistance, simulations, virtual reality activities, educational robots, massive open online courses (MOOCs), for tertiary education and numerous other innovations. The value of AI in addressing the challenges of educational disparity in Nigeria needs to be recognized. Technology can be highly beneficial in response to demands for improved access to education. AI can simplify enrolling as many learners as necessary for schools and colleges, regardless of their location.

AI-powered educational robots play a significant role in various aspects of human life, including education; according to Fawaz (2023), these robots possess a physical presence that can actively engage learners in real-world activities to enhance learning. They are intelligent machines capable of fulfilling multiple educational roles, including teaching and tutoring. Notably, there are instances where a robot, acting as a tutor, demonstrates a more profound knowledge base than human teachers, underscoring the substantial role of AI in teaching and learning. Educational robots have become invaluable in broadcasting pedagogy for individuals who lack access to traditional educational institutions or physical classrooms. These robots enable learners to engage with peers and instructors in real time, fostering synchronous interaction. Unlike learning from a screen, educational robots are physically present, capturing the learner's attention more effectively. This heightened engagement contributes to the overall efficiency of the learning process within educational settings (Alhabbash et al., 2016).

Educational Broadcasting in Nigeria: The Journey So Far

Nigeria has a rich history of utilizing educational broadcasting to support its education system (Obot & Inwang, 2017). Over the years, educational broadcasting has evolved and been integrated into different educational levels, primary, secondary, and tertiary education. The journey of educational broadcasting in Nigeria has been marked by significant milestones, with radio and television playing a pivotal role in reaching a broad audience of students and educators.

In primary education, educational broadcasting has been employed to support teaching and learning by delivering curriculum-based content and lessons (Obot & Inwang, 2017). Radio programs, for example, have been developed to teach core subjects like mathematics, English, and science. These programs utilize engaging and interactive formats to capture the attention of young learners and facilitate their understanding of critical concepts. Similarly, educational broadcasting has been integrated with secondary education to supplement classroom instruction and expand students' knowledge (Olumorin et al., 2018). Television broadcasts have been utilized to showcase educational content, documentaries, and school programs. These broadcasts provide students access to various educational resources, fostering critical thinking skills and promoting independent learning.

Even in tertiary education, educational broadcasting has made significant contributions (Omosekejimi et al., 2019). It has provided access to specialized courses, lectures, and expert opinions. Broadcasting platforms have facilitated distance education programs, enabling individuals to pursue higher education despite physical limitations. Integrating educational broadcasting in tertiary education has broadened academic horizons and enhanced student learning opportunities across Nigeria.

New Trends in Broadcasting in the AI Era

The digital era has democratized the production and dissemination of educational content. With the rise of user-generated content and open educational resources, individuals and organizations can create and share educational materials, further enriching the educational broadcasting landscape (Adeoye, 2020). This decentralization of content creation promotes diverse perspectives and allows for the customization of educational materials to meet specific learning needs. Another significant trend in broadcasting in the digital era is the shift toward mobile learning. The widespread adoption of smartphones and tablets has made educational content more accessible on the go (Ijeh & Ojebode, 2023). Learners can access educational broadcasts and resources anytime and anywhere, facilitating continuous learning beyond traditional classroom settings.

Social media platforms have also emerged as influential channels for educational broadcasting. Educators and educational institutions can leverage social media to reach and engage with a broader audience (Martens et al., 2020). These platforms provide interactive discussions, collaboration, and knowledge-sharing opportunities among learners, creating a virtual learning community. Furthermore, integrating AI in data analytics and learning analytics in educational broadcasting offers insights into learner behavior, progress, and preferences (Salihu & Umar, 2020). This data-driven approach allows for personalized learning experiences and targeted interventions to support learners' individual needs and optimize their learning outcomes.

The digital era has ushered in new trends in broadcasting, revolutionizing educational broadcasting in particular. The digitalization of information has expanded the possibilities for instructional delivery and content creation, offering greater flexibility, accessibility, and interactivity.

Emerging AI technologies such as virtual, extended, and augmented reality have enhanced the immersive and interactive nature of educational broadcasting. The democratization of content creation and the rise of mobile learning have made educational content more accessible and personalized. Social media platforms and data analytics have opened new avenues for engagement, collaboration, and personalized learning experiences (Adeoye, 2020). By embracing these new trends, educational broadcasting in the digital era can enhance pedagogical effectiveness, promote lifelong learning and advanced education in Nigeria.

Role of Artificial Intelligence in Effective Pedagogy in Education

Effective pedagogy in educational broadcasting involves using multimedia resources, interactive tools, and learner-centered approaches (Adeoye, 2020). These elements help create an engaging and dynamic learning environment catering to student's diverse needs and preferences. By incorporating visual and auditory aids, educational broadcasting captures students' attention, stimulates their senses, and facilitates comprehension and retention of information. Furthermore, effective pedagogy in educational broadcasting promotes active participation and collaboration among students. It encourages students to interact with the educational content, ask questions, and engage in discussions (Bello et al., 2020). This interactive approach fosters critical thinking skills, promotes creativity, and encourages students to contribute to their learning process actively.

Primary Education

Effective teaching practices in educational broadcasting can enhance students' foundational knowledge and skills in Nigeria's Primary education system (Bello et al., 2020). It can provide visual representations, real-life examples, and engaging activities that facilitate understanding and retention of concepts. By aligning educational broadcasting with pedagogical principles via Artificial Intelligence, educators can create a supportive and stimulating learning environment for young learners. In Nigeria, educational broadcasting in the Primary level of education has been known to facilitate improvement in literacy levels (Ijeh, 2011). The AI will have to be used to conceive and produce programs that will be accessible to the target audience and appealing enough to attract and meet the needs of learners at this level. The poor electricity supply in Nigeria makes it difficult for consumers of educational broadcast programs. Thus, with the use of AI technology, these programs can be designed to be so enticing that learners will be compelled to watch them, even with electricity-generating sets for those with them.

In both the Primary and Secondary levels of education, AI can aid in identifying exceptional talents and recognizing learning challenges students face. Learning within the AI system is characterized by technology-based personalization, fostering students' independence and enhancing their overall learning experience (Cukurova et al., 2020). AI can identify areas of difficulty for students at these levels, enabling subsequent adjustments to be made to develop new and more effective methods for facilitating their learning.

Additionally, educational broadcasting in primary education fosters a student-centered approach, where learners actively participate in the learning process. It encourages students to engage with the educational content, ask questions, and explore concepts beyond the confines of the classroom (Olumorin et al., 2018). This active engagement promotes profound understanding, critical thinking, and problem-solving skills among young learners. AI systems are valuable resources for teachers, providing them with supplementary materials, lesson plans, and teaching strategies (Bello et al., 2020). By incorporating educational broadcasts into their instruction, teachers can enhance their lessons and cater to the diverse learning needs of their students. Integrating AI in educational broadcasting and pedagogy creates a more comprehensive and practical learning experience for primary school students.

Furthermore, using AI systems in primary education can offer standardized content that ensures consistency in curriculum delivery. It provides access to various subjects and topics, covering disciplines such as mathematics, science, language, and social studies (Holmes et al., 2018). This standardized approach helps to overcome the challenges associated with limited resources and variations in teaching quality across different schools and regions. In the digital era, educational broadcasting has expanded its reach and accessibility through online platforms and digital technologies. Integrating digital resources and interactive tools in educational broadcasting further enhances pedagogical effectiveness in primary education (Martens et al., 2020). It allows for personalized learning experiences, where students can engage with educational content at their own pace and revisit materials as needed. Moreover, AI platforms will enable teachers to monitor students' progress, provide feedback, and tailor instruction to individual needs, promoting individualized learning.

Secondary Education

In secondary education, effective pedagogy in educational broadcasting can reinforce classroom instruction and expand students' knowledge (Tukur et al., 2020). It can provide supplementary resources, expert interviews, and documentaries that enrich students' understanding of various subjects. Moreover, educational broadcasting can encourage independent learning, critical thinking, and the development of digital literacy skills. Educational broadcasting in secondary education supports the development of essential twenty-first-century skills. By integrating AI technology and multimedia resources, students gain experience navigating digital platforms, critically evaluating information, and effectively utilizing digital tools for learning (Tira, 2021). This digital literacy is vital for their future academic and professional pursuits. Educational broadcasting also addresses the challenges of limited resources and variations in teaching quality across different secondary schools in Nigeria. Standardized educational content ensures consistency and quality in curriculum delivery (Olumorin et al., 2018). Students from different regions and backgrounds have equal access to high-quality educational materials, bridging the educational divide and promoting educational equity.

Furthermore, educational broadcasting in secondary education cultivates independent learning skills. AI systems encourage students to explore educational broadcasts, engage in self-directed research, and pursue their interests beyond the scope of the curriculum (Bello et al., 2020). This self-directed learning fosters autonomy, creativity, and a lifelong passion for learning. Moreover, integrating AI technologies in educational broadcasting opens up new possibilities for personalized learning experiences in the digital era. Adaptive learning platforms, virtual reality simulations, and multimedia presentations enhance student engagement and comprehension (Bukola, 2020). These innovative pedagogical approaches provide students with immersive and interactive learning experiences, enabling them to grasp complex concepts and develop critical thinking skills.

In all, educational broadcasting plays a significant role in enhancing pedagogical effectiveness in Nigeria's secondary education. By providing supplementary resources, promoting independent learning, and leveraging digital technologies, educational broadcasting enriches the learning experiences of secondary school students. It fosters critical thinking, digital literacy, and independent research skills, preparing students for higher education and the demands of the modern workforce. Embracing educational broadcasting in secondary education contributes to the holistic development of students and empowers them with the knowledge and skills necessary for their future success.

Tertiary Education

In tertiary education, effective pedagogy in educational broadcasting can enhance students' higher-order thinking skills and prepare them for the complexities of their chosen fields (Bukola, 2020). It can provide access to specialized courses, lectures, and discussions that deepen students' understanding and broaden their perspectives. Furthermore, educational broadcasting can support distance education programs, enabling individuals to pursue higher education regardless of geographical location. Educational broadcasting in tertiary education goes beyond traditional classroom settings and provides students access to many educational resources and opportunities (Bukola, 2020). Through specialized courses, lectures, and expert opinions, students can delve deeper into their interests and gain industry professionals' insights. This exposure to diverse perspectives enhances their learning experience and broadens their understanding of the subject matter.

Higher and Adult Education students in Nigeria can become users of global courses. They can search for and enroll in online courses from around the world. The course platform can intelligently recommend courses aligned with one's interest based on the keywords used. Individuals can explore diverse free and open courses featuring engaging interactions, structured content, and exciting topics. Examples of platforms incorporating AI into their course offerings include MOOCs Udemy, Google AI, Alison, Khan Academy, edX, Udacity, and Coursera (Zhang, 2021). Massive open online courses provided by MOOCs provide learners with a foundational pedagogical experience typically comprising video lectures and quizzes. The innovation in these adaptations of large lecture-style classes makes the educational materials developed accessible to learners all around the world (Fawaz, 2023). The AI-powered platforms also offer virtual mentorship to monitor and track student's progress.

While it is acknowledged that human teachers possess a deeper understanding of student needs, instant feedback from a virtual tutor should not be underestimated.

Moreover, educational broadcasting platforms in tertiary education promote lifelong learning and professional development (Tukur et al., 2020). Professionals seeking to expand their knowledge or acquire new skills can benefit from the convenience and flexibility of AI platforms. They can access various educational content including online courses, webinars, and workshops. AI caters to their needs and interests. This continuous learning approach enables individuals to stay up-to-date with the latest advancements in their fields and adapt to the evolving demands of their professions (Holmes et al., 2018). In Higher Education, AI-powered applications can allow individuals to study during their free moments, dedicating just ten or fifteen minutes without physically attending a class; furthermore, students can receive direct feedback from tutors or instructors through these AI-driven solutions. Additionally, AI-based systems like intelligent tutoring platforms can be customized to align with a student's existing knowledge level, areas of interest, and more (Aleven et al., 2016). The system is designed to assist students with weaknesses by providing learning material tailored to address those areas. For instance, students may take an initial assessment through the app, which analyzes their performance and delivers appropriate assignments and course recommendations, thus disseminating effective pedagogy.

Overall, educational broadcasting in Nigeria's tertiary education system empowers individuals to pursue their educational goals, whether seeking higher qualifications or professional development. Educational broadcasting enhances pedagogical effectiveness by offering specialized courses, promoting lifelong learning, and integrating digital technologies. It equips students with the knowledge and skills necessary for personal and professional growth.

Prospects of Integrating AI in Educational Broadcasting in Nigeria

The prospects of educational broadcasting in Nigeria are promising. Lessons from other nations have shown the benefits educational broadcasting in the digital era can bring to education systems. Countries like the United States, Canada, and the United Kingdom have successfully leveraged educational broadcasting to enhance pedagogical effectiveness, improve educational outcomes, and bridge educational gaps (Endong, 2015). Specific steps must be taken to fully tap into the potential of AI-powered educational broadcasts in Nigeria. First, there is a need for increased investment in infrastructure and technology to expand the reach of broadcasting platforms and ensure reliable access to educational content (Endong, 2015). Improved internet connectivity, availability of devices, and digital literacy initiatives will contribute to a more inclusive educational broadcasting landscape.

Secondly, partnerships and collaborations among stakeholders are crucial for the success of educational broadcasting initiatives. Collaboration between broadcasting organizations, educational institutions, policymakers, content developers, and Programmers can ensure the development of high-quality, relevant, and engaging educational content (Endong, 2015). These partnerships also facilitate the sharing of best practices, resources, and research findings to improve technology and pedagogical approaches in educational broadcasting continually.

However, the technological awareness divide may inhibit the effective use of AI to provide access and equity in education through broadcasts. Most Nigerian teachers' educationists and educational institutions from Primary to Tertiary levels of education need to be made aware and familiar with digital technologies available for disseminating teaching and learning of educational content and the process of integrating AI facilities to improve educational access.

Ethical Challenges

The use of AI in education raises a lot of ethical considerations. From plagiarism to cheating, AI technologies need to be carefully considered to guarantee they are used responsibly and ethically. The technology's algorithms can be biased and discriminatory if not carefully designed. In addition there is a general concern about the ethical implications of the use of AI for tasks that are traditionally meant for the teachers which could affect education quality And the teachers' role in the classroom (Fawaz, 2023).

Conclusion

The article has also explored the role of educational broadcasting in enhancing pedagogical effectiveness across educational levels in Nigeria. By highlighting the theoretical framework of goal-oriented consumption of mass media in which AI can benefit Nigerian learners more significantly if it is directed to their unique needs and the universal goal of education in Nigeria. By embracing the opportunities offered by AI technologies in educational broadcasting, Nigeria can unlock the full potential of educational broadcasting and pave the way for a brighter future in education. Integrating AI in educational broadcasting has the potential to not only lead to greater access to quality and effective pedagogy but also give rise to more profound advancement in learning and educational service delivery across educational levels in Nigeria. However, poor technological awareness is a significant challenge to using these systems.

However, the challenges of digitization in broadcasting and the evolving trends in the AI era present both opportunities and complexities for educational broadcasting, with strategic investments, partnerships, research, and a commitment to disseminating pedagogical excellence.

Nigeria can harness the potential of AI technology in educational broadcasting to bridge educational disparities, improve learning outcomes, and empower learners at all levels with the knowledge and skills necessary for overall educational advancement.

Recommendations

Several recommendations can be made to optimize the dissemination of education with AI in Nigeria. Firstly, research is needed to guide the development and implementation of AI educational broadcasting initiatives. Evidence-based practices and insights can inform AI-powered educational content design, platforms, pedagogical approaches, and dissemination.

Secondly, continuous professional development programs should be provided for teachers and educators to enhance their digital literacy skills and pedagogical competencies in utilizing educational broadcasting effectively. Training programs can empower teachers with the knowledge and skills to implement AI in educational broadcasting platforms and maximize their pedagogical impact.

Lastly, policymakers and stakeholders should collaborate to develop policies void of ethical constraints to using AI to support and promote educational broadcasting. These policies should also address funding, infrastructure development, licensing, and content regulations to ensure the sustainable advancement of AI-supported educational broadcasting initiatives. By implementing these recommendations, Nigeria can unlock the full potential of educational broadcasting and pave the way for a more functional, inclusive, equitable, and effective education system resulting from the AI era.

References

Abidoye, J. A., Adelokun, A. K., & Aderele, S. O. (n.d.). *Broadcast media: A veritable tool for effective teaching and learning in Nigerian schools.* https://www.globalacademicgroup.com/journals/teacher%20perspective/BROADCAST%20MEDIA%20A%20VERITABLE%20TOOL%20FOR%20EFFECTIVE.pdf

Adeoye, B. (2020). *The era of digital technology in teaching and learning in Nigeria educational institutions review.* https://www.semanticscholar.org/paper/The-Era-of-Digital-Technology-in-Teaching-and-in-Adeoye/c2b9b4fb3d35b4433242c3ddb0c97bedb610beb6

Aleven, V., Roll, I., McLaren, B. M., & Koedinger, K. R. (2016). Help helps, but only so much: Research on help-seeking with intelligent tutoring systems. *International Journal of Artificial Intelligence in Education, 26*, 205–223.

Alhabbash, M. I., Mahdi, A. O., & Naser, S. S. A. (2016). An intelligent tutoring system for teaching grammar English tenses. *European Academic Research, 4*(9), 1–15.

Bello, H. S., Idris, S. U., & Bappayo, A. (2020). Media and educational technology in Nigeria: Managing the broadcast programs of Radio Nigeria Globe FM towards girl child education. *International Journal of Innovative Research in Education, 7*(1), 20–30. https://doi.org/10.18844/ijire.v7i1.4715

Bukola, O. (2020). Digitization of broadcasting in Nigeria: A mirage or a possibility. *The International Journal of Humanities & Social Studies, 8*(3), 109–118. https://doi.org/10.24940/theijhss/2020/v8/i3/hs2003-023

Cukurova, M., Luckin, R., & Kent, C. (2020). Impact of an artificial intelligence research frame on the perceived credibility of educational research evidence. *International Journal of Artificial Intelligence in Education, 30*, 205–235.

Endong, F. (2015). *Digitization of media broadcast in Nigeria: The journey so far and challenges.* https://semanticscholar.org/paper/31a8e8fd0aeb09c66f4db99f8000be660d6cd551

Fawaz, O. I. (2023). *Impact of emerging AI technologies on Nigerian education*. https://susafrica.com/2023/04/05/the-impact-of-emerging-ai-technologies-on-nigerian-education/:

Fitria, T. N. (2021a). Grammarly as AI-powered English writing assistant: Students' alternative for writing English. *Metathesis: Journal of English Language, Literature, and Teaching, 5*(1), 65–78.

Fitria, T. N. (2021b). QuillBot as an online tool: Students' alternative in paraphrasing and rewriting English writing. *English: Journal of Language, Education, and Humanities, 9*(1), 183–196.

Holmes, W., Bialik, M., & Fadel, C. (2018). Artificial intelligence in education: Promises and implications for teaching and learning. Center for Curriculum Redesign, pp. 65. https://www.researchgate.net/publication/332180327_Artificial_Intelligence_in_Education_Promise_and_Implications_for_Teaching_and_Learning

Ijeh, P. N., & Ojebode, A. (2023, February). *Managing educational broadcasting in Nigeria: Reflections on concept, prospects and challenges*. https://www.researchgate.net/publication/368751269_MANAGING_EDUCATIONAL_BROADCASTING_IN_NIGERIA_REFLECTIONS_ON_CONCEPT_PROSPECTS_AND_CHALLENGES

Ijeh, P. N. (2011). Media uses and gratification theory in educational broadcasting: A theoretical analysis. In D. Wilson (Ed.), *Communication for social change and development* (pp. 91–108). African Council for Communication Education.

Katz, E., Blumler, J. G., & Gurevitch, M. (1974). Utilization of mass communication by the individual. In J. G. Blumler & E. Katz (Eds.), *The uses of mass communications: Current perspectives on gratifications research* (pp. 19–31). Sage Publications.

Katz, E., Blumber, J. G., & Gurevitch, M. (1995). Utilization of mass communication by the individual. In O. Boyd-Barrett & C. Newbold (Eds.), *Approaches to media: A reader* (pp. 164–173). Arnold.

Marcus, N. (2020). Personalized learning dan multimedia Berbasis Komputer Masih Perlukah Guru? *JINOTEP (JurnalInovasi Dan TeknologiPembelajaran): Kajian DanRisetDalamTeknologiPembelajaran, 1*(1), 50–57.

Miao, M. E., & Holmes, W. (2021). *Intelligence unleashed: An argument for AI in education*. UCL Knowledge Lab.

Martens, M., Hajibayova, K., & Jeonghwa, O. (2020). Being on the wrong side of the digital divide: Seeking technological interventions for North East Nigeria Technological Interventions for Nigeria. *Aslib Journal of Information Management, 72*(6). https://doi.org/10.1108/AJIM-05-2020-0172

Obot, C. D., & Inwang, I. I. (2017). Broadcasting among communication practitioners and educators in Uyo. *African Journal of Media and Communication Studies, 3*(2), 11–23. https://doi.org/10.30958/AJMMC.3.2.2

Olumorin, C., Aderoju, M. A., & Onojah, A. (2018). Students' awareness and utilization of educational broadcasts to learn in Ogbomoso, Oyo State. *The Turkish Online Journal of Distance Education, 19*(3), 107–119. https://doi.org/10.17718/TOJDE.445122

Omosekejimi, A. F., Brume-Ezewu, S., & Ejiro, G. (2019). ICT and digital literacy skills: A mechanism for efficient teaching in Nigerian colleges of education. *Information Impact: Journal of Information and Knowledge Management, 9*(3), 39–52. https://doi.org/10.4314/IIJIKM.V9I3.5

Salihu, G. A., & Umar, N. S. (2020). ICT as a tool to foster teaching and learning in Nigeria. *European Journal of Electrical Engineering and Computer Science, 4*(4), https://doi.org/10.24018/ejece.2020.4.4.228

Tira, N. F. (2021). Artificial Intelligence (AI) in education: Using AI tools for teaching and learning process. *Proceeding seminar nasional, institute knologibisnisaas Indonesia.*

Tukur, M., Bebeji, G. U., & Suleiman, M. M. (2020). The impact of ICT in adult and nonformal education in Nigeria: A review. *International Journal of Business, Law, and Education, 1*(2), 77–86.

Zhang, Z. (2021). The impact of digital technologies on entrepreneurship education. Literature review for Progress and Prospects. *6th International Conference on Social Sciences and Economic Development* (ICSSED) (pp. 448–452). https://doi.org/10.2991/assehr.k.210407.088

CHAPTER 10

Leveraging on 4IR for an Effective Educational Broadcasting in Nigeria

Gertrude Kanayo Ezekoka

Introduction

The term broadcasting evolved from its use as an agricultural method of sowing seeds in a field by casting them broadly about. It was later adopted for describing the widespread distribution of information by printed materials or by telegraph. Ogunmilade as cited in Babalola (2012, p. 43) says: "broadcasting is the mode of spreading information widely by sound and or vision to a group of people either in their homes or at the listening or viewing centers and in schools through electronic devices of several kinds." Contributing Onabajo in Nkwam-Uwaoma and Onu (2017) sees broadcasting as the transmission of information through radio waves from a radio or television station to the audience in far and near places through their receivers, which help in decoding such information. It is the spreading of audio and visual information or content to a dispersed audience through any electronic mass communication medium.

G. K. Ezekoka (✉)
Faculty of Education, Imo State University, Owerri, Imo State, Nigeria
e-mail: gertrudeezekoka@gmail.com

U. S. Akpan (ed.), *Educational Broadcasting in Nigeria in the Age of Artificial Intelligence*,
https://doi.org/10.1007/978-3-031-68530-9_10

It can simply be referred to as the transmission of signals through electronic agent wares which convert audio and video signals in a form in which they can be received in the audiences' homes, offices and places of meeting.

The broadcast media aids education through educational broadcasting. The post-independence Nigerian government understood that education was the key to a better future for Nigerians, so they strategically used the mass media in educating her citizens. According to Nwabueze (2018) educational broadcasting is defined as a process of teaching, training or learning through the broadcast media with a view to improving knowledge or developing skills of the audience. Educational broadcasting is a type of programme that covers educational subjects with specific teaching and learning purposes through television and radio media. The use of television and radio for promoting learning or as a supplement for classroom teaching continues to attract much attention because of the major role educational broadcasting plays in contemporary society.

We are at the dawn of the Fourth Industrial Revolution (4IR), where cutting-edge technologies reshape our lives and work. From artificial intelligence (AI) to blockchain, 3D printing to robotics, these innovative advancements are transforming industries worldwide at an unprecedented pace. According to Schwab, the fusion of these technologies and their interaction across the physical, digital, and biological domains fundamentally make the 4IR different from previous revolutions. Businesses that embrace these disruptive technologies are set to thrive in this exciting new age, while those who fail to adapt risk being obliterated.

The fourth industrial revolution is driven by several groundbreaking technologies that provide innovative solutions to complex problems. The Internet of Things (IoT) connects devices and machines, enabling them to communicate and share data in real time. This technology helps businesses optimize operations, automate processes, reduce costs, and increase efficiency. Robotics is another critical technology driving the 4IR. Robots are increasingly replacing monotonous manual labour in manufacturing, logistics, healthcare, mass communication and other industries. With artificial intelligence (AI), advancements in creating thinking machines, robots can now perform more complex tasks autonomously.

AI has also been a game changer for various industries, enabling the automation of processes that would have otherwise required human intervention. Machine learning algorithms help organizations predict consumer behaviour patterns based on big data-tailored training, while chatbots improve customer service experiences. Also, Blockchain technology has shown significant potential for disrupting traditional financial systems with its decentralized nature, providing enhanced security measures combined with transparency across transactions made through a distributed ledger system. Finally, 3D printing stands out among the 4IR technologies as it creates customized products at a scale without compromising quality or increasing production time substantially- this allows companies from various sectors such as healthcare, mass communication, agritech, aerospace, or automotive to make more efficient use of resources while creating higher value-added products than previously possible. "Today, manufacturing is changing faster than ever before, and the drivers for this include globalization, individualization, time to market, and sustainability"-Brian Holliday.

Artificial Intelligence (AI)

Handley (2018, p. 43) defines AI "as a non-human device or algorithm being able to do behaviours and actions that are possible only for a person of human intelligence, or maybe not even possible for humans, so above human intelligence." According to Makridakis (2017), artificial intelligence or machine intelligence can be said to be the process of making machines intelligent and that intelligence can be seen as the quality that enables an entity to function appropriately and with foresight in its environment. Jackson (2019) referred to Artificial Intelligence as the ability of a digital computer or computer-controlled robot to perform tasks commonly associated with intelligent beings. AI is also defined as, an intelligent entity created by humans, capable of performing tasks intelligently without being explicitly instructed. AI is an artificially created human-like intelligence that can learn, reason, plan, perceive, or process natural language among other things in a machine.

Artificial Intelligence is now applied to almost all aspects of human endeavour, including journalism, and it is playing an increasingly major role in modern society. According to Guanah (2021), AI brings about better and faster service delivery and more efficient ways of work performance that are mostly cheaper to execute, apart from labour-saving. Guanah et al., (2020, p. 12) noted that the emergence of Artificial Intelligence is gradually having effects in most facets of the society and no area tends to be exempted from this AI bug; "all these indicate that AI has the potential to cause significant disruptions to many hitherto known and established ways of doing things all over the world, including Nigeria."

Types of Artificial Intelligence

There are 3 types of artificial intelligence (AI)

1. Narrow or weak AI
2. General or strong AI
3. Artificial super intelligence

Narrow or weak AI

Artificial Narrow Intelligence (ANI) also referred to as weak AI or narrow AI is the only type of artificial intelligence we have successfully realized to date. Narrow AI is goal-oriented, designed to perform singular tasks—like facial recognition, speech recognition/voice assistants, driving a car, or searching the internet and is very intelligent at completing the specific task it is programmed to do. While these machines may seem intelligent, they operate under a narrow set of constraints and limitations, which is why this type is commonly referred to as weak AI.

Narrow AI doesn't mimic or replicate human intelligence.

Examples of Narrow AI

1. Rank brain by Google/Google search
2. Siri by Apple, Alexa by Amazon, and other visual assistants.
3. Image facial recognition software
4. Disease mapping and prediction tools
5. Self driving cars, etc.

Artificial general intelligence (AGI)/strong AI/Deep AI

Artificial General Intelligence (AGI) also referred to as strong AI or deep AI, is the concept of a machine with general intelligence and/or behaviours, with the ability to learn and apply its intelligence to solve any problem. AGI can think, understand, and act in a way that is indistinguishable from that of a human in any given situation. AI researchers and scientists have not yet achieved strong AI. To succeed, they would need to find a way to make machines conscious, programming a full set of cognitive abilities. Strong AI uses a theory of mind AI framework, which refers to the ability to discern needs, emotions, beliefs and thought processes of other intelligent entities. The lack of comprehensive knowledge on the functionality of the human brain has researchers struggling to replicate basic functions of sight and movement. It is difficult to determine whether or not strong AI will be achieved in our foreseeable future. As image and facial recognition technology advances, it is likely we will see an improvement in the ability of machines to learn and see.

Artificial Super Intelligence (ASI)

Artificial Super Intelligence (ASI), is the hypothetical AI that doesn't just mimic or understand human intelligence and behaviour. ASI is where machines become self aware and surpass the capacity of human intelligence and ability. Super intelligence has long been this muse of science fiction in which robots overrun, overthrow and enslave humanity. ASI would theoretically be exceedingly better at everything we do; math, science; sports, art, medicine, etc. ASI has a greater memory and a faster ability to process and analyse data and stimuli. Consequently, the decision-making and problem solving capabilities of super intelligent beings would be far more superior to those of human beings.

Application of AI in Educational Broadcasting

Clearly, AI has also introduced a paradigm shift in the learning and practice processes of journalism where it is now being used to speed up research, gather and disseminate information, cross reference data, and boost quality outcomes by enhancing the journalistic process. AI is also being used to summarize complicated write-ups into bite-sized content for social media and to create short videos from text in seconds or collect information from various sources. The co-founder of Narrative Science predicts that up to 90% of articles will be written by AI within 15 years (Hall, 2018). AI has the ability to deepen news coverage and personalize it for individual or group of readers or viewers. The adaptation of AI in journalism is sometimes referred to as "automated journalism." This is a situation whereby, with little or no human input after programming, algorithmic processes convert data into narrative news texts. Some AIs can even write and broadcast news independent of the human journalist, and also improve the quality of news. Hence, Guanah et al., (2020) argue that "just as the advent of AI has impact on various sectors of the society, it also affects journalism practice in numerous ways, especially now that journalists can use AI-generated smart templates to gather and disseminate news reports easily on various issues." When there is clean, accurate and structured data for AI to process, it can generate routine news stories for repetitive topics. Hitherto, it may be compulsory for a news reporter to be physically present to cover a news event, sometimes at the risk of his life, but today, with AI-powered drones, a reporter can even cover a war situation while not being present at the theater of war. This agrees with Ladi Ojora's assertion as cited in Ndiomewese (2017) that, "True Artificial Intelligence is the empowerment of computer systems with the ability to independently learn and make decisions exclusively of the programmer or system that created it". The advent of AI technology is causing disruptions, both positively and negatively, in all aspects of human life, including journalism studies and practice. Though it has the propensity to displace people from their jobs, yet it enhances efficiency. Majority Discourses on Communication and Media Studies in Contemporary Society 155 of the journalism training schools and media houses in Nigeria are yet to fully inculcate AI into their operations (Guanah et al., 2020) even though it has come to stay. Earlier, Adeniyi (2011) has observed that Mass communication schools in Nigeria do not imbibe e-learning as much as it is required in their curricular, and this makes students to graduate without acquiring the adequate skills needed to enable them to be E-reporters. AI is an integral part of E-learning. Now that AI is a global phenomenon, how does it impinge on journalism studies/educational broadcasting and practice in Nigeria? What are the practical steps that can be taken to prepare Nigeria's media industry for the utilization of AI in its tasks? This study serves as a call for the recognition of the inevitability of AI in media practice and by extension on educational broadcasting in Nigeria.

In recent years, artificial intelligence technology has developed rapidly, among which intelligent voice technology is the most outstanding. At present, it has realized the functions of fast information input and convenient man–machine interaction, which can convert speech recognition into text, convert text into voice through speech synthesis, understand the meaning of speech and execute corresponding commands and operations.

At present, AI voice technology has been widely used in government and enterprise, education, medical care, automobile, finance and other fields. In the future, the development of radio and television should make use of scientific and technological innovation to promote the intelligent development of radio and television program production, content production, safety supervision and other aspects. The rapid development of artificial intelligence in recent years has provided possibilities for the future development of radio and television. As a brand new technology, intelligent voice technology can realize functions such as rapid input of information and human interaction, and is currently involved in many industries such as education, medical care and automobiles.

Intelligent Voice Technology Classification

According to Hu, Xiang, & Li (2021), Intelligence Voice Technology can be classified into three namely: Speech recognition technology, speech transcribe technology and speech synthesis technology.

Speech Recognition Technology

Speech recognition technology mainly refers to the technology that translates spoken words into the corresponding text using closed captions to enable a person with hearing loss to understand what others are saying. This is a new type of information input technology. Speech recognition technology first detects the endpoint of the audio, determines the position of speech, and then recognition processing. It intelligently judges the punctuation and other relevant information of the input information by recognizing the dialogue context of the statement. In the process of input, the system selects the corresponding words preferentially by identifying the user-defined words.

Speech Transcribe Technology

Speech transcribe technology refers to the recognition or translation of the speech signal into text content through computational linguistics. At the same time, some large databases and historical data of users can be used to translate speech, and then the relevant semantic context, pauses, tone, and so on are summarized, and sentences and paragraphs are distinguished and analysed to solve problems such as distant noise.

Speech Synthesis Technology

Speech synthesis refers to the output text, the text is processed by the computer, captured into fluent text and sentences, but also can use this stage of the language to play, language navigation and voice prompt many applications. The main content of language combination is to judge the order of words, to data process words, to derive language wave signals, and finally to put the unit sequence into waveform series, and finally to output the complete signal. It consists of the artificial production of human voices. The main use is the ability to translate a text into spoken speech automatically.

The application of the intelligent voice technology: speech recognition technology, speech transcribe technology and speech synthesis technology into today's radio and television educational broadcasting will go a long way in enhancing its speed and quality.

Challenges of Artificial Intelligence

The following are some challenges confronting the use of AI for educational broadcasting:

1. **Limited Knowledge**: Apart from technology enthusiasts, college students, and researchers, there are only a limited number of people who are aware of the potential of AI.
2. **Data scarcity**: The working of an AI system depends on trained data. The ability to obtain this quality data can be challenging for the new applications or start-up companies.
3. **Job Displacement for broadcasters**: The automation potential of AI raises concerns about job displacement for broadcasters. While AI can streamline administrative tasks, it cannot replace the unique insights, creativity, and adaptability that humans bring to the studio. Therefore, integrating AI should complement, not replace, human broadcasters.
4. **Expensive Implementation costs**: Implementing AI in industries, involves significant costs for them. Not all industries may have the financial resources to adopt advanced AI solutions, potentially leading to unequal opportunities for students.

Other challenges include:

1. Infrastructure limitations
2. A prevailing skill gap
3. Concerns over data privacy and ethics, and the need for appropriate policy and regulation.
4. Difficulty accessing capital
5. Limited access to qualified human capital
6. Limited internet access and developing infrastructure
7. Government policy
8. Job loss problems
9. The dependencies of human beings on such technologies make humans lazy.
10. There is always a fear with AI that if it gets advanced, it may be harmful to humanity.
11. If inputs are not fed correctly to AI systems, then it may cause harmful results.

Conclusion

Artificial Intelligence is undoubtedly a trending and emerging technology. It is growing very fast day by day, and it is enabling machines to mimic the human brain. Due to its high performance and as it is making human life easier, it is becoming a highly demanded technology among industries. Intelligent voice technology has been found to have a great impact on broadcasting and can be applied for a more effective educational broadcasting. However, there are also some challenges and problems with AI. Many people around the world are still thinking of it as a risky technology, because it will be dangerous for humanity, as shown in various Sci-fi movies. People also feel that with time, it will overtake humans. However, the day-to-day development of AI is making it a comfortable technology, and people are connecting with it more.

Recommendations

1. Broadcasters and teachers in our schools should be trained on the use of AI for a more effective use of the same for lesson delivery. This training should also help them overcome the fear of being replaced by AI.

2. Government should make annual budgetary allocations for the high financial resources required for the application of AI in schools and media houses.
3. Data with high bandwidth should be made available by appropriate companies to schools and media houses to enhance the use of AI.

References

Adeniyi, G. (2011). Empowering newsmen for modern journalism practice. *The Punch*, p.12

Babalola, B. K. (2012). Educational broadcasting in Nigeria. A historical development perspective. *Journal of Communication and Culture, 3*, 14–18.

Guanah, J. S. (2021). Mainstream media and artificial intelligence awareness amongst residents of Asaba metropolis, Delta State, Nigeria. *Journal of Contemporary Social Research, 5*(1), 65–79.

Guanah, J. S., & Akumabor, N. T. (2022). Chapter 20- application of AI in the learning and practice of journalism in Nigeria. In E. S. Asemah, D.O. Ekhareafore & T. Santas (Eds.), *Discourses on communication and media studies in contemporary studies.* University of Jos Press.

Guanah, J. S., Agbanu, N. V., & Obi, I. (2020a). Artificial intelligence and journalism practice in Nigeria: Perception of journalists in Benin City, Edo State. *International Review of Humanities Studies, 5*(2), 698–715.

Guanah, J. S., Obi, I., & Ginikachukwu, A. C. (2020b). Artificial intelligence and its reportage in select Nigerian newspapers: A content analysis. *International Journal of Language and Literary Studies, 2*(2), 45–61.

Hall, S. (2018). Can you tell if this was written by a robot? 7 challenges for AI in journalism. https://www.weforum.org/agenda/2018/01/can-you-tell-if-this-article-was-written-by-a-robot-7-challenges-for-ai-in-journalism/.

Handley, L. (2018). Experts cast doubt on whether China's news anchor is really A.I. https://www.cnbc.com/2018/11/16/experts-cast-doubt-on-whether-chinas-news-anchor-is-really-ai.html

Jackson, P. C. (2019). *Introduction to Artificial Intelligence.* Courier Dover Publications.

Hu, M., Xiang, Z., & Li, K. (2021). *Application of Artificial Intelligence voice technology in radio and television medi*a.

Makridakis, S. (2017). The forthcoming Artificial Intelligence (AI) revolution: Its Impact on Society and Firms. *Futures*, (90), 46–60

Ndiomewese, I. (2018). *Experts answer 9 questions on the state of artificial intelligence in Nigeria*. https://techpoint.africa/2017/09/26/artificial-intelligence-nigeria/.

Nkwam-Uwaoma, A.O., & Onu, D. M.(2017). *Educational broadcasting in contemporary society*. Gabtony Prints.

CHAPTER 11

Adapting Radio Broadcasting as a Tool Against Teachers Tendency for Resisting AI Technology

Thelma U. Ekukinam

Introduction

Artificial intelligence (AI) in a layman's sense is technology employed to enhance the human mental ability just like different kinds of technology are employed to enhance our physical abilities. The amount of work our hands or legs would have achieved with difficulty is made easy with maximum results within a short period through the application of technology. Similarly the amount of work the brain could achieve within a set time frame can be maximized by employing technology. That is why for instance, it is easy to do large amounts of calculations effortlessly through the use of technological devices and applications (Subrahmanyam & Swathi, 2018). AI is seen as 'raw data, received from any user, filtered by a device, made meaningful, and processed' before

T. U. Ekukinam (✉)
University of Uyo, Uyo, Akwa Ibom State, Nigeria
e-mail: thelmaekukinam@gmail.com

U. S. Akpan (ed.), *Educational Broadcasting in Nigeria in the Age of Artificial Intelligence*,
https://doi.org/10.1007/978-3-031-68530-9_11

finally becoming consumed by end users', while Nilsson (2018, p. 54), defines AI 'as the entirety of an algorithmic construction copying human intelligence'. Simply thus, AI is a technology that enables machines to perform tasks that would typically require human intelligence such as mental processes like reasoning, perception, generalization, and learning from past experiences (Goksel, & Bozkurt, 2019).

Objectives

Specifically, it will highlight the Nigerian teacher's position regarding by answering the following questions:

1. Does the professional development of teachers enhance integration of AI?
2. What are the factors that create teachers' resistance to AI integration and the consequences?
3. What are the implications and suggestions for using Radio broadcast for AI awareness among teachers?

Artificial Intelligence and its Adoption in the Nigerian Educational System

Generally, AI applications are utilized to make daily tasks easier and less time consuming. These include: Google Maps for easy and safe navigation, facial detection and recognition for security purposes, text editors or autocorrect applications to enhance our writing skills, e-payments for easy bank and financial transactions, social media platforms, etc. (Oshodi, 2021). However, as knowledge on AI continues to abound in various aspects of life, education has received its fair share of AI inventions and applications which have already been adopted into the formal educational system in some countries while some other countries are yet to embrace it formally. Despite the extent of AI awareness created through Information and Communication Technology (ICT) outlets, the Nigerian educational system still has a lot of work to do in regard to making decisive statements and policies to integrate AI into the mainstream of educational technologies (Ebubechukwu, 2023). This implies that the educational sector cannot rely on such ICT outlets to create adequate awareness regarding

AI among teachers. This approach might be out of the reach of certain categories of educational stakeholders especially the teachers.

The existence of the technological divide between the developed and underdeveloped countries would be an understatement regarding AI when even issues regarding access to computers have not been resolved. This becomes worrisome for some underdeveloped countries that lack the financial capacity to keep pace with emerging technologies. Several reviews of the status of educational technology (ET) adoption in Nigeria only reveal a sporadic kind of implementation that cannot cater for the greater Nigerian community. For instance, some significant attempts have been made in a few higher institutions and also in the National Open University of Nigeria (NOUN) yet the utilization of ET in Nigeria is still rated as being poor (Oshodi, 2021). In Obafemi Awolowo University, a Remote Lap was built by Ishola Babatunde (Ogbonnia, 2017). Also in consonance with the directives of the Federal Government, the Nigerian Educational Research and Development Council (NERDC) took steps to ensure that robotics and artificial intelligence are incorporated into the basic education curriculum in the country. The Federal Government Girls College, Ogun State has also set up a ROBOTIC Centre. They have succeeded in building a robot that can be operated to perform some locomotive acts (Idoko, 2023).

AI Content for the Teacher

The National Policy of Education in Nigeria (2004), emphasizes the integration of ET as a subject matter and as a means of instructional delivery in its curriculum development plan. This highlights the need for the teachers to be properly grounded in its content and usage. The high cost of textbooks has made information seekers, including teachers, to resort to the use of internet facilities as a shortcut to gaining knowledge on areas of concern. Apart from content development, AI has brought in lots of assistive innovations to make the work of teachers easier. A professional teacher needs to constantly research to update both knowledge and skills.

AI tools and applications are numerous and cannot be fully discussed in this article. However, the major types of AI technologies include machine vision, expert systems, machine learning, natural language processing, deep learning, and robotics (Obla, 2020; Olafare, 2023). There are different kinds of AI applications that are useful for educational purposes such as Plagiarism Detection, Exam Integrity, Chatbots for Enrollment and Retention, Learning Management Systems, Transcription of Faculty Lectures, Enhanced Online Discussion Boards and Analyzing Student Success Metrics. These are utilized at the higher education levels for effective instructional delivery, control and assessment. Some other examples include: 'Palitt', which enables a teacher to personalize instructional plan and content; 'Cram101', a summarized smart guide to aid learners' revision on a particular subject and 'JustTheFacts101', a highlighter that can detect and mark out salient facts similar in usage to a yellow marker and Grammarly language structural correction tool, etc. (Karyuart et al., 2018; Martin, 2019). These and many others can be utilized by any instructor for personal use and (or) assessment of students' work.

Benefits of AI for Teachers

Generally, the workload of a teacher concerning the needs of the students and being able to identify and tailor instruction to suit the needs has been reduced through the use of AI. Specifically thus:

i. AI can establish students' previous knowledge and determine preferred learning style.
ii. AI does not only mark and grade multiple choice tests but does the same for essays.
iii. AI produces reliable feedback from previous assessments for the purpose of improving instructional content and approach.
iv. Provides useful on the spot tips and feedback that can easily be accessed by students.
v. There is time reduction in administrative tasks and more time for teachers' interaction with the students.

Thus considering the benefits of AI to the educational system, this paper will generally examine the place of teachers regarding integration of AI into the educational system.

Research Question 1

The Teacher's Professional Development: A teacher must acquire formal education with at least National Certificate of Education (NCE), a Bachelor of Science in Education or Bachelor of Arts in Education depending on which level of education one intends to teach. One can still aspire to a higher status with a Master's degree and Doctoral Degree. The teacher receives an all-round exposure to the rudiments of becoming a professional teacher through training in educational psychology, philosophy, technology, general studies, special methods and body of knowledge in specific subjects or disciplines. After graduation and employment, the teacher has the opportunity of attending government organized in-service training for professional updates in current pedagogical skills and innovation. It is assumed that a course in Educational Technology should expose the teachers to basic knowledge about AI and its applications. Apart from government interventions regarding training and retraining of teachers, in pedagogical skills it is the duty of the teacher to personally engage in personal research to remain relevant to current educational trends. A teacher who fails to stay updated becomes obsolete in knowledge and skills. This in turn breeds the tendency for resistance and total avoidance. Obla, (2020) opines that these negative tendencies can be avoided by making the teachers work environment more enhancing and comfortable (Ekukinam & Monday, 2020). AI does not leave out any category of teachers, starting from the nursery, primary, secondary and higher institutions, there are AI tools that can be utilized at each level. Thus there is a need to create more awareness on AI technologies for teachers.

Research Question 2

Factors that Could Create Resistance to AI Integration: The teacher's exposure to a conducive environment while in training and in practice will determine their level of interest in or resistance to utilizing current pedagogical skills and applications. Some of these factors are discussed below:

(i) Lack of Exposure During Professional Training

In the first place, institutions providing teacher's professional development lack facilities for exposing teacher trainees to ICT skills. Some teacher trainers lack training skills in utilization of ET and as such only deliver contents without practical backups and demonstrations. The trainee teachers acquire certificates that cannot be backed up with practical skills. Some that do have the opportunity of interacting with such facilities, graduate and get employed in schools that lack facilities for utilizing acquired skills.

(ii) Inadequate Financial Back up to Ensure Proper Implementation of Educational Policies on the Integration of Technology

Educational policies are clearly stated on the application of ICT to instructional delivery (NPE, 2004) but the financial backup provided by the government is outstandingly inadequate to ensure proper interpretation and implementation of educational goals. Thus some teachers see an opportunity to shift the blame of their poor performance on the government with no attempt at self-development in current technologies (Ekukinam & Monday, 2020). A clear pointer to the fact that the teachers totally depending on the government to provide ET facilities for continuous professional development may not have adequate exposure to technologies in education. Nonetheless, many still work at keeping abreast with technological developments through personal mobile gadgets, which is still limited due to their meager resources for data subscriptions for in-depth internet engagement.

(iii) Tendency for Resistance and Total Avoidance of ET

According to Okoye & Okwo resistance to ICT is a feeling of discouragement from the use of Educational communications technology. Some for lack of familiarity with use of technologies develop phobia and resistance towards utilization of ET (Christopoulos & Sprangers, 2021) which if left unchecked can result in complete avoidance. This author is of the opinion that such a category of teachers may ignore or lose interest completely from any attempts to seek for enlightenment on emerging concepts. This may occur as a result of lack of skills in the basic aspects of ET and not necessarily as a result of lack of facilities as they prefer the traditional method to instructional delivery instead of using technological tools (Christopoulos & Sprangers, 2021). The teachers having avoidance tendency resort to the expository method. Okoye and Okwo (2019) employ the fact that the tendency for avoidance can be nipped in the bud through enlightenment on the workings and benefits of emerging technologies. Ekukinam and Monday (2020) are of the opinion that teachers' preparedness for integration of technology can be sharpened through workshops that actually demonstrate and apply the use of technology for training on instructional delivery as it is done in Jolly Phonics training workshops for Primary school teachers. The problem that could arise here is the Government's inability to sponsor teachers regularly to workshops where their knowledge and skills can be updated. In a situation where the efforts of the government are not yielding expected outcome in terms of placing the teachers at an advantaged position for integration of ET, the consequence is that teachers are left with no other option but avoidance for lack of skills (Obla, 2020). As such, the need to think out of the box regarding integration of AI. The concern should be on ways of increasing awareness for teachers on AI for the purpose of creating interest in AI for the instructional delivery processes. Hence the suggestion of the broadcast media as an effective medium for creating awareness on AI.

Consequences of Total Avoidance of AI Technologies in Education by Teachers

There have been several arguments as to the possibility for AI applications to have a negative impact on the learners' attitude towards personal adaptation and improvement. For instance, Grammarly application earlier mentioned as a suitable content for both teacher and student permits the user to make use of pre-arranged structural language patterns for writing their essays and compositions. This suggests the fact that one may not have to study the basics of English Language structural patterns as it is directly possible to have correct versions. This can have an adverse effect on the user's study habits. Karyuart et al. (2018), suggest that these tendencies can be checked through dictating homogenous answers, stereotype answers and personal cross checking. Teachers' lack of skills in ET can allow such negative tendencies to remain unchecked. Below are some consequences of resistance to AI integration:

1. Complete reliance on the expository method to the detriment of the learners.

2. The fact that the younger generation is more proactive when it pertains to the use of technology can give them an edge over their teachers.
3. Learners may also develop negative tendencies without teachers' guidance and monitoring.
4. Teachers assessment of class assignments will lack credibility as the teacher is not in a position to detect quick fixes by some AI knowledgeable learners.
5. Learners will lose confidence in the teacher's ability to deliver sound instructions.
6. Learners stand to lose a chance of competing favorably with their mates who have early exposure to AI.

Research Question 3

Implications for the Broadcast Media (Radio): The broadcast media has a major role to play in creating awareness for AI in Nigerian society. The choice of broadcast media, especially radio, is significant at this point because it is a means of reaching out to the larger society in both urban and rural areas. The core basis is that people tend to use their sense of hearing when other options fail or are not forthcoming. The visuals may be hard to come by, the audiovisuals may be expensive to operate and maintain. The characteristics and benefits of the audio medium as a means of disseminating information to the larger community of people that may not assess other media forms are quite significant (Patrick, 2023). Radio sets abound in sizes and capacities that can meet the needs of the consumers. Maintenance and operation are also within the reach of the lowest cadre of workers and small business people in the society. These workers live among and also associate with other groups who may not consider the importance of the radio as a means of gaining information but do rely on verbal communication. Radio are manufactured in sizes that are tailored to meet the needs of the customers. The more portable ones are carried around as can be seen publicly done by people who have developed the habit and also derive pleasure in listening to the radio. In this vein, the broadcast media should take advantage of this situation to purposefully work towards reducing if not totally closing the gap between those with and without the awareness of AI.

Suggestions for Creating Awareness on Educational Benefits of AI Through Radio Broadcast

i. The name tagged to the broadcast unit should be one that captures the interest of the teachers as the target audience while giving them a sense of relevance and importance.
ii. Other interested members can benefit from the series but it should not be junked up with the general enlightenment of the public on issues relating to technology in education.
iii. Make prior announcements and advertisements for a wide coverage to keep them alert in preparation for listening.
iv. The content on AI should be broadcast on specific objectives for teacher development.
v. The broadcast should be delivered by qualified experts in the field preferably educational technologists who are versed in the applications of AI in education.
vi. Present the broadcast in predetermined chunks that can aid easy understanding and logical buildup of the knowledge base of the teacher.
vii. Choose a suitable period for the teachers' convenience especially away from school hours.
viii. Include life tune-in for slots for listeners who may have questions or would like to interact with the presenter.
ix. Invite experienced teachers for a radio talk show that will encourage other teachers.
x. The broadcast media can provide references that will aid the teachers' personal study.
xi. Some content can be broadcast in the local language of the community.

Conclusion

It is necessary to advance the use of the broadcast media, especially the radio which has a far greater outreach for the purpose of increasing awareness on AI integration. AI has made its impact on the educational system and whether it is formally or informally utilized, there is an ardent need to check the negative impact of misuse by the learners and also resistance to use by teachers. In a situation where the younger generation are more proactive to the use of technology, the teachers stand at a disadvantage of not being able to check misuse. Thus, the earlier the teachers can be encouraged to develop interest in AI integration, the better. This can be advanced through the use of radio broadcasts.

References

Christopoulos, A., & Sprangers, P. (2021). Integration of educational technology during the Covid-19 pandemic: An analysis of teacher and student receptions. *Cogent Education, 8*(1), 1964690.

Ebubechukwu, F. C. (2023). *Revolutionizing education in Nigeria: Harnessing AI for equitable access and quality learning*. Bookcraft.

Ekukinam, T. U., & Monday, J. S. (2020). Appraising jolly phonics models for technology integration in a continuous professional development through workshops. *Journal of Nigeria Association for Educational Media and Technology(JEMT), 26*(2), 213–221.

FGN. (2004). *The National Policy on Education.*

Goksel, N., & Bozkurt, A. (2019). Artificial Intelligence in education: Current insights and future perspectives. In S. Sisman-Ugur, & G. Karabacak (Eds.), *Handbook of research on learning in the age of transhumanism* (pp. 224–236).

Idoko, C. (2023, August 8). FG urges integration of AI in basic education curriculum. In *The Nigerian Tribune.*

Karyuart, L., Rizqan, M. D., & Darayani, N. A. (2018). Grammarly as a tool to improve students' writing quality (free online proofreader across the boundaries). *Jurnal Sains Sosial Dan Humaniora, 2*(1), 83–89.

Martin, I. B. (2019). Using padlet for collaborative learning, 5th International Conference on Higher Education Advances (HEAd'19). Universitat-Polit'cnicade Valencia.

Obla, M. E. (2020). Inspiring teaching and learning through technology inclusion for sustainable national development. *Journal of Nigeria Association for Educational Media and Technology (JEMT), 26*(2).

Ogbonnia, O. O. (2017). Artificial Intelligence as an imperative to the effective delivery of instructional materials' content. *International Journal of Advanced Research and Publications, 1*(5), 323–327. www.ijarp.org

Okoye, A. N., & Okwo, F. A. (2019). Teachers resistance to the use of educational communications technology in state owned tertiary institutions in Enugu State, Nigeria. In T. I, Asino. & F. O. Moprmah (Eds.), *ADAECT, 2019 Conference Proceedings*.

Olafare F. O. (2023). Artificial intelligence in education: Challenges and way forward. *Nigerian Online Journal of Educational Sciences and Technology (NOJEST)*, (51), 1–8.

Oshodi, I. K. (2021). *A review of the impact of education technology in developing countries: A case study of Nigeria*. Concept Books.

Patrick, N. I. (2023). *Managing educational broadcasting in Nigeria: Reflection on Concepts*. Spike Books.

Subrahmanyam, V., & Swathi, K. (2018). Artificial Intelligence and its implications in education. International Conference on Improved Access to Distance higher Education Focus on Underserved and Uncovered Regions, Kakatiya University, Telangana, India.

CHAPTER 12

Artificial Intelligence (AI) Influence in Educational Media Broadcast in Individualized Instruction in the Twenty-first Century

Idongesit Akan Udi

Introduction

Today's world in the twenty-first century is witnessing radical transformation in technology now tagged Artificial Intelligence. Technological development is never static, but keeps advancing and changing as human innovators are still searching for ways of solving problems in a technological way using computers and its electronic peripherals. Udi and Nwosu (2023) assert that all levels of education and every facet of life have been transformed through the use of technological devices which has become very eminent and essential in human capacity building and development. Artificial Intelligence (AI) has emerged as a revolutionary technology with

I. A. Udi (✉)
Department of Educational Technology, University of Uyo, Uyo, Nigeria
e-mail: idongesitaudi@gmail.com

U. S. Akpan (ed.), *Educational Broadcasting in Nigeria in the Age of Artificial Intelligence*,
https://doi.org/10.1007/978-3-031-68530-9_12

transformative implications across various industries, including education. AI refers to the simulation of human intelligence in machines that can perform tasks requiring human-like cognitive abilities. Its applications in education have grown exponentially, impacting how knowledge is delivered and acquired in educational settings. AI-driven technologies, such as natural language processing, machine learning, and computer vision, have paved the way for personalized and adaptive learning experiences, content creation, assessment, and much more. Harve (2023) asserts that AI is becoming significant in almost all phases of our lives such as surveillance (exposing criminal activities), executing art works, research capabilities, transcribing languages, logistic matters, education sectors, in medical diagnosis and media broadcasting, etc.

Educational media broadcast plays a crucial role in disseminating knowledge, reaching a broader audience, and enhancing the learning experience. With the advent of the internet and digital technologies, educational content can now be accessed anytime and anywhere. AI's integration in educational media broadcasts holds the potential to revolutionize how information is presented, making it more engaging, interactive, and tailored to individual learners' needs. This integration enables educators to cater for diverse learning styles, preferences, and paces, leading to improved learning outcomes. This research explores the influence of AI in educational media broadcasts during the twenty-first century, analyzing its role in personalized learning, content creation, assessment, and addressing challenges and concerns. Through case studies and future prospects, we delve into the concept of media broadcast and the potential of AI to reshape education, while acknowledging the importance of human educators in this evolving landscape.

Concept of Media Broadcast

Media in this case is for the instructional broadcast which falls within the range of audio to audio- visual media such as radio, television, smart phones, computer, video clips, etc., or any media that can transmit information orally from source (encoder) to receiver (decoder). Rosencrance (2023) opines that media could fall into any kind of graphic, photographic, electronic or mechanical mode that can process and transmit visual and oral information. A television or radio becomes an educational media when it has to do with broadcasting instruction for learners/ users. At this point the instructor who is obviously distant has to select the appropriate media for the broadcast knowing that these encoded messages must reach the individual learners who have to decode these messages. Gruetzemacher (2023) The messages used in media broadcast must have fixative, manipulative and distributive properties that the media must allow capture, preservation and reconstitution of objects and events. This means that the objects or events such as the voice note can be captured and preserved and can be built up again from parts (reconstituted) at any time or whenever desired. That is to say that objects or events could be transformed in several ways like slow mode or fast mode and there must be an ability to multiply or reproduce items in several locations at any time desired (Marr, 2023). This means it does not have time bounds. This research is in agreement with these qualities of media broadcast and views it as strongly related to this study of individualized instruction which enables the individual learner to have a good access to learning instructions in a flexible way with little or no stress.

The Historical Development of AI

It is of essence the study discusses the historical development of AI that could have paved the way to its impact on educational media broadcast. The Evolution of AI in Educational Media Broadcast can be linked to its development in education. The roots of AI in education can be traced back to the twentieth century, but significant advancements were witnessed in the twenty-first century, driven by improved computing power and data availability. Early educational AI applications involved intelligent tutoring systems that provided personalized feedback to students. Opentext (2023) asserts that education has adapted and adopted technology for quite some ages, viewing the past and recent developments as being so precedential that one is often very expectant of what is going to come. The most recent technology rarely replaces the previous ones, rather it stays with those who are used to using it. However the influence of the internet on education can be viewed as it pertains to educational technology. Over time, AI algorithms became more sophisticated, allowing for data-driven decision-making and personalization at scale in educational media broadcasts. Advancements in AI technology and its impact on media broadcast cannot be overemphasized.

The proliferation of AI technologies, such as natural language processing and machine learning, has fueled innovative approaches in educational media broadcast. AI-powered chatbots can engage with learners, answering questions and providing support. Sentiment analysis enables educators to gauge learners' emotions and tailor content accordingly. AI-driven recommendation systems suggest relevant educational content, encouraging continuous learning. This study discusses all of these and also highlights the benefits of AI technology in media broadcast as well as the challenges faced, in terms of the inability of underdeveloped countries like Nigeria in catching up with these global trends. The paper draws a conclusion that there is a need for under-developing countries such as Nigeria to ensure they catch up with the global world, as well as mentioning recommendations required in order not to be left out of the scheme of things in this technologically advanced era of the twenty-first century.

Components of AI Media Broadcast in Individualized Instruction

AI could be categorized into five major components which includes Machine Learning, Natural Language Processing, Computer vision, Robotics and Expert systems. These will be discussed as it pertains to individualized instruction through media broadcast.

1. Machine Learning: Computer vision algorithms could be engaged to recognize the learner, objects or videos thereby allowing more detailed information to be released about them at a particular time. Learning (2023). Such probably would provide detailed descriptions of people, things viewed on the camera during the broadcast. With AI-Driven Personalization in Educational Media, there will be the use of adaptive learning and personalized content delivery which enables educational content that is dynamically adjusted to suit each learner's strengths and weaknesses. By analyzing data on learners' interactions, assessments, and progress, AI algorithms can identify learning gaps and tailor content to fill those gaps. Personalized content delivery enhances motivation and promotes self-directed learning.

   According to Bhatia (2023) AI has the capacity to enhance independent learning processes. Once the system is put in the right place in terms of adequate facilities like internet connections and functionality it can deliver education efficiently and effectively to accommodate an individual learner. It accommodates the learner's needs and characteristics and ensures the flow of individualized instructional resources. One of the merits accrued to AI is its capability to enhance individualized studies in such a way that it can analyze large data on independent learners, taking cognizance of their preferred learning styles, lapses and strengths. This enables AI systems delivery instructions with learning contents based on learners characteristics with specification for effective education outcomes. This takes the discussion to the very important role of AI because of its ability to recognize, understand, translate and transmit spoken language which plays a vital role in media broadcast as it pertains to individualized instruction.

2. Natural Language Processing (NPL): NPL has to do with the communication style of AI which is associated with intelligence. According to Deng and Liu (2018) NLP is divided into three categories such as; Speech recognition, Natural language understanding and Natural language generation.

    a. Speech recognition; this is the translation of spoken language into oral language and text. The computer receives the natural language and translates it into a machine readable form (language). This is the first step to the process known as speech recognition. Speech recognition in individualized instruction as viewed could be used to help students learn languages. It has the capacity to enable students to learn pronunciation by speaking into the App. It is also capable of assessing students' skills in oral language in terms of pronunciation of words. There are two types of speech recognition namely; Speaker- dependent software and the other is speaker-independent software. The latter is commonly used for dictation software, while speaker-independent is more commonly found in telephone applications. According to Doty (2023) speech recognition can make provision for class discussion, transcription, etc., especially for those impaired learners and non-natives who may find it difficult to grasp every word of the lecture.
    b. Natural language understanding (NLU): This has to do with the computer capacity to understand our spoken language. NLU is noted as the most difficult aspect of NLP because of the processes involved in it. The process starts with the computer interpreting

the word as it is a noun or a verb, past or present tense, etc. This is referred to as part of a speech tagged POS. Because there are several words that could mean the same thing; at this point developers use codes in the NLU system and train. According to Qualtrics (2023) natural language understanding is an area of computer technology that examines the actual meaning of human language not just about the saying in words. The concern is about the meaning behind the saying such as intent, feeling or emotions, the energy released from that statement or better still the outcome of the spoken statement or what is to be achieved as an end result of the statement made. The question that comes to mind is, "in what ways could NLU improve individual instruction as it pertains to educational media broadcasts?" NLU has added advantages on instructional technology with the capabilities of correcting grammatical and typing errors and many other applications such as internal and external email responses, chat boat, internet search engines, social media comments, interactive voice response (IVR) system for calls, voice assistant, auto correct, etc. NLU is an application that has multiple language support capabilities. Individual instruction could require processing of data in several languages. Ability to have more than just the English language could create efficiency and effectiveness in education delivery.A larger community of students could be reached for media broadcasts for individualized instruction.

c. Natural Language generation (NLG): This has to do with a computer software procedure that outputs natural language. NLG makes use of AI programmed to produce written or oral narratives from structured data into human readable text. This method of transmission enables multiple generation of data-driven narratives in a very short space of time as long as the right data has the right information. NLG is the AI technology driven force behind text content automation with the ability to turn data into written words or journals or film scripts. Gruetzemacher (2023) affirms that AI has tremendously transformed. the potential of technology in an unbelievable manner for instance by its abilities such as being used in writing articles, for cognitive capabilities like generating instruction for humans. NLG also works with such potentials as content determination the amount of data required in the information); data interpretation (specifications or detailed information); document planning (could be used in research, writing articles and generating instructions for students); sentence aggregation, grammaticalization, language implementation, and so on. The researcher adopts these views and is of the opinion that all of these potentials of AI are required in the effectiveness of education delivery of individualized instruction through media broadcast systems (Dilmaghani, 2023).

3. Computer Visions; IBM This has to do with the aspect of AI known as machine learning and neural networks that enables the computer to dictate defeats and issues that could affect the operations of the system. These allow actions to be taken and recommendations to be made. Computer vision works pretty much like human vision, with the exception that machines are faster and can use a much lesser time and at the same time can detect issues in several or thousands of products within a short space of time. A few examples of computer vision include; image classification (seeing image and classifying it, example a cat); object detection (ability to detect damages); object tracking—can track detected objects and can browse, search and retrieve images; content—based images retrieval (International Business Machine Corporation. (IBM, 2023)
4. Robotics; Robotics is a field of artificial intelligence that focuses on the design, development, and implementation of robots, which are machines capable of performing tasks autonomously or semi-autonomously. Robotics involves the integration of various AI technologies, such as computer vision and natural language processing, to enable robots to interact with the world around them. Ameen (2019) asserts that Robots are rapidly increasing globally and its effect will soon be felt academically. It is estimated that over 800 millions jobs will be threatened by 2030. Innovation in AI is still on going so more potentials are yet to be tapped although its influence on teaching and learning is expected to be enormous as far as lecturing is concerned.

   Robot teachers are putting teaching on a higher level of demand for smartness. This infers that the regular teacher without digital skills will likely lose his/her place for Robot teachers. Robots plus AI enhanced teachers enable improved individualized learning, purposes and grading without delay. With the capabilities of recognizing the weaknesses and strengths of learning, Robots create more awareness for academic success in higher institutions (Ameen, 2019). These views are adopted and the position of this study is that the use of Robot tutors for educational media broadcast in individualized study will enable a higher level of effectiveness in academic achievements for individual students.

5. Expert System; This is a computer programme that provides solutions to complex problems by making decisions like human experts. It extracts knowledge from the computer database by reasoning and inference rules as directed by the user. These knowledge bases are designed for specific fields such as engineering, social sciences, economics, etc. The knowledge base depends on what content of knowledge was stored in the first instance (Point, 2023)AI ability to generation of learning contents using natural language processing and machine learning algorithms has enabled instructors and lecturers to save time thereby reducing the workload while still offering effective education delivery (Bhatia, 2023). The predictive and intervention capabilities of the AI system enable it to recognize weaknesses of learners and those at risk of failure or behind academic expectations. This is noticed with the early warning signs through analyzing data patterns and educators are expected to act immediately for the rescue of such students.

Benefits of AI Media Broadcast Instruction for Individualized Study

1. Enhancing Content Creation with AI in Educational Media broadcast for individual instruction. AI-powered content generation tools can automate the creation of educational materials, such as quizzes, exercises, and summaries. This efficiency reduces the burden on educators and allows them to focus on higher-order tasks like facilitation and mentorship. AI-generated content can also be customized for specific learning objectives and target audiences, such as individualized learners' media broadcast instruction.
2. Examples of successful AI integration in educational media include AI-driven language learning apps that adapt content difficulty based on learners' proficiency levels. Virtual reality (VR) and

augmented reality (AR) applications supported by AI facilitate immersive learning experiences. Educational platforms leveraging AI have made content more interactive, incorporating ramification and simulations to enhance engagement and knowledge retention.

3. Case studies showcasing personalized learning through AI in broadcast could demonstrate how learners progress at their own pace, leading to improved language proficiency. Another case study might explore an AI-powered educational video platform that tailors content based on learners' interests, resulting in increased engagement and retention rates. These examples highlight the potential of AI in revolutionizing educational media broadcasts by catering to individual learners' unique needs.
4. The role of AI in automating content creation and delivery could enable a vast amount of educational content available online, selecting the most appropriate and reliable resources for learners. Furthermore, AI-powered content delivery systems can adapt content formats and presentations based on learners' preferences, making it more accessible and engaging. AI system enables a high cognitive level of virtual tutoring with learning strategies that suit the instructional delivery. Lapses are noticed on time and necessary interventions are put in place while monitoring the development process. AI tutors not only supply immediate support and necessary anchor and individualized instruction at the learner's pace or time, but also have the ability to understand students' feedback for required adaptations. The professionalism associated with AI technology in grading student's work cannot be overemphasized. Students' work, assignments and continuous assessment are automatically scored with high accuracy reducing the workload on the teacher who has extra time for other necessary engagements. The system is such that it allows responses or feedback from students in order to make improvements on weaknesses for greater academic achievements.
5. AI strength in content determination is yet another milestone achieved in individualized instruction. For instance in individualized instruction the instructor /teacher has to determine the needs, strength and area of student's interest. The instructor must identify the strategies and instructional approaches purposefully that will deliver effective and efficient learning. According to Regina (2023) quoting Glickman (1991) asserting that effective teaching has to do

with context-driven decisions about teaching and that the teacher's decision should be based on practices that show that students are learning and that it should be adjustable based on the observation rather than being static and insisting on everyday lesson delivery. Regina (2023) views instructional framework as something to do with instructional approaches that when properly used are believed to be in line with sound education practice. These instructional approaches encompass instructional models, strategies, methods and skills. Instructional models are concerned with the broadest level of instructional practices and philosophical aspect to the instruction used in selecting teaching strategies, method, skills and students activities. Therefore content determination in AI for individualized instruction in media broadcast is concerned with the amount of data that should be allowed in the information taking into consideration the data interpretation, document planning (narrative structure) and so on which could enable delivery of an efficient education system.

6. AI system enables machine to act like humans through such applications as chatbots and virtual assistant (the ability to understand and respond to human language considering the nature and feeling of the user experience); sentiment analysis (ability to monitor the user's feedback and make improvements); language translation (communication is enabled between people that do not speak the same languages) and information retrieval (information is retrieved from data, search engines and quizzes or question and answering system).

Conclusion

The twenty-first century has witnessed the influential impact of AI in educational media broadcast, revolutionizing personalized learning experiences, content creation, and assessment. AI-powered recommendation systems, adaptive learning algorithms, and automated feedback mechanisms have transformed how knowledge is delivered and acquired. Reflection on the transformative potential of AI in educational media broadcast AI's transformative potential in educational media broadcast is undeniable. It enables tailored learning experiences, promotes self-directed learning, and optimizes educational content delivery. As AI technologies continue to evolve, it is essential to address challenges like data privacy, bias, and equitable access. Responsible and ethical AI use is crucial to ensure the benefits of AI accessibility to all learners, regardless of their background or location. AI is a powerful tool no doubt, but human educators remain central to the learning process. Their guidance, empathy, and understanding are irreplaceable, nurturing learners' holistic growth and development. Collaboration between AI and educators can create an educational ecosystem that maximizes the potential of both technology and human expertise. AI's influence on educational media broadcasts has redefined how education is approached and delivered. By embracing AI's capabilities responsibly and leveraging it alongside human educators, we can shape a future of learning that empowers learners to thrive in an ever-changing world.

Recommendations

1. Overcoming Challenges and Concerns about privacy and data security in AI-driven educational media is paramount to the successful integration of the system where there are various vices such as scammers, hackers, etc., polluting the twenty-first-century driven technology. As AI systems collect and analyze vast amounts of learner data, ensuring data privacy and security becomes paramount. Implementing robust data protection measures and adhering to privacy regulations is critical to maintain learner trust and confidentiality.
2. Addressing bias and fairness in AI algorithms where AI can perpetuate existing inequalities and stereotypes. To address this, developers and educators must prioritize fairness in AI design, evaluation, and deployment, conducting regular audits to detect and mitigate biases.
3. Ensuring equitable access to AI-powered educational content is of essence to ensure the education delivery works efficiently. While AI holds the promise of personalized learning experiences, it is essential to address the digital divide and ensure equitable access to AI-integrated educational media. Ensuring affordability and availability of AI-driven tools in diverse educational settings can promote inclusivity and bridge the digital gap.
4. AI-powered recommendation systems analyze learners' behavior, interests, and previous interactions with educational content to suggest relevant materials. These should be recommended in instructions to foster exploration and serendipitous learning while expanding learners' knowledge horizons. Moreover, these systems

empower educators by providing insights into learners' preferences, enabling them to make informed decisions about content selection.

References

Ameen, N. (2019). *What robots and AI may mean for University lecturers and students*. https://theconversation.com/what-robots-and-ai-may-mean-for-university-lecturers-and-students-114383

Bhatia, D. (2023). *India redefining the globalization Blueprint*. https://community.nassocom.in/communities

Deng, L., & Liu, Y. (2018). *Deep learning in natural language processing*. https://books.google.com.ng/books?id-y

Dilmaghani, C. (2023). *Natural language generation (NLG) in 2023*. https://researchaimultiple.com

Doty, C. (2023). *Top 7 uses for speech to text in education*. https://deepgram.com

Great Learning. (2023). *What is machine learning, definition, types, application and more*. mygreatlearning.com/blog/what-is-machine-learning

Gruetzemacher, R. (2023). *AI and machine learning. The power of natural language processing*. https://hbr.org/2022/04/the-power-of-natural-language-processing

Harve, A. (2023). *7 roles of artificial intelligence in learning and development*. https://hurix.com/role-of-artificial-intelligence-in-learning-and-development

International Business Machine Corporation (IBM) (2023). *What is a computer?* https://ibm.com/topics/computer-vision

Marr, B. (2023). *7 amazing examples of computer and machine vision in practice*. https://aorbes.com/site/bernardmarr

Opentext, B. C. (2023). *A short history of educational technology-teaching in the digital age*. https://opentextbc.ca/teachinginadigitalage/chapter/section-8-1-a-short-history-of-educational-technology/

Point, J. T. (2023). *What is an expert system?* https://javatpoint.com/expert-systems-in-artificial-intelligence

Qualtrics, X. M. (2023). *What is natural language understanding?* https://qualtrics.com/experience-management/costumer/natural-language

Regina, S. K. (2023). *Teaching as decision making instructional approaches: A frame work for professional practice*. https://webpages.uidoho.edu/cte492/modules/m3/methods-strategies.htm

Rosencrance, L. (2023). *What does the media mean?* https://technopedia.com/definition/1098/media

Udi, I., & Nwosu, K. (2023). Integrating technologies in education for teaching and learning of fine art in Nigeria. *Journal of Education Media and Technology, 28*(1), 205–211.

CHAPTER 13

Promoting Educational Broadcasting in the Digital Era for Effective Teaching and Learning in Nigerian Schools

Teresa Chinasa Anyanwu

Introduction

Education is the vehicle through which knowledge, skills and attitude are transferred to the learner for societal and national development. These are achieved through formal education. Equally, informal and non-formal education helps learners to acquire knowledge, skills and attitudes. Education; again is the process by which deliberately transmits accumulated knowledge, skills and values from one generation to another. Education in this modern and technological age, is the process of making it possible for a country like Nigeria to have a steady supply of highly creative citizens who help to keep improving the processes of teaching and learning (Falabe 2010). Plato, as cited by Adedipe (2005, p. 65) argues that "every society should always consider the education of her citizens paramount in

T. C. Anyanwu (✉)
Faculty of Education, Imo State University, Owerri, Nigeria
e-mail: anyanwuteresachinasa@yahoo.com

U. S. Akpan (ed.), *Educational Broadcasting in Nigeria in the Age of Artificial Intelligence*,
https://doi.org/10.1007/978-3-031-68530-9_13

order to have reliable and intelligent leadership for sustainable development, in the same vein, teaching and learning at all levels in corporate a rarity media. The most sustainable way of meeting the improved quality of life is to invest in education.

Concept of Broadcasting

Broadcasting is the transmission of powerful electromagnetic waves through the air, Ogunmilade (1988) viewed broadcasting as the art of spreading information widely through sound and vision to a group or groups of people either in their homes, classrooms, at listening or viewing centers and through electronic devices of several kinds. Therefore broadcast media are the agencies through which messages, information, knowledge, are transmitted to certain persons within a specific place.

When such broadcast is primarily concerned with educating the people of the audiences may be through the formal setting, i.e., in an established institution or informal way, (mounting of literacy campaigns by media houses on health, agriculture and family planning, school programme, etc., and learnt by the audience through observation or imitation), it is known as educational broadcasting. Educational broadcasting engages two important media communications. They are television and radio educational broadcasting. The emphasis here is on radio broadcasting, as it concerns educational instruction.

Objectives of Educational Radio Broadcasting in the Nigerian School System

- To strengthen the nation's education enterprise by reducing imbalances and improving educational opportunities in rural schools handicapped by lack of qualified staff and equipment.
- To improve the quality of education through the use of sound teaching methods (as can be seen in Interactive Radio Instruction (IRI) and supplementary audio materials.
- To assist in teaching subjects where trained school/subject teachers are in short supply.
- To improve attendance rates at all levels by motivating learners by means of interesting programme materials, audio techniques and increased personal attention in large classes.
- To assist in curriculum reforms through speedy and effective delivery.

- To promote civic consciousness and national unity through civic programmes in both primary and secondary level through the phased introduction and use of indigenous or national language.
- To disseminate information of interest.
- To promote and keep teachers up-to-date on curricula activities and practices.
- To assist in teacher training programmes both pre-service and in-service, through employment of new media techniques (NPE, 2013).

Brief History of Radio in Nigeria

The Federal Radio Corporation of Nigeria was founded in 1933 by the British colonial government named the Radio Diffusion Services (RDS). It allowed the public to hear British Broadcasting Corporation's foreign radio service, broadcasting public locations over loudspeakers. In April 1980, the RDS became the Nigerian Broadcasting Service and introduced radio stations in Lagos, Kaduna, Ondo, Ibadan and Kano. This service was reorganized into the (NBC) on April 1, 1997, by the act of parliament LPS mission which was provided as a public broadcasting service. By 1962, the NBC expanded its broadcast station into many other states in Nigeria. Each of these stations was considered as a subsidiary in late 1960, the Federal parliament amended the NBC ordinance to all the sale of commercial advertisement. The first ads ran on October 31, 1961 and were broadcast by 4 pm in Lagos. By 1962 regional and other broadcasting began selling ads to local businesses; the goal of allowing station advertisement was to help provide additional funding to NBC stations.

The Federal Parliament approved the creation of the Voice of Nigeria (VONT) External hardware service in 1961, LPS initial operations were limited to two hours per day to West Africa, but by 1963 VONT had expanded both coverage and transmission times. In April 1961, with financial assistance from the ford foundation and technical assistance from British Broadcasting Corporation NBC began the National school broadcasting service in April, 1961. FRCN's medium wave service, Radio Nigeria has 25 stations located throughout the country and together with voice of Nigeria and considers itself to have the largest radio network in Africa.

Currently, radio stations are almost evenly divided between two broadcast spectrums; amplitude modulation (AM), which comprises the dial range from 540 to 1700 kilohertz (kHz); and frequency modulation (FM), from 88 to 108 megahertz (MHz). AM broadcasting, which allows a transmitter to have greater geographical reach, consists mostly of talk programming, including telephone call-in shows, all news formats, religious evangelism, and sports coverage. FM, developed in the 1930s by Edwin Howard Armstrong, has several advantages over AM. It is nearly free of static and can be broadcast in stereo- two simultaneous sound waves that yield more realistic reproduction of music and other sounds. From Armstrong's earliest demonstrations, it was obvious that FM offered a richer, fuller sound than AM. But the millions of radio sets already sold to the public could not receive FM broadcasts, so companies heavily invested in AM technology suppressed FM for decades. FM did not reach a large audience until in the 1960s, when the public immediately embraced it; most FM stations are dedicated to presenting music. They tend to establish specific, easily identifiable formats, such as rock, country, rap, or other genres that appeal to particular audiences. New broadcast delivery system continues to be developed. In the increasing number of homes equipped with digital cable systems, broadcast radio stations must now compete against scores of commercial-free digital music channels, each offering round-the-clock delivery of a single style or genre of music. Radio broadcasting remains a significant method of mass communication, all over the country and beyond.

Application of Radio in the Classroom Instruction

The radio is a type of wireless communication device in which sound waves in a broadcasting studio are charged into electrical waves by the broadcasting transmitter and radiated into space. The radio set (receiver) picks the electrical waves and converts them to sound unlike television; the radio set is not connected to any external cable (Anyanwu, 2018). The procedures for using the radio as a medium of instruction do not vary much from those of the instructional television. However when using the radio as a instructional medium, the following procedures must be followed:

- Radio sets should be made available in the schools and put in the special listening classroom.

- Other media which should be used along with broadcast should also be provided. These media may include maps, globes, demonstration materials, photographs, projected materials depending on the topic to be programmed.
- The teacher should get a copy of the broadcasting schedule to enable him to select the appropriate and relevant programmes which his students will listen to.
- When using the radio, the teacher should ensure that the radio is in a good working condition.
- As the broadcast goes on, the teacher should be able to write difficult words or concepts on the chalkboard and take note of how the students react to the programme.
- The teacher should be able to devise means of finding out the extent to which the students followed the lesson.

Advantages of the Instructional Radio

Anyanwu (2018) gave the following as advantages of the instructional radio:

- The cost of producing radio programmes is cheaper when compared with that of television.
- Radio broadcast reach the audience wider and faster than those of the television
- Radio brings up-to-date information as it is happening to the listeners, unlike the television which may not be broadcast until the studio house opens later in the day.
- Radio broadcasts have emotional impacts on the listeners. In other words, it makes the listener feel the presence of the presenter, especially if the voices and musical accompaniment are clear.
- It can be used to bring the exact words and voice of the expert teacher into the classroom.
- Like the television, radio broadcasts encourage team teaching demonstration.
- It enables students to acquire listening skills, especially when they form the habit of listening to radio programmes.
- Radio can stimulate the imagination without the interference of visuals.

- Radio programmes can provide a vista of knowledge to the classroom if properly organized.

Disadvantages of Instructional Radio

The disadvantages of instructional radio include:

- Radio broadcasts present one-way communication. However, in an ideal instructional radio, provisions are made for feedback facilities.
- It does not encourage face-to-face interaction between the learners and the presenter.
- In radio instruction, you cannot stop a radio broadcast in order to repeat or review a particular point not initially understood.
- The time of the radio broadcast does not fit into the normal school time table.

Challenges of Instructional Radio Broadcasting in the Digital Era

The word digital is being used in almost every sector of the economy. It is common to hear people say everyone is going digital, why are you still doing things in analog manner. This suggests that there is a shift in the way or methods of doing things better. Obviously, when changes occur in organizations such changes are expected to bring about improvement or add value to the organization. So it is believed that going digital which is currently highly advocated is valued. In the case of instructional radio broadcasting, the radio systems transmit sounds to paid subscribers rather than to the general public and self-programmable system. Despite these innovations, in the first years of the twenty-first-century broadcasting remained the single most important component of mass communication.

- There is limited usage of instructional radio broadcasting in the villages due to lack of electricity.
- Numerous conflicts arise due to poor business through radio and public services.
- There is also the problem of reaching everybody at the same time.

- Some communities do not receive radio broadcasts along with others, they only receive noise instead of sound.
- The shifting from analogue to digital is a big burden to the government in terms of finance. Government lacks the capacity to finance schools at all levels to apply Information Communication Technology (ICTs) facilities for teaching and learning.
- Most schools at all levels can not afford broadcasting programmes in their school except private schools that are rich.

Conclusion

This chapter has examined educational radio broadcasting and its relevance in the school system. Objectives of radio broadcasting with advantages and disadvantages were discussed. Also application of radio broadcasting in the classroom instructional was discussed. It equally outlined challenges of radio broadcasting and how to improve educational radio broadcasting in the schools by the government. The guidelines for the incorporation of the broadcast media were also cleared.

Recommendations

In promoting radio broadcasting in schools, the following recommendations are hereby stated:

- The government should supply functioning radio equipment into schools with the focus of making use of them to enhance the teaching and learning process.
- In-service training should be organized for teachers in Nigerian schools to enhance the usage of the equipment and to complement the chalk and talk method.
- Technicians who will be in charge of the equipment should also be employed by the government to make the promotion of radio broadcasting a successful one in schools.
- National Educational Technology center, Kaduna should intensify radio broadcasting programmes or out-ful for educational broadcasts.
- There should be regular electric power supply to all nooks and crannies of the country.

- Every school at all levels should have functional tape-recorder and recording system and powerful radio transistor.
- Every information about the broadcast should be collected by each school ahead of time and studying the teaching guides, lesson, topics and teachers notes, time-table and scripts.
- The school libraries should have a catalog of the audio-tape for replay at convenient times by entire schools.
- Radio broadcasting in schools can be used through integration, to make the communication of knowledge an exciting experience in schools with class work, assignment or class projects.
- Radio clubs in the school should have tape recorded short-wave broadcasts and use them in foreign language and other instruction.
- Teachers of special subjects may have students record broadcasts of interest outside the class, to be played back during regular class instruction.

References

Adedipe, Y. O. (2005). *Challenges of globalization on education and leadership in Africa*. Nigeria Perspectives. Walex Prints.

Anyanwu, T. C. (2018). *Fundamental concept in educational technology*. Uzopieto Publisher.

Falabe, A. A. (2010). *Promoting radio/audio/broadcast/media for effective teaching and learning in schools*. Oyo, College of Education Walex Print.

Federal Republic of Nigeria. (2013). National Policy on Education Lagos NERDC.

Ogunmilade, A. (1988). *Educational technology in curriculum and instruction*. Solomon Publishing Ltd.

CHAPTER 14

Artificial Intelligence and Educational Broadcasting: Digitizing Higher Education (HE) in Nigerian Context

Harriet Akudo Agbarakwe and Olorunfemi Adedeji

Introduction

Educational broadcasting refers to the use of broadcast media, such as radio and television, to deliver educational content to learners (Tadesse & Muluye, 2020). It has been used as leverage to address inequalities between the urban and rural settlements in regard to access to quality education and as an approach to tackle the inadequacy of trained personnel (Zhou & Xiong, 2017). In recent years broadcast technology has evolved from the traditional and more linear radio and television media formats to the more dynamic possibilities offered by the internet with its accompanying geometric modes of information channeling and

H. A. Agbarakwe (✉) · O. Adedeji
University of Port Harcourt, Choba, Nigeria
e-mail: haret.agbarakwe@uniport.edu.ng

O. Adedeji
e-mail: olurunfemi_adedeji@uniport.com

U. S. Akpan (ed.), *Educational Broadcasting in Nigeria in the Age of Artificial Intelligence*,
https://doi.org/10.1007/978-3-031-68530-9_14

instant feedback. We can now broadcast educational content live via Social Media Networks (SMN), independent live-streaming platforms, and a myriad of other new and emerging platforms. This has made it possible for the implementation of more robust Open and Distant Learning (ODL) frameworks for both synchronous and asynchronous systems of communication. However, because of this evidence of a strong connection between ODL broadcasting and technology, the rapid evolution of technological trends also affects the interactions, roles, and content delivery methods within ODL (Aydemir et al., 2015). A crucial part of this rapid change is Artificial Intelligence (AI).

Recent research has shown how digital educational technology innovations have been influenced by the advent of artificial intelligence, particularly the Large Language Models (LLMs). LLMs refer to generative artificial intelligence models that have undergone extensive training with text data widely sourced from the internet. These models are capable of producing text content that resembles human language, based on natural language inputs (Yan et al., 2023). Apart from finding relevance in content creation and curation in educational broadcasting workflow, these new LLMs have also been found to be useful in personalized learning systems, intelligent tutoring models, computational speed, assessment and feedback management. There have also been used cases for language translation and learning content localization, data analytics for improved forecasting, learning content engagement tracking and overall improvement of an interactive educational broadcasting scenario (Owan et al., 2023). AIs can thus be seen as robotic contributors to content creation, curating and dissemination processes in educational broadcasting. This paper is thus limited to reviewing the extent to which AI and LLM models affect the workflow and processes within the educational use-case subset of instructional broadcasting.

Aim and Objectives of the Paper

AI has far-reaching implications for every technological implementation in the world today; hence it also affects the mode of interaction, roles and content delivery methods in educational broadcasting. This paper is intent on examining the implications and reviewing best practices on the use of AI in educational broadcasting as a means of digitizing Higher education in Nigeria's educational systems. Basically, this paper shall assess the practicality and ethics of existing LLMs-based innovations using established frameworks and provide suggestions to support future studies in developing AI-based innovations that can practically and ethically promote authentic educational broadcasting.

Literature Review

New and Emerging Media Production and Broadcast Approach in AI

AI has been present in most technologies used within closed systems and applications in recent years. The concept of machine learning, which is an integral idea within AI, has been implemented within media production tools to a good extent. Design, production and post-production tools like Adobe Creative Suites employ AI to track user inputs and use the same to improve the efficiency of users within the software (Esler, 2019). Also, following the transition of Google to Alphabet in 2015, there were conscientious efforts to reposition the Google Search services beyond just word search. By implication, Google Search no longer just provides pure search results. Instead, with the help of artificial intelligence and big data, it suggests results based on internet trends and previous user behavior. This leads to a faster and easier search experience for the user (Hanson, 2019). Other tools like Unity3D now widely used in broadcast technologies have also introduced AI to simplify computational challenges within the engine and enhance user experience (Li, 2017).

However, with the explosion of open AI implementation after the launch of OpenAI's ChatGPT (Generative Pre-trained Transformer) Dall-E generative AI model in 2021, individual educational technology innovators and developers have been using the solution's Application Programming Interface (API) to create a proliferation of AI products (Hashemi-Pour, 2023).

This study is important because it explores how AI is affecting educational broadcasting. With AI changing so many different sectors, it is crucial to understand how it is impacting the way students and teachers interact, the people involved, and how information is delivered. Some of these are:

1. *Determining Implications:* Delving into the implications of AI on educational broadcasting sheds light on how this technology alters knowledge dissemination. Educators, policymakers, and stakeholders need to adapt and harness AI's potential responsibly.

2. *Guiding Best Practices and Ethical Frameworks:* The use of AI in educational broadcasting can be optimized through the examination and review of best practice models. Practitioners and institutions can gain valuable insights to integrate AI into their educational strategies while ensuring alignment with effective pedagogical approaches and ethical considerations. A structured approach to evaluating the moral and technical aspects of AI-driven educational solutions can be achieved through the assessment of the practicality and ethics of existing LLMs-based innovations using established frameworks. Maintaining transparency, fairness, and accountability when deploying AI in educational contexts is crucial.
3. *Contributing to Educational Technology:* The research paper puts forward suggestions for forthcoming studies on educational technology, with a focus on practical and ethical advancements based on AI. The recommendations aim to promote responsible and effective integration of AI in education.
4. *AI helps to enhance best practices in educational broadcasting by* fostering more engaging, personalized, and efficient learning experiences within the field of educational broadcasting which will in turn lead to improved educational outcomes and an overall more enriched educational environment.

Pedagogical Implications of AI and LLM in Educational Broadcasting

The following considerations are areas of interest around the implication of AI and LLM in educational broadcasting:

i. *LLM for Generative Image, Speech and Video Production:* The use of LLMs for generative multimedia production opens new possibilities in educational broadcasting. LLMs can create texts, images, human-like speeches, and videos to supplement educational content, enhancing visual and auditory learning experiences and creating engaging presentations. They can even facilitate language learning through speech generation, subtitling and in-video help. This drastically removes the time and cost limitation of implementing the same requirements within the traditional post-production workflow. An interesting interplay between traditional media production tools and AI is the newly introduced Fireflies AI by Adobe (2023). This ground-breaking innovation allows media production experts to implement AI/LLM prompts within the conventional user interface as an everyday industry-standard tool. Other image-generative tools in this genre include Midjourney and Craiyon (Hutson & Lang, 2023)

ii. *Adaptive Digital Platforms for Personalized Content Curating and Broadcasting:* Adaptive learning technology allows teachers to create personalized learning opportunities for each learner, no matter where or when they're studying (Kem, 2022). This learner-centered approach leverages technology to achieve a self-paced learning environment. Real-time data science is a centerpiece of this system and it is driven by machine learning and artificial intelligence.

iii. *AI Suggestive Algorithm in Content Accessibility:* During a conference, YouTube's Chief Product Officer Neal Mohan disclosed that over 70% of the videos watched on YouTube are recommended by AI-driven suggestions. This is particularly relevant for mobile viewers who spend more than 60 minutes per viewing session. With these lengthy viewing sessions, YouTube's AI has plenty of opportunities to suggest videos to the average viewer. (Geyser, 2019). This is an example of the present-day reality in content archiving and broadcasting - using user-generated data to determine the structure and pattern of individual preferences and needs. This has found its usefulness in other structured Learning Management Systems (LMSs) and learning environments.

iv. *AI-enabled Content Localisation Systems:* AI-enabled Content Localisation Systems are a powerful tool that can greatly enhance various aspects of content localization. These systems leverage AI techniques to improve the accuracy and efficiency of translating content from one language to another (Devlin, 2018). One key technology that has been instrumental in advancing AI-enabled Content localization Systems is the use of deep learning models. One such model is BERT (Bidirectional Encoder Representations from Transformers), which is designed to pretrain deep bidirectional representations from unlabeled text (Devlin, 2018). BERT has been shown to be highly effective in a wide range of natural language processing tasks, including question-answering and language inference.

v. *Interactive and Conversational AI/LLM Systems:* Interactive and Conversational AI/LLM (Language Learning Model) systems have gained significant attention in recent years due to their potential to enhance human–computer interactions and language learning experiences. These systems utilize advanced AI techniques, such as deep reinforcement learning and natural language processing, to enable interactive and engaging conversations between users and virtual agents. Deep reinforcement learning algorithms have been employed to train dialogue generation models that exhibit useful conversational properties, including informativity, coherence, and ease of answering. By rewarding sequences that display these properties, the models can generate more interactive responses and foster sustained conversations. This approach represents a step toward developing neural conversational models that can simulate realistic and engaging dialogues.

Ethical Frameworks in AI and LLM Use in Education

The IEEE Global Initiative on Ethics of Autonomous and Intelligent Systems: The IEEE Global Initiative on Ethics of Autonomous and Intelligent Systems is a program initiated by the Institute of Electrical and Electronics Engineers (IEEE), one of the world's largest professional organizations dedicated to advancing technology for humanity. This initiative focuses on addressing ethical issues and concerns arising from the development and deployment of autonomous and intelligent systems, including AI and LLMs (Chatila & Havens, 2019). It provides a framework and guidelines for the responsible design, development, and use of these technologies. The IEEE initiative can provide valuable resources and guidelines to help educators and institutions incorporate ethical discussions and considerations into AI technology-enhanced educational programmes.

The Fairness, Accountability, and Transparency in Machine Learning (FAT/ML) Framework: This framework is a set of principles and guidelines aimed at ensuring that Machine Learning (ML) systems are developed and deployed in a manner that is fair, accountable, and transparent (Shen et al., n.d.). A key index of this framework is that it encourages efforts to identify and mitigate biases in data used for training ML models.

In educational broadcasting, this means being aware of potential biases in the content and data used for personalization and making efforts to reduce or eliminate these biases. This helps ensure that learners receive a balanced and unbiased educational experience.

The CSTA K-12 Computer Science Standards: The Computer Science Teachers Association (CSTA) developed this as a set of standards for computer science education to guide K-12 educators in the United States in designing and delivering effective computer science curricula (CSTA, 2023).

Conclusion

The implication of AI in educational broadcasting in higher education at the moment appears to be controversial. For some, it is very profitable while for some it is a disaster and should be deployed with utmost caution. In spite of the varied opinions by different scholars and schools of thought, the education system must perceive it as a welcome technology that has come to assist both the learner and instructor to optimize learner-instructor interaction in Open Distance Learning, especially in online learning for supportive and effective communication.

Conclusively, the evolution of educational broadcasting from traditional radio and television to encompass the digital landscape, including Social Media Networks (SMN) and live-streaming platforms, has paved the way for innovative Open and Distant Learning (ODL) frameworks. At the core of this transformation lies Artificial Intelligence, which has rapidly advanced into educational technology innovations. LLMs, harnessed by extensive training with internet-sourced text data, have become instrumental in content creation, curation, personalization, intelligent tutoring, assessment, and language localization. AI has the potential to bridge educational inequalities and redefine how knowledge is disseminated in Nigeria.

Suggestions

In attempt to digitize educational broadcasting through deploying of AI and LLMs in Nigeria's Higher Education, the following are hereby put forward for responsible and effective integration:

1. Integration of AI and LLMs in Educational Broadcasting: Educational institutions and broadcasting platforms should explore the integration of AI and LLMs for content creation, curation, and personalization. This can enhance the quality of educational materials, save time and resources and adapt them to the needs of individual learners.
2. Adaptive Learning Platforms: Educational broadcasters should develop and implement adaptive learning platforms that leverage AI to personalize content delivery. These platforms can assess learners' strengths and weaknesses and provide tailored resources and activities to support their learning journey.
3. Content localization: Governments and learning organizations should Invest in AI-enabled Content localization Systems to make educational content accessible to learners in different languages and regions. This can facilitate the global reach of educational broadcasting platforms.
4. Interactive and Conversational: Educational broadcasters should explore the use of interactive and conversational AI/LLM systems to engage learners in meaningful dialogues and language learning experiences. These systems can be used for language practice, virtual tutoring, and improving conversational skills.
5. Ethical Considerations and Bias Mitigation: Educators should prioritize ethical considerations when implementing AI and LLM technologies in educational broadcasting, and adhere to ethical frameworks like the IEEE Global Initiative on Ethics of Autonomous and Intelligent Systems and the FAT/ML Framework to ensure fairness, transparency, and accountability. They should also implement measures to identify and mitigate biases in AI algorithms. Regularly auditing and reviewing the algorithms will ensure they do not perpetuate discrimination or stereotypes.
6. Collaboration and Research: There should be encouraged collaboration between educational institutions, technology developers, and AI researchers to conduct research on the effectiveness of AI-driven educational broadcasting. Share best practices and insights to improve the integration of AI in education.

References

Adobe (Nasdaq:ADBE). (2023). *Adobe unveils future of creative cloud with generative AI as a creative co-pilot in photoshop.* https://news.adobe.com/news/news-details/2023/Adobe-Unveils-Future-of-Creative-Cloud-with-Generative-AI-as-a-Creative-Co-Pilot-in-Photoshop-default.aspx/default.aspx

Aydemir, M., Ozkeskin, E. E., & Akkurt, A. (2015). A theoretical framework on open and distance learning. *Procedia—Social and Behavioral Sciences, 174*, 1750–1757. https://doi.org/10.1016/j.sbspro.2015.01.833

Chatila, R., & Havens, J. C. (2019). The IEEE global initiative on ethics of autonomous and intelligent systems. In M. I. Aldinhas Ferreira, J. Silva Sequeira, G. Singh Virk, M. O. Tokhi, & E. E. Kadar (Eds.), *Robotics and well-being* (Vol. 95, pp. 11–16). Springer International Publishing. https://doi.org/10.1007/978-3-030-12524-0_2

CSTA. (2023). *The CSTA K-12 computer science standards*. Computer Science Teachers Association. https://csteachers.org/k12standards/

Devlin, J. (2018). Bert: Pre-training of deep bidirectional transformers for language understanding. https://doi.org/10.48550/arxiv.1810.04805

Esler, B. (2019). Adobe releases AI-centric Photoshop 2020, *Photofocus*, https://photofocus.com/software/adobe-releases-ai-centric-photoshop-2020/

Geyser, W. (2019, June 12). *How does the YouTube algorithm work: A peek into its changes in 2023.* Influencer Marketing Hub. https://influencermarketinghub.com/how-does-the-youtube-algorithm-work/

Hanson, F. (2019). *Google's AI mission, Medium*, https://medium.datadriveninvestor.com/googles-ai-mission-17cd8b61c415

Hashemi-Pour, C. (2023). What is OpenAI? Definition and History from TechTarget, *Enterprise AI*, https://www.techtarget.com/searchenterpriseai/definition/OpenAI

Hutson, J., & Lang, M. (2023). Content creation or interpolation: AI generative digital art in the classroom. *Metaverse, 4*, 1–13. https://doi.org/10.54517/m.v4i1.2158

Kem, D. (2022). Personalised and adaptive learning: Emerging learning platforms in the era of digital and smart learning. *International Journal of Social Science and Human Research, 5*. https://doi.org/10.47191/ijsshr/v5-i2-02

Li, Y. (2017). Artificial Intelligence in Unity Game Engine, Oulu University of Applied Sciences.

Owan, V. J., Abang, K. B., Idika, B. O., Etta, E. O., Basse, B. A. (2023). Exploring the potential of artificial intelligence tools in educational measurement and assessment. *Eurasia Journal of Mathematics, Science and Technology Education, 19*(8), Article No: em2307. https://doi.org/10.29333/ejmste/13428

Shen, J. H., Fratamico, L., Rahwan, I., & Rush, A. M. (n.d.). *Darling or babygirl? Investigating stylistic bias in sentiment analysis.*

Tadesse, S., & Muluye, W. (2020). The impact of COVID-19 pandemic on the education system in developing countries: A review. *Open Journal of Social Sciences, 8*(10), 159–170. https://doi.org/10.4236/jss.2020.810011

Yan, L., Sha L., Jin, Y., Gasevic, D. (2023). Practical and Ethical Challenges of Large Language Models in Education: A Systematic Scoping Review. *British Journal of Educational Technology*.

Zhou, Y., & Xiong, Y. (2017). Live broadcast classroom: A feasible solution for Chinese rural weak education. *International Journal of Distance Education Technologies, 15*, 31–46. https://doi.org/10.4018/IJDET.2017070103

PART II

AI and Educational Instruction

CHAPTER 15

Artificial Intelligence in Educational Technology: Panacea to Efficient Instructional Delivery

Festus Oladimeji Olafare

Introduction

Artificial Intelligence (AI) and educational technology have become integral components of modern education, offering new possibilities for efficient instructional delivery. As educators and institutions strive to meet the diverse needs of students in the digital age, AI-driven tools and technologies have emerged as potential panaceas for enhancing the teaching and learning process. The role of AI and educational technology in revolutionizing instructional delivery gives benefits to educators and learners alike. AI-driven educational technology offers the potential for highly personalized and adaptive learning experiences. These systems can analyze individual student data, track progress, and adjust content and assessments accordingly. Research by Nouri (2021) demonstrates that this adaptability can significantly enhance engagement and learning

F. O. Olafare (✉)
University of Lagos, Lagos, Nigeria

U. S. Akpan (ed.), *Educational Broadcasting in Nigeria in the Age of Artificial Intelligence*,
https://doi.org/10.1007/978-3-031-68530-9_15

outcomes, providing students with tailored content that caters to their unique learning needs.

AI-powered tools can assist educators in various administrative tasks, allowing them to focus more on teaching. For instance, AI chatbots can handle routine student queries, while grading automation tools can expedite the assessment process. UNESCO (2019) shows that such tools enable teachers to allocate more time to developing meaningful instructional content and providing one-on-one support to students. The integration of AI in educational technology provides educators and institutions with access to valuable data insights. This data can inform decisions related to curriculum design, resource allocation, and instructional strategies. Siemens (2013), leveraging data-driven insights enables education stakeholders to make informed choices for the benefit of both educators and students. AI-driven technologies have the potential to make education more accessible to individuals with disabilities. Innovations like speech recognition, text-to-speech, and captioning tools assist learners with diverse needs. Zeng et al. (2020) underscores the role of AI in promoting inclusivity, breaking down barriers to education for all. AI's capacity for real-time feedback and analysis contributes to continuous improvement in educational delivery. Rizvi (2023), opined that educators can use AI-generated insights to adjust their instructional methods, ensuring that content remains up-to-date and effective. The online nature of many AI-driven educational technologies enables students to access high-quality education globally. This is particularly vital in regions with limited educational resources. A report by Johnson et al. (2020) highlights how AI-powered online courses have extended educational opportunities to underserved populations worldwide.

Artificial Intelligence Tools That Serve as EdTech Tools

Artificial Intelligence (AI) tools have increasingly become indispensable in education, serving as powerful teaching, and learning tools. These tools offer innovative ways to engage students, enhance learning outcomes, and streamline educational processes. The AI tools that serve as EdTech tools for teaching and learning are classified as Intelligent Tutoring Systems (ITS), Natural Language Processing (NLP), Machine Learning-Enhanced Content Delivery, and Virtual and Augmented Reality (VR/AR).

Intelligent Tutoring Systems (ITS): ITS are AI-driven platforms that provide personalized instruction, feedback, and assessment to students. They adapt to the individual learning needs of students, offering targeted content and support. Koedinger and Corbett (2006) found that ITS can significantly improve learning outcomes by providing immediate, customized feedback and guidance.

Natural Language Processing (NLP): NLP-based AI tools help students improve their language and communication skills. These tools can analyze written or spoken language and provide feedback on grammar, style, and content. For example, Grammarly, an NLP tool, is widely used by students to enhance their writing skills. Vajjala and Meurers (2014) demonstrated the effectiveness of such tools in supporting language learning.

Machine Learning-Enhanced Content Delivery: AI-driven content recommendation systems, such as those used by popular e-learning platforms like Coursera and Netflix, use machine learning algorithms to suggest relevant content to students. These systems help learners discover new materials aligned with their interests and needs. Rokach, L. and Maimon, O. (2005) discuss the application of recommendation systems in education and their impact on personalized learning.

Virtual and Augmented Reality (VR/AR): VR and AR technologies powered by AI have gained traction in education. These immersive technologies offer students an interactive and engaging learning experience. Zhang et al. (2019) highlight the potential of AI-driven Virtual reality and Augmented Reality tools to improve comprehension and retention, particularly in subjects like science and engineering, by providing students with hands-on simulations and visualizations. Incorporating these AI tools into education not only enhances the learning experience but also empowers educators to better understand and cater to individual student needs. As AI continues to evolve, these tools are expected to play an increasingly central role in modern pedagogy, ensuring that students receive a more personalized and effective education.

Advantages and Disadvantages of Artificial Intelligence to Instruction

Artificial Intelligence (AI) has made significant inroads into education and instructional methods, bringing both advantages and disadvantages to the field.

Advantages

Personalized Learning: AI allows for personalized learning experiences by analyzing individual student data and adapting content and assessments to meet their unique needs. Vanlehn (2011) noted that personalized learning can lead to improved learning outcomes as it caters to each student's pace and learning style. Automation and Efficiency: AI can automate administrative tasks, such as grading and data analysis, freeing up teachers to focus on instructional activities. Also, Benaissa (2019) underscores the potential of AI in reducing the burden of routine tasks, increasing efficiency, and allowing educators to dedicate more time to teaching. Enhanced Accessibility: AI-driven tools can make education more accessible to learners with disabilities. Speech recognition, text-to-speech, and other AI-driven technologies can support individuals with diverse needs. Kizilcec (2018) demonstrated how AI can be used to create more inclusive and accommodating learning environments.

Disadvantages

Artificial Intelligence brings technological barriers as one of its major disadvantages. The digital divide shows that not all students have equal access to AI-powered educational tools. This can exacerbate educational inequalities. Warschauer and Matuchniak (2010), the lack of access to technology can hinder the potential benefits of AI in instruction for underserved populations. AI in education raises significant ethical concerns, especially regarding data privacy and algorithmic bias. As highlighted in a report by UNESCO (2020), the collection and use of student data by AI systems must be closely monitored to protect individuals' privacy and prevent discrimination based on algorithms.

Accessibility and Inclusivity in Instructional Delivery using Artificial Intelligence

Artificial Intelligence (AI) integration into instructional delivery can significantly enhance accessibility and inclusivity in education. By providing personalized learning experiences, language support, assistive technologies, real-time accessibility features, and diverse learning environments, AI contributes to breaking down barriers and ensuring that all students, regardless of their abilities or backgrounds, have equal access to education. However, it is crucial for educators and institutions to actively leverage AI's potential to create more inclusive learning environments and continually monitor and address any potential biases in AI systems to ensure equitable outcomes. Artificial Intelligence (AI) has the potential to greatly enhance accessibility and inclusivity in instructional delivery, making education more equitable and accommodating to diverse learner needs.

Personalized Learning: AI-driven educational tools can adapt to individual learning needs, offering customized content and support. This personalization benefits students with varying learning styles and abilities, allowing them to learn at their own pace. For example, AI can provide alternative formats, such as text-to-speech, for students with visual impairments or dyslexia, making the content more accessible (Vajjala & Meurers, 2014).

Language Support: AI-powered language translation and interpretation tools break down language barriers, facilitating access to education for non-native speakers. These tools can translate lectures and materials into the student's preferred language, improving comprehension and inclusivity in multilingual classrooms (UNESCO, 2019).

Assistive Technologies: AI can serve as a bridge to assistive technologies that aid students with disabilities. Speech recognition, predictive text, and captioning tools can be integrated into AI-driven platforms, enabling learners with disabilities to engage with the content effectively (Zeng et al., 2020).

Real-time Accessibility Features: AI can generate real-time accessibility features, such as automatic transcription and sign language interpretation, during live lectures or presentations. This ensures that students with hearing impairments can actively participate and understand the content (Kasprzak & Stach, 2021).

Diverse Learning Environments: AI-driven virtual and augmented reality can create more immersive and interactive learning experiences. This benefits students who may struggle with traditional teaching methods. For instance, AI-enhanced simulations can provide a hands-on approach to learning in science and engineering, catering to various learning preferences and abilities (Zhang et al., 2019).

Conclusion

Artificial Intelligence and educational technology play a pivotal role in reshaping instructional delivery, making education more personalized, efficient, and inclusive. The adaptability of AI-driven tools, personalized learning experiences, and efficient administrative support enhance the educational process. Data-driven decision-making and accessibility innovations further improve educational outcomes. However, ethical considerations, privacy concerns, and potential technological barriers must be addressed to maximize the benefits of AI in education. As AI continues to evolve, educators and institutions should harness its potential to ensure that all students receive a high-quality, inclusive, and efficient education.

Recommendations

The study recommends the establishment and adherence to clear ethical guidelines for the use of AI in education, ensuring that privacy and data security are prioritized, and potential biases are addressed. Provision of educators with training in AI and educational technology to maximize their effectiveness in using these tools for personalized instruction. Address the digital divide by advocating for policies and initiatives that ensure equitable access to AI-powered educational tools for all students.

References

Benaissa, S. (2019). Artificial intelligence and education: Promises and pitfalls. *Education and Information Technologies, 24*(3), 1583–1592.

Johnson, T., Smith, K., & Garcia, M. (2020). AI for Personalized Learning: Unlocking the Potential. *Journal of Educational Technology, 48*(3), 325–340.

Kasprzak, R., & Stach, R. (2021). The importance of live captioning in online education for the deaf. *European Journal of Open, Distance and E-Learning, 24*(1), 181–196.

Koedinger, K. R., & Corbett, A. (2006). Cognitive tutors: Technology bringing learning science to the classroom. In *The Cambridge Handbook of the Learning Sciences* (pp. 61–78).

Nouri, J. (2021). The promises and perils of AI in education. *Technology, Knowledge and Learning, 26*(2), 181–193.

Rizvi, M. (2023). Investigating ai-powered tutoring systems that adapt to individual student needs, providing personalized guidance and assessments. *The Eurasia Proceedings of Educational & Social Sciences (EPESS), 31*, 67–73.

Rokach, L., & Maimon, O. (2005). *Data mining and knowledge discovery handbook*. Springer.

Siemens, G. (2013). Learning analytics: The emergence of a discipline. *American Behavioral Scientist, 57*(10), 1380–1400.

UNESCO. (2019). *I'd blush if I could: Closing gender divides in digital skills through education*. UNESCO.

UNESCO. (2020). *Steer, don't veer: Data privacy in education*. UNESCO.

Vajjala, S., & Meurers, D. (2014). An empirical study on the effectiveness of grammar checkers for non-native English language learners. *CALICO Journal, 31*(2), 253–273.

Vanlehn, K. (2011). The relative effectiveness of human tutoring, intelligent tutoring systems, and other tutoring systems. *Educational Psychologist, 46*(4), 197–221.

Warschauer, M., & Matuchniak, T. (2010). New technology and digital worlds: Analyzing evidence of equity in access, use, and outcomes. *Review of Research in Education, 34*(1), 179–225.

Zeng, M., Liu, D., & Yun, H. (2020). Assistive technology and artificial intelligence: Benefits and challenges in education. *Educational Technology & Society, 23*(3), 53–69.

Zhang, L., Duan, X., & Luo, W. (2019). Augmented reality in education and training: A literature review. *British Journal of Educational Technology, 50*(4), 1707–1728.

CHAPTER 16

Artificial Intelligence (Speechify App) for Dyslexia on Students' Performance and Retention in Reading in Port Harcourt Metropolis, Rivers State, Nigeria

Chinwe Joyce Chukwuemeka and Harriet Akudo Agbarakwe

Introduction

Artificial Intelligence (AI) has been defined as the ability of a digital computer or computer-controlled robot to perform tasks commonly associated with intelligent beings (Britannica, 2023). Artificial intelligence (AI) refers to computer systems capable of performing complex tasks that historically only a human could do, such as reasoning, making decisions, or solving problems. Artificial intelligence

C. J. Chukwuemeka (✉) · H. A. Agbarakwe
Department of Curriculum Studies and Educational Technology, Faculty of Education, University of Port Harcourt, Choba, Nigeria
e-mail: chukwuemeka_chinwe@uniport.edu.ng; chyjoyce23@yahoo.com

H. A. Agbarakwe
e-mail: haret.agbarakwe@uniport.edu.ng

U. S. Akpan (ed.), *Educational Broadcasting in Nigeria in the Age of Artificial Intelligence*,
https://doi.org/10.1007/978-3-031-68530-9_16

is an umbrella term that encompasses a wide variety of technologies, including machine learning, deep learning, and natural language processing (NLP). However, for individuals with dyslexia some tasks such as searching and extrapolating information from literature sources can be more challenging compared with neurotypical individuals. Artificial intelligence (AI) has now entered what has been deemed as the stage of intelligent cognition. Artificial intelligence has potential to mimic brain processes similar to those of humans. There is scope for such approaches to provide another layer of 'reinforcement' when used correctly, potentially having a positive impact on learning (Barua et al., 2022). Artificial intelligence could be a potentially valuable assistive tool for those with dyslexia. Speechify App which now encompasses artificial intelligence has the potential to enhance the learning environment and make it a more pleasant experience for those with dyslexia. Language has a significant impact on the human brain's capacity to process color and make moral judgments. Language determines how events are interpreted and remembered, how we classify things, how smells and musical tones are encoded, how we maintain focus, and how our visual attention is distributed. To put it another way, it is impossible to comprehend the human brain without comprehending the contributions that language has made, both as a forming force during earlier learning and experience and in the present day. The brain is reorganized even when written language is learned later in life. Consequently, the researcher investigated the subfield of language research known as Psycholinguistics.

Psycholinguistics is the study of the mental aspects of language and speech. It focuses primarily on how language is represented and processed in the brain. Psycholinguistics is a field of study within cognitive science. David Carrol writes, "At its core, psycholinguistic work consists of two questions" in "Psychology of Language." What language abilities are necessary for communication? Knowing something about a language is necessary before we can use it. What kinds of mental processes are going on when we use language every day? Understanding a lecture, reading a book, writing a letter, and having a conversation are all examples of "ordinary use of language," according to the researcher. The processes of perception, performance, memory, retention, and thinking are referred to as "cognitive processes" by the researcher. We discovered that these two tasks required significant cognitive processing, despite the fact that some students complete them more frequently and with greater ease than others. The researcher, therefore, investigated the language and brain of dyslexic students in Reading as one of the language skills, utilizing Speechify App as seen in the National Policy on Education.

The National Policy on Education stipulated under special educational needs that schools shall be required to arrange regular sensory, medical, and psychological screening assessments to identify any incidence of disability such as dyslexia, autism, dyscalculia, aphasia, dysgraphia, dyspraxia, attention deficit hyperactivity disorder (ADHD), etc. This is to enable students with learning disabilities to fully contribute their quota to national development. The English language plays an essential role in communication and it becomes an indispensable tool for communication in various aspects of society, economy, and culture. The English language is widely used in our daily lives and it is necessary to use effective pedagogies in its delivery as a subject in schools. Under the New National English Curriculum Standards, students living with dyslexia should be encouraged to interact with a lot of English Reading software and also to use emerging technologies. Technology can help students of all ages work around their reading challenges.

Assistive technology is defined as any tool, device, or item designed to help people with learning disabilities perform better and encourage them to become more independent and self-reliant such as Reading, taking notes, Mathematics, organizing ideas, managing time, Writing, Spelling, etc. Many assistive technological tools work on digital devices but some of the most useful tools are digital. Assistive technology can play an important role in special education because many students with disabilities need special instructional treatment. Assistive technology for dyslexia like Speechify App (Read Out Loud), dyslexia quest, optical readers, smart pens, text-to-speech, speech-to-text, amplification systems, audiobooks, grammar check software, magnification, and tracking supports. Speechify App (Text-to-speech) and audiobooks are two examples of assistive technology for reading. For students who struggle to read text, technology can be a lifeline for dyslexics. An audiobook, for example, allows dyslexics to read a story they might not be able to read with a traditional book. A highlighter can make a text passage understandable and Speechify App is one of the assistive technologies explored.

Speechify App is for readers with dyslexia and the most widely used text-to-speech application which aids students who are dyslexic in addition to those who suffer from ADHD, autism, and other learning disabilities. Speechify App lets dyslexics listen to PDF files, articles, emails, web pages, and other electronic documents. To improve comprehension and retention, read alongside the highlighted features or while performing other tasks, like housework, yard work, or other tasks. Speechify can assist you if you require reading assistance. However, if you are still unsure, the benefits of the app are listed below.

By converting text into speech, Speechify assists students in developing their reading fluency. Dyslexics can read emails, web pages, ebooks, PDF files, and more. A natural voice reads to students living with dyslexia while using the app. The highlight feature allows dyslexics to highlight text as dyslexics follow along while reading. As the app reads to dyslexics, reading skills, sight words, and letter sounds are bound to improve.

As the app reads the text aloud to the user, Speechify helps them better understand what dyslexics are reading. Speechify App stimulates dyslexics' visual and auditory systems which aids in comprehension. Reading comprehension is crucial to academic and life success. Reading is the foundation for the majority of what students learn in school. To be independent, dyslexics need to be able to read. A person's success in life is severely hindered by illiteracy. When you learn to read, you can be free. One of the greatest gifts you can give someone is to assist them in learning to read. If you give the Speechify App to someone who has dyslexia or another learning disability that brings solutions for dyslexics to read, you are giving dyslexics the key to getting out of illiteracy.

A student's desire to read more grows when they are better able to comprehend what they read. Dyslexics want to read more and more once they realize how many doors reading opens. Speechify App helps them become more motivated to read by improving their Reading Comprehension. Dyslexics can move around as the text is read to them, or dyslexics can follow along as the text is read to them. Because of this adaptability, dyslexics are not constrained to read the text at their own pace or, worse, to struggle to read it without assistance.

When dyslexics struggle with a skill, the process of mastering it becomes much more difficult. Additionally, students are significantly less motivated to attempt to master it when they struggle with it. Speechify directs students to the content and lets them choose the pace and tone of their learning. Many people enjoy reading and are lifelong learners. It all comes down to how you present the material and interact with dyslexics in order to entice them to learn. Teachers should look into the Speechify App because of students who struggle to read due to dyslexia or another learning disability.

The Speechify App is compatible with the majority of browsers, digital devices, and operating systems. In the app, which can be customized to meet your learning needs, dyslexics can choose between a fast speaker so dyslexics can listen to what is being read and a slower speaker so dyslexics can follow along. Speechify App is currently available for free trial, allowing teachers to evaluate Speechify potential to enhance Reading Comprehension and retention. Give dyslexics the gift of reading, and work on dyslexics' Reading Comprehension skills.

Statement of the Problem

According to observations, the majority of teachers and school administrators fail to promptly identify dyslexic students. According to research, dyslexic students are subjected to ridicule, bullying, and other forms of abuse from both their teachers and peers, making the school atmosphere unbearable for them. Teachers and other students frequently use derogatory terms like "stupid," "lazy," "fool," and "slow learner" to describe students who are unable to read or write correctly. These students, who bring dysfunctional language skills to the classroom, are wished away, or ignored because teachers lack the necessary motivation and resources. Dyslexics may struggle to comprehend written material without a lot of rereading, but easily distracted while reading, not be able to retain information in a form that can be retrieved for the task at hand, make a lot of mistakes when reading aloud, misspell words, and have poor phonological awareness.

After working with dyslexics, the researcher became interested in students with disabilities. The stigma that is associated with dyslexia, a lack of awareness, early assessment, qualified remedial teachers, and a lack of early intervention put many children at risk of dropping out of school and becoming socially excluded. Little research has been done on how dyslexia affects learning in Nigerian schools, despite the possibility that dyslexia contributes to Nigeria's poor English language performance. This study looked at how dyslexic students' performance and retention were affected by Speechify App. The study likewise saw homeroom rehearsals in this manner utilizing Speechify Apps. Digital learning tools and the appropriate learning environment are unavailable to dyslexic students. The gap was filled by this study.

Aim and Objectives of the Study

This study aimed at investigating the effect of Speechify App for dyslexia on secondary school students' performance and retention in Reading in Port Harcourt Metropolis, Rivers State. The specific objectives of the study were to:

1. investigate the effect of Speechify App, collaborative learning and discussion method on the performance of dyslexic students in Reading.
2. determine the effect of Speechify App, collaborative learning and discussion method on the retention of dyslexic students in Reading.
3. examine the influence of gender on the performance of dyslexic students in Reading.

Research Questions

The understated research questions guided this study:

1. What is the effect of Speechify App, collaborative learning and discussion method on the performance of dyslexic students in Reading?
2. What is the effect of Speechify App, collaborative learning and discussion method on the retention of dyslexic students in Reading?
3. What is the gender effect on the performance of dyslexic students in Reading?

Hypotheses

For this study to establish and determine the stated objectives, research hypotheses that are testable and analyzable based on data collected therefore need to be formulated. The following research hypotheses were formulated to guide the study.

$H0_1$: There is no significant difference among dyslexic students taught using Speechify App, collaborative learning and discussion method in their performance in Reading.

$H0_2$: There is no significant difference among dyslexic students taught using Speechify App, Collaborative learning and discussion method in their retention of Reading.

$H0_3$: There is no significant difference between the performance of male and female dyslexic students in Reading.

Significance of the Study

This study will be beneficial to special educational needs teachers in secondary schools if they adhere to the hybrid learning approach of the twenty-first century which is the integration of Speechify App into teaching and learning. Teachers will understand that their duty has changed from “one who knows all” to a facilitator who is also a student in the learning process. The Special Educational Needs (SEN) teachers also knew that one size does not fit all and differentiated the learning of the dyslexics based on their abilities. This study created awareness of the need for SEN teachers to upgrade themselves and also integrate emerging technologies into their lessons. Based on the International Society for Technology in Education (ISTE) there are responsibilities stipulated for teachers such as teachers should engage in professional development and leadership, demonstrating computer-age work and learning, facilitate and show computer citizenship and responsibility. The teachers mentioned here include; English language teachers, English lecturers, primary school teachers, secondary school teachers and speech pathologists/therapists. More so, the utilization of assistive technology for Reading Comprehension can serve as a catalyst for English language teachers to emulate. It can also guide them on a better approach to introducing dyslexics to Reading via assistive technology.

The findings of this study can as well improve dyslexics’ knowledge of Reading and the importance of interactive learning which is trending globally. This study encouraged the students living with dyslexia to always be ready for Reading Comprehension lessons as it is fully activity based which can arouse students’ interest and led to better performance in speaking and reading skills. Interest and engagement which are two levels of interactivity via Speechify App were revealed to dyslexic students; Speechify App helped them judge their recent level so that they will re-adjust if they actually want to enjoy Reading via Speechify App.

Methodology

This study adopted a quasi-experimental nonequivalent pretest–posttest control group design to identify the effectiveness of Speechify App on dyslexic students' learning performance and retention in Reading. This plan was viewed as most fitting since it was without randomization utilizing intact class. Dyslexic students that participated in this study got treatment in their various classes without reshuffling the class arrangement.

The population of this study comprised two hundred and five (205) senior secondary school students (one) (S.S.1) in selected public secondary schools in Port Harcourt Metropolis. The sample size was two hundred and five (205) senior secondary school one (S.S.1) dyslexic students in Port Harcourt Metropolis, Rivers State. They were chosen through the census method or technique. This was done after the preliminary study to determine students who are dyslexic. The researcher used all the senior secondary students one (S.S.1) identified as dyslexic. Utilization of explicit qualities like web offices through computers, interactive whiteboards (IWB) smart boards, iPads, (tablets) iPhones, and smartphones. These gadgets served as a prerequisite to take the Reading Comprehension course utilizing Speechify App and the dyslexics must have access to the internet. Therefore, the experimental groups were made up of dyslexics who have smartphones; computers and can access the internet while the control group did not have access to the Read-Out-Loud Speechify App and the internet.

The criteria that were utilized for the proper representation of male and female dyslexic students were; public schools with ICT offices for Speechify App or strategy consent of dyslexic students and trained and qualified Special Education Needs (SEN) facilitators. The instruments that were utilized to gather data for the study are: (1) Dyslexia Screening Questionnaire (DSQ). (2) Reading Performance Test (RPT) and Reading Retention Test (RRT). The research instruments were designed by the researcher and were validated by the researcher's supervisors, experts in Measurement and Evaluation and Language Education.

Dyslexia Screening Questionnaire (DSQ) was used as a preliminary study for identification of students with Dyslexia. Dyslexia Screening Questionnaire (DSQ) had four segments labeled alphabetically A, B, C, and D with 20 items (see Appendix). The dyslexics were permitted to demonstrate their level of acceptance or rejection on the number of positive and negative statements on Phonological awareness and Reading. Its questions probed dyslexics' skills, qualities, motivation, behavior, and feelings. The researcher applied critical thinking skills to formulate the items which were relevant to ascertain the skills of the dyslexics. Section A was for demographic data in which the dyslexic students wrote their names and gender. Secondly, Sections B, C and D were on phonemic sounds, feelings, level of acceptance and rejection of the lessons taught and the method utilized for the lessons. Likert scale of Strongly Agree (SA), Agree (A), Disagree (D), and Strongly Disagree (SD) was utilized to score the response of the dyslexic students. The following values were allotted to the responses: SA = 4, A = 3, D = 2, SD = 1. The criterion that was utilized to assess the dyslexic students' skills in Reading was the average of the response figures: $(4 + 3 + 2 + 1)/4 = 10/4 = 2.5$. In this way, dyslexic students who scored below 2.5 had poor Reading skills while dyslexic students who scored above 2.5 exhibited high Reading skills, meaning the absence of dyslexia. The instruments were given to two secondary school English Language teachers and an expert in measurement and evaluation for validation. The test–retest method was used to generate two sets of scores from students outside the sample of this study and the scores were correlated using the PPMC to determine their internal consistency. The reliability coefficients of the instruments were 0.89 for Dyslexia Screening Questionnaire (DSQ) and 0.77 for Reading Performance Test (RPT). The researcher carried out the data collection procedure in stages for three weeks. The researcher visited the selected schools for permission in using their students and some of the school facilities. Afterward, the dyslexic students were identified utilizing Dr Warren's Dyslexia Screening Questionnaire (DSQ). The control and experimental groups were exposed to the Reading Performance Test (RPT) before the experimental treatment (pre-test). This is to empower the researcher to set up the standard information of the dyslexic students in the control and experimental groups before the learning environment changed from face-to-face to web-based learning for experimental group 1. The items from the instruments were reshuffled utilizing a yellow paper to print the questions but the content remained the same for the post-test and retention test. The data of the post-test and post-posttest were utilized for the study. The post-test was scored and used to generate quantitative data which was analyzed using Analysis of Covariance (ANCOVA). The significance level of 0.05 was used to test the null hypotheses.

Results

Research Question One: What is the effect of Speechify App, collaborative learning, and discussion method on the performance of dyslexic students in Reading?

Table 16.1 and Fig. 16.1 show the effect of Speechify App, collaborative learning, and discussion method on the performance of dyslexic students in Reading. The results indicated that dyslexic students taught Reading Comprehension utilizing Speechify App instructional strategy (Pretest; $\overline{x}$ = 5.13, SD = 2.25, Post-test; $\overline{x}$ = 20.33, SD = 1.53, Mean Gain = 15.20) performed better than dyslexic students taught Reading Comprehension utilizing collaborative learning instructional strategy (Pretest; $\overline{x}$ = 6.91, SD = 1.83, Post-test; $\overline{x}$ = 17.12, SD = 17.12, Mean Gain = 10.21), followed by dyslexic students taught Reading Comprehension using the discussion instructional strategy (Pretest; $\overline{x}$ = 5.73, SD = 2.80, Post-test; $\overline{x}$ = 13.99, SD = 1.93, Mean Gain = 8.26).The implication of these results is that the performance of dyslexic students taught Reading Comprehension utilizing Speechify App instructional strategy is higher than those of their counterparts taught using collaborative learning and discussion instructional strategies.

Research Question Two: What is the effect of Speechify App, collaborative learning and discussion method on the retention of dyslexic students in Reading?

Table 16.2 show the effect of instructional strategy on the retention of dyslexic students in Reading Comprehension. The results indicated that dyslexic students taught Reading Comprehension utilizing Speechify App instructional strategy (Posttest; $\overline{x}$ = 20.33, SD = 1.53, Retention; $\overline{x}$ = 20.89, SD = 1.86, Mean Gain = 0.56) had higher retention

Table 16.1 Mean score and standard deviation of the effect of Speechify App, collaborative learning, and discussion method on the performance of dyslexic students in Reading

Instructional strategies	n	*Pretest*		*Posttest*		*Mean gain*
		$\overline{x}$	*SD*	$\overline{x}$	*SD*	
Discussion	88	5.73	2.80	13.99	1.93	8.26
Speechify App	60	5.13	2.25	20.33	1.53	15.20
Collaborative Learning	57	6.91	1.83	17.12	2.77	10.21

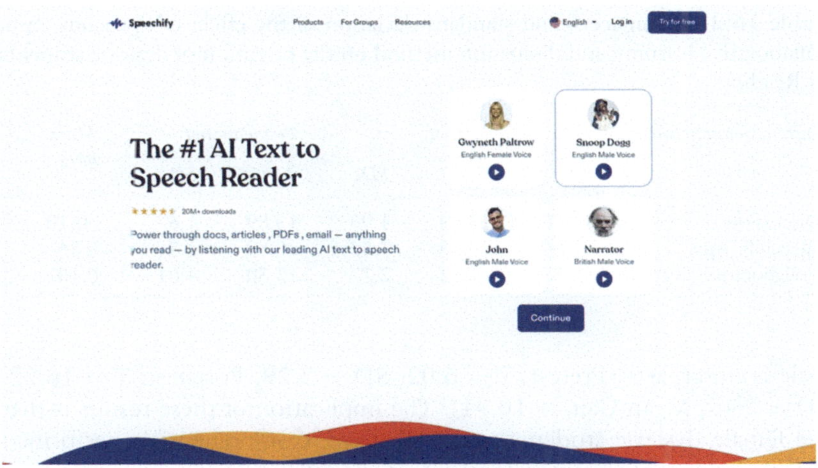

Fig. 16.1 Interface of Speechify App (*Source* https://speechify.com/blog/best-chrome-extensions-fordyslexia/?landing_url=https%3A%2F%2Fspeechify.com%2Fblog%2Fbest-chrome%20Extensions-for-Dyslexia%2F)

than dyslexic students taught Reading Comprehension utilizing collaborative learning instructional strategy (Posttest; $\overline{x}$ = 17.12, SD = 2.77, Retention; $\overline{x}$ = 17.30, SD = 4.01, Mean Gain = 0.18), followed by dyslexic students taught Reading Comprehension utilizing the discussion instructional strategy (Posttest; $\overline{x}$ = 13.99, SD = 1.93, Retention; $\overline{x}$ = 13.89, SD = 1.67, Mean Gain = –0.10). The implication of these results is that the retention of dyslexic students taught Reading Comprehension utilizing Speechify App instructional strategy was higher than those of their counterparts taught utilizing collaborative learning instructional strategy. Conversely, dyslexic students taught Reading Comprehension utilizing discussion instructional strategy showed negative retention. In other words, dyslexic students have forgotten what they learned after two weeks.

Research Question Three: What is the gender effect on the performance of dyslexic students in Reading?

Table 16.3 show how gender influences the performance of dyslexic students in Reading. The results indicated that male dyslexic students taught reading comprehension (Pretest; $\overline{x}$ = 5.78, SD = 2.63, Post-test; $\overline{x}$ = 16.72, SD = 3.45, Mean Gain = 10.94) performed better than their

Table 16.2 Mean score and standard deviation of the effect of Speechify App, collaborative learning and discussion method on the retention of dyslexic students in Reading

Instructional strategy	n	*Posttest*		*Post-Post test*		*Mean gain*
		$\bar{x}$	*SD*	$\bar{x}$	*SD*	
Discussion	88	13.99	1.93	13.89	1.67	–0.10
Speechify App	60	20.33	1.53	20.89	1.86	0.56
Collaborative Learning	57	17.12	2.77	17.30	4.01	0.18

male counterparts (Pretest; $\bar{x}$ = 6.02, SD = 2.29, Post-test; $\bar{x}$ = 16.72, SD = 3.45, Mean Gain = 10.94). The implication of these results is that the female dyslexic students taught Reading Comprehension performed slightly better than their male counterparts did.

Hypothesis One: There is no significant difference among dyslexic students taught utilizing Speechify App, collaborative learning and discussion method in their performance in Reading.

Table 16.4a shows that there is a significant difference in the effect of instructional strategy on the performance of dyslexic students in reading ($F_{2, 201}$, = 164.37, $P = 0.00 < 0.05$). Thus, null hypothesis one is rejected at 0.05 alpha level. The implication of this result is that the performance of the dyslexic students taught Reading Comprehension using Speechify App, collaborative learning and discussion instructional strategies differed significantly.

Table 16.4b shows the extent to which the difference in the effect of instructional strategies on the performance of dyslexic students in Reading differed. For the pre-test performance, the interaction between the discussion strategy (DS) and Speechify App strategies (SA) was not significant

Table 16.3 Mean and standard deviation of the effect of gender on the performance of dyslexic students in Reading

Gender	n	*Pretest*		*Posttest*		*Mean gain*
		$\bar{x}$	*SD*	$\bar{x}$	*SD*	
Male	85	6.02	2.29	16.72	3.32	10.70
Female	120	5.78	2.63	16.72	3.45	10.94

Table 16.4a Summary of Analysis of Covariance (ANCOVA) of the effect of Speechify App, collaborative learning and discussion on the performance of dyslexic students in Reading

Dependent variable: Post-test

Source	*Type III Sum of squares*	*df*	*Mean square*	F	*Sig*
Corrected Model	1449.13[a]	3	483.04	109.04	0.00
Intercept	8372.33	1	8372.33	1889.85	0.00
Strategies	1441.26	2	720.63	162.67	0.00
Pretest	0.00	1	0.00	0.00	0.98
Error	890.46	201	4.43		
Total	59,629.00	205			
Corrected Total	2339.59	204			

[a]R Squared = 0.619 (Adjusted R Squared = 0.614)

(MD = 0.59, Sig = 0.34 > 0.05), while the interaction between DS and collaborative learning strategy (CLS) was significant (MD = –1.19, Sig. = 0.02 < 0.05). Also, the interaction between the SA and DS was not significant (MD = –0.59, Sig = 0.34 > 0.05), while the interaction between SA and CLS was significant (MD = –1.78, Sig. = 0.00 < 0.05). Furthermore, the interaction between the CLS and DS was significant (MD = 1.19, Sig = 0.02 < 0.05), and the interaction between CLS and SA was significant (MD = 1.78, Sig. = 0.00 < 0.05). For the post-test performance, the interaction between the DS and SA was significant (MD = –6.35, Sig = 0.00 < 0.05), and the interaction between DS and CLS was significant (MD = –3.13, Sig. = 0.00 < 0.05). Also, the interaction between the SA and DS was significant (MD = 6.35, Sig = 0.00 < 0.05), while the interaction between SA and CLS was significant (MD = 3.21, Sig. = 0.00 < 0.05). Furthermore, the interaction between the CLS and DS was significant (MD = 3.13, Sig = 0.00 < 0.05), and the interaction between CLS and SA was significant (MD = 3.21, Sig. = 0.00 < 0.05).

Hypothesis Two: There is no significant difference among dyslexic students taught utilizing Speechify App, collaborative and discussion method in their retention in Reading.

Table 16.5a shows that there is a significant difference in the effect of instructional strategy on the retention of dyslexic students in Reading

Table 16.4b Scheffe Post Hoc analysis on the difference in the effect of Speechify App, collaborative learning and discussion instructional strategies on the performance of dyslexic students in Reading

Multiple comparisons

Scheffe

Dependent Variable	*(I) Strategy*	*(J) Strategy*	*Mean Difference (I-J)*	*Std. Error*	*Sig*	*95% Confidence Interval*	
						Lower Bound	*Upper Bound*
Pre-test	Discussion	SA	0.59	0.40	0.34	−0.40	1.59
		CLS	−1.19*	0.41	0.02	−2.19	−0.18
	Speechify App	DS	−0.59	0.40	0.34	−1.59	0.40
		CLS	−1.78*	0.45	0.00	−2.88	−0.68
	Collaborative Learning	DS	1.19*	0.41	0.02	0.18	2.19
		SA	1.78*	0.45	0.00	0.68	2.88
Posttest	Discussion	SA	−6.35*	0.35	0.00	−7.21	−5.48
		CLS	−3.13*	0.36	0.00	−4.01	−2.25
	Speechify App	DS	6.35*	0.35	0.00	5.48	7.21
		CLS	3.21*	0.39	0.00	2.25	4.17
	Collaborative Learning	DS	3.13*	0.36	0.00	2.25	4.01
		SA	−3.21*	0.39	0.00	−4.17	−2.25

*The mean difference is significant at the 0.05 level

($F_{2,\,201}$, = 118.20, $P = 0.00 < 0.05$). Thus, null hypothesis two is rejected at 0.05 alpha level. The implication of this result is that the retention of the dyslexic students taught Reading Comprehension using Speechify App, collaborative learning and discussion instructional strategies differed significantly.

Table 16.5b shows the extent to which the difference in the effect of instructional strategies on the retention of dyslexic students in Reading differed. For the post-post-test, the interaction between the DS and SA was significant (MD = −6.60, Sig = 0.00 < 0.05), and the interaction between DS and CLS was significant (MD = −3.41, Sig. = 0.00 < 0.05). Also, the interaction between the SA and DS was significant (MD = 6.60, Sig = 0.00 < 0.05), while the interaction between SA and CLS was significant (MD = 3.19, Sig. = 0.00 < 0.05). Furthermore, the interaction between the CLS and DS was significant (MD = 3.41, Sig = 0.00 <

Table 16.5a Summary of ANCOVA on the effect of Speechify App, collaborative and discussion method on the retention of dyslexic students in Reading

Dependent variable: Retention					
Source	*Type III Sum of squares*	*df*	*Mean square*	F	*Sig*
Corrected Model	1606.353[a]	3	535.45	81.88	0.00
Intercept	584.891	1	584.89	89.44	0.00
Strategies	403.691	2	201.85	30.87	0.00
Posttest	31.369	1	31.37	4.80	0.03
Error	1314.408	201	6.54		
Total	60,545.000	205			
Corrected Total	2920.761	204			

[a]R Squared = 0.550 (Adjusted R Squared = 0.543)

0.05), and the interaction between CLS and SA was significant (MD = –3.19, Sig. = 0.00 < 0.05).

Hypothesis Three: There is no significant difference between the performance of male and female dyslexic students in Reading.

Table 16.5b Scheffe Post Hoc analysis on the difference in the effect of instructional strategies on the retention of dyslexic students in Reading

Multiple comparisons							
Scheffe							
Dependent variable	*(I) Strategy*	*(J) Strategy*	*Mean difference (I–J)*	*Std. error*	*Sig*	*95% Confidence interval*	
						Lower bound	*Upper bound*
Post Posttest	Discussion Strategy	SA	–6.60*	0.43	0.00	–7.66	–5.53
		CLS	–3.41*	0.44	0.00	–4.49	–2.33
	Speechify App	DS	6.60*	0.43	0.00	5.53	7.66
		CLS	3.19*	0.48	0.00	2.01	4.36
	Collaborative Learning	DS	3.41*	0.44	0.00	2.33	4.49
		SA	–3.19*	0.48	0.00	–4.36	–2.01

*The mean difference is significant at the 0.05 level

Table 16.6 Summary of ANCOVA on the difference between the performance of male and female dyslexic students in Reading

Dependent variable: Post-test

Source	*Type III Sum of squares*	*df*	*Mean square*	F	*Sig*
Corrected Model	4.782E-01[a]	1	4.782E-01	0.00	1.00
Intercept	55,620.02	1	55,620.02	4826.00	0.00
Gender	4.782E-01	1	4.782E-01	0.00	1.00
Error	2339.59	203	11.53		
Total	59,629.00	205			
Corrected Total	2339.59	204			

[a] R Squared = 0.00 (Adjusted R Squared = −0.01)

Table 16.6 shows that there is no significant difference in the influence of gender on the performance of dyslexic students in Reading ($F_{1,\ 201} = 0.00$, $P = 1.00 > 0.05$). Hence, null hypothesis three is retained at 0.05 alpha level. The implication of this result is that the performance of male and female dyslexic students taught Reading Comprehension did not differ significantly.

Discussion of Findings

The study investigated the effect of Speechify App on dyslexic students' performance and retention in Reading in Port Harcourt Metropolis. From the data gathered, and analysis carried out, the findings of research question one showed that the performance of dyslexic students taught Reading Comprehension utilizing Speechify App instructional strategy is higher than those of their counterparts taught utilizing collaborative learning and discussion instructional strategies. Furthermore, the result of hypothesis one showed that there is a significant difference in the effect of instructional strategy on the performance of dyslexic students in reading. The finding is consistent with the findings of Marsh (2012), which revealed that the speech recognition group significantly performed better than the control group in word recognition, spelling, and reading comprehension. Furthermore, the finding is supported by Smith (2017), whose study revealed that the use of assistive technology seems to have transfer effects on reading ability and to be supportive, especially for students with the most severe difficulties.

Also, the findings of research question two showed that the retention of dyslexic students taught Reading Comprehension using assistive technology instructional strategy was higher than those of their counterparts taught using collaborative learning instructional strategies. Conversely, dyslexic students taught Reading Comprehension using discussion instructional strategy showed negative retention, in other words, the students forgot what they have been taught. Furthermore, the result of hypothesis two showed that there is a significant difference in the effect of instructional strategy on the retention of dyslexic students in reading. These findings are consistent with the findings of Bogi et al. (2017), which revealed that assistive interventions proved overall beneficial, but the most commonly used interventions were unexpectedly not the most effective. Interventions based on word processing, multimedia and hypertext proved the most effective, while smart pens and text-to-speech systems presented mixed results. Speech-to-text systems had a small positive effect. The finding is supported by Ghazizah and Fatemipour (2021), whose study revealed that assistive technology influenced their reading proficiency at a statistically significant level.

The findings of research question three showed that the female dyslexic students taught Reading Comprehension performed slightly better than their male counterparts did. Furthermore, the result of hypothesis three showed that there is no significant difference in the influence of gender on the performance of dyslexic students in Reading. These findings are corroborated by Virginia et al. (2020), which revealed that there was no significant difference in the mean scores of the two groups.

Conclusion

The study investigated the effect of Speechify App on dyslexic students' performance and retention in reading in Port Harcourt Metropolis, Rivers State. Consequently, the study revealed that the performance of dyslexic students taught Reading Comprehension using Speechify App instructional strategy is higher than that of their counterparts taught utilizing collaborative learning and discussion instructional strategies, while the retention of dyslexic students taught Reading Comprehension utilizing Speechify App instructional strategy is higher than that of dyslexic students taught utilizing collaborative learning and discussion instructional strategies. Furthermore, dyslexics taught utilizing Speechify App instructional strategy was higher than those of their counterparts taught utilizing collaborative learning instructional strategy, among others.

The gender comparison revealed that there was no significant difference in the performance and retention of dyslexic students taught using Speechify App, collaborative learning, and discussion instructional strategies, which implied that male and female dyslexic students' performance and retention did not differ significantly. Therefore, it can be deduced that dyslexic students are weak in not only reading and writing but also in comprehension, memory, and other higher-order mental processes that are necessary for accurate reading and understanding.

Based on the findings of the study, it was concluded that the provision of appropriate text-to-speech app would reduce the challenges faced by dyslexic students; as such technology allows them to effectively navigate the environment, increasing their ability to read and understand the content. This is because; Speechify App instructional strategy requires students to participate in a collaborative setting, whereas collaborative learning and discussion require individuals to work together on self-directed tasks.

Recommendations

Considering the findings, discussion, and conclusions of this study, the following recommendations were proffered:

1. The Rivers State Ministry of Health should carry out intensive diagnosis and remediation programmes in public schools in Port Harcourt Metropolis, as many male and female dyslexic students are not aware of their predicament.
2. The Government should provide Speechify App free of charge to dyslexic students to help them participate fully in the teaching and learning process, as well as influence their performance in Reading Comprehension.
3. Parents of dyslexic students should know that early intervention with explicit and intense instruction in the sound structure of language (phonemic awareness) and how sounds relate to letters (phonics) is the key. They should provide a Speechify App for their wards to enable them to gain the ability to retain what is learned extensively.

References

Barua, P. D., Vicnesh, J., Gururajan, R., Oh, S. L., Palmer, E., Azizan, M. M., Kadri, N. A., & Acharya, U. R. (2022). Artificial intelligence enabled personalized assistive tools to enhance education of children with neurodevelopmental disorders: A review. *International Journal of Environmental Research and Public Health, 19*(3)c, 1192.

Bogi, P., Mutter, K. K., McGregor, K., & Gordon, R. (2017). Assistive technology interventions for adolescents and adults with learning disabilities: An evidence-based systematic review and meta-analysis. . https://doi.org/10.1016/j.compedu.2017.06.005

Britannica. (2023). Artificial intelligence. https://www.britannica.com/technology/artificial-intelligence

Ghazizah, T., & Fatemipour, H. (2021). The effect of blended learning on EFL learner proficiency. *Journal of Language Teaching and Research, 8*(3), 606–614. https://doi.org/10.17507/jltr.0803.21

Marsh, D. (2012). Blended learning: Creating learning opportunities for language learners.

Smith, C. R. (2017). *Learning disabilities: The interaction of learners, task, and setting*. Allyn and Bacon. https://speechify.com/blog/best-chrome-extensions-for-dyslexia/?landing_url=https%3A%2F%2Fspeechify.com%2Fblog%2Fbest-chrome-extensions-for-dyslexia%2F

UMBC. Computing machinery and intelligence by A. M. Turing, https://redirect.cs.umbc.edu/courses/471/papers/turing.pdf."

Virginia, W. K., Doo, H. L., & Michael, L. M. (2020). Online vs blended learning: Differences in instructional outcomes and learner satisfaction. *Journal of Asynchronous Learning Networks, 11*(12), 27–24. www.eric.ed.gov

CHAPTER 17

Modern Aspects of Communication for Pedagogic Knowledge and Skills Development in Human Kinetics, Sports and Health Education Students in Lagos State University, Lagos, Nigeria

Bidemi Bilkis Lafiaji-Okuneye and Adeyinka Joseph Babajide

Introduction

The goal of sustainable development to achieve holistic development such as social progress, environmental equilibrium and economic growth remains a tall dream for developing countries such as Nigeria till date. This is because it is difficult for any nation to enjoy sustainable development when a sizeable number of her youth population, who, naturally should drive sustainable development indulge in drug use and abuse

B. B. Lafiaji-Okuneye (✉) · A. J. Babajide
Lagos State University of Education, Lagos, Nigeria
e-mail: bbidowu2000@yahoo.com

U. S. Akpan (ed.), *Educational Broadcasting in Nigeria in the Age of Artificial Intelligence*,
https://doi.org/10.1007/978-3-031-68530-9_17

that ultimately result in stagnancy, unproductivity, retrogression and intimate partner violence, among others (Lafiaji-Okuneye, 2023). Although almost every country in the world is affected by one or more drugs being abused by citizens (UNODC, 2018), it is disheartening that 40 per cent of Nigerian youths are on hard drugs, with Oyo, Lagos, and Gombe states having a high prevalence each. The southwest zone has the highest prevalence of drug addiction with approximately 22% compared to the north-central zone at about 10% prevalence rate. In another development, there has been an unprecedented increase in the number and non-medical use of synthetic psychoactive substances between 2005 and 2015 (UNODC, 2018).

The problem of drug abuse poses a significant threat to the social, health and economic status of the families, society and the entire nations (Oshodi et al., 2010). The abuse of psychotropic drugs like *rephenol, codeine, tramadol and comorado*, with *cannabis*, pharmaceutical opioids and cough syrups being the highest abused substances is prevalent among the youth across the country. Thus, there are growing concerns that there has been a consistent rise in the number of cases especially among young adults between the ages of 25 and 39 despite several efforts of the Nigerian Government and the National Drug Law Enforcement Agency (NDLEA) to stem the tide.

While a majority of the Nigerian youths ignorantly depend on one form of drug or the other for their various daily activities, the young ones from well-to-do homes increasingly abuse hard drugs like heroin and cocaine. Other substances like Indian hemp, methamphetamine and tablets with codeine capable of intoxication are mostly found in schools (Oliha, 2021). With the involvement of such a high percentage of Nigerian youths addicted to drugs with the resultant negative effect on their well-being, behaviours, output and sustainable development remains elusive. At the core of the nuisance is the breakdown of societal values and the attendant waste of human capital. This is because such substance abusers lose their capabilities, potentials and positive contributions to national growth and development (Lafiaji-Okuneye, 2023).

Sadly, there has been an overwhelming report on the correlation between risky sexual behaviour and drug abuse (Adeyemo et al., 2016). This has led to several unwanted pregnancies, sexually transmitted diseases, among others. However, the common challenge of drug addiction appears to be intimate partner violence (IPV). Intimate partner violence occurs worldwide and its occurrence is not affected by race, culture, religion or socioeconomic status (Oliha, 2021). IPV perpetration is significantly higher among those who abuse drugs compared to those who do not and males who abuse substances are more likely to be IPV perpetrators (Adeyemo et al., 2016). The challenges associated with this neuro-bio behaviour vary from one geographical location to the other. IPV could be perpetrated against both sexes. However, women are more commonly victims rather than men. When perpetrated against men, it is commonly in self-defense (Ipinmisho, 2016). It affects both young and older persons of reproductive age in the intimate relationship whether married or not (Ipinmisho, 2016; Oliha, 2021). IPV affects the victims' physical and mental health adversely, causing physical injuries and long-term chronic medical conditions including severe depression and suicide (Nigerian Drug Law Enforcement Agency, 2007).

A report in 2010 established a link between cultism/violent behaviour and drug abuse in secondary schools and tertiary institutions in Nigeria (Oshodi et al., 2010). Ironically, a higher percentage of the youth who are supposed to be the major agents of change and development in Nigeria remain stagnated and unproductive, having been negatively impacted by drug addiction, with the resultant negative outcomes, including sexually frequent behaviours, and intimate partner violence. It is a serious issue: a global issue; a major public health challenge; a social misdemeanor; and an individual problem that persistently aggravates economic crises and entrenches Nigeria's poverty status(Lafiaji-Okuneye, 2023).

It is worrisome that despite government efforts through the establishment of NDLEA and other institutional-based interventions, drug abuse is on the rise with over 40% of Nigerian youths abusing various types of drugs. Thus, there is the need to change the drum beat to effect a change in the dance step for a better result. Adopting the modern aspects of communication to teach the undergraduates in the Department of Human Kinetics, Sports and Health Education in our universities on how to combat the issues of drug use and abuse may yield positive results.

Interestingly, information and communications technology has offered a series of possibilities of modern aspects of communication in the education system. The word communication, in general, indicates the presence of two or more parties between which communication occurs for a specific reason and in the presence of the main communication factors so that the communication process takes place correctly (Babajide & Olatunji, 2022). Education about the new forms of communication represents a basic skill of individual learning and intellectual growth of each individual, using collaboration and communication in the education process. The development of communication competence of teachers by means of new technologies therefore represents an essential breakthrough in education (Adomi, 2010; Kosoko-Oyedeko & Tella, 2010). With the new forms of communication, development in the quality of education, educational institutions and learning outcomes becomes significant. In addition, learners' personality, skill in decision-making, assuming responsibility, finding solutions by sharing, discussing ideas and accepting others are greatly enhanced. They also facilitate strong and effective exchange of information and knowledge, ensure transfer and exchange of cultures and languages and facilitate effective learning about different societal customs and traditions (Babajide, 2012).

It appears that adopting Computer-Assisted Instruction (CAI) will make a wholesome difference in teaching undergraduates about the issues of drug use and abuse.Computer-Assisted Instruction (CAI) is a computer-based teaching tool used in the teaching and learning of educational activities (Brophy, 2009). CAI enables the students to learn by self-evaluating and reflecting on their learning process. It motivates children to learn better by providing them with immediate feedback and reinforcement and by creating an exciting and interesting game-like atmosphere. Studies in the field reveal that the students' achievements increase when the CAI technique is provided as a supplement to the classroom education (Çepni et al., 2006; Senemoğlu, 2003). CAI is more effective on less successful children. The reason for this is that CAI enables the children to progress at their own pace and provides them with appropriate alternative ways of learning by individualizing the learning process. Student learning rate is faster with CAI than with Traditional instruction. CAI provides an opportunity for experimentation, and builds realism and relevance into the learning situation. One of the most challenging techniques used in CAI is problem solving. It helps students develop skills in logic, solving problems and following directions. It is generally used to augment higher order thinking skills. Computer-Assisted assessment can be used to initially place and then monitor students' progress within a curriculum.

Statement of the Problem

With the world moving rapidly into digital media and information, the role of ICT in education is becoming more and more important. It has been suggested that information and communications technology (ICT) can play a number of roles in education such as developing the kind of graduates and citizens required in an information society; improving educational outcomes and enhancing the quality of teaching and learning (Watkins & Mortimore, 2017). Garrison and Anderson (2006) had argued that the application of ICTs in the teaching–learning process can enhance the quality of education in several ways such as increasing learner motivation and engagement, facilitating the acquisition of basic skills, and enhancing teacher training. The impact of ICT on various fields of human endeavour such as medicine, tourism, business, law, banking, engineering and architecture over two or three decades has been enormous. Although ICT has begun to have a presence in education, its impact has not been as extensive as in other fields (Cornu, 2015). It is against this backdrop that this study investigates the influence of Computer-Assisted Information (CAI) in the teaching of drug use and abuse in sports courses in Lagos State University, Lagos, Nigeria.

The gains in this exercise are expected to effect a major correction in the control of drug use and abuse that appears to be hell-bent on destroying the Nigerian youths who by nature are supposed to drive sustainable development in the nation. Since Drug Use and Abuse is one of the major subjects being offered at both secondary and tertiary levels, its relevance and sustenance in the twenty-first century requires the adequate application of ICT. This application must include video tapes, television and multimedia computer software that combine text, sound and colourful moving images which can be used to provide challenging and authentic content that will not only engage the student in the learning process but as well make learning concrete. While the aim of this study is to assess the influence of Computer-Assisted Information (CAI) in the teaching of Drug Use and Abuse in Sports course in Lagos State University, Lagos, Nigeria, the study's specific objectives are to:

1. Find out if there is a significant difference in the academic achievement of students in Drug Use and Abuse in Sports in Lagos State University when taught using CAI and traditional method of teaching; and

2. Assess the statistical significant difference (if any) between the academic performance of male and female students in Lagos State University when taught Drug Use and Abuse in Sports using Computer-Assisted Instruction (CAI).

To achieve the objectives of this study, the specific objectives are converted to the following research hypotheses:

$H_0 1$: There is no significant difference in the academic achievement of students in Drug Use and Abuse in Sports in Lagos State University when taught using CAI and traditional method of teaching; and

Ho2: There is no significant difference between the academic performance of male and female students in Lagos State University when taught Drug Use and Abuse in Sports Using Computer-Assisted Instruction (CAI).

This study will be relevant in many ways, given its theoretical significance, academic value and practical relevance. Theory of Reasoned Action (TRA) and Technology Acceptance Model (TAM) are used to explain the variables in this study and put them into proper perspectives. Researchers, various sports bodies, organizations and policy makers will benefit from this study. Also, the study will add value to the existing body of knowledge and trigger further studies on some researchable issues which will be raised in the study but not exhausted as they did not constitute the main focus of the study.

Research Design

The Quasi-experimental design was adopted in this study because of its aptness to assess cause and effect relationship (Osuala, 2011). Other reasons for its use included its economy, rapidity to collect data, getting a good amount of responses from a wide range of population, and ability to understand the characteristics of the population under study (Agburu, 2011). This design is a useful method for assessing attitudes or opinions towards programmes, individuals, organizations and events. Finally, surveys, when properly constructed and administered, could constitute important sources of high-quality data (Agburu, 2011).

Population of the Study

The population for this study was 822 regular undergraduate students in the Department of Human Kinetics, Sports and Health Education in the Faculty of Education, Lagos State University, Ojo. The figure comprised 208 students in 100 level; 206 students in 200 level; 205 students in 300 level; and 203 students in 400 level. Students' enrolment figures were established from the ICT centers of the institution.

Sample Size and Sampling Procedure

Both probability and non-probability sampling techniques were used to pick 90 participants from the Department of Human Kinetics, Sports and Health Education. These students were divided into experimental and control groups.

Instrumentation

Basic Teaching Achievement Test (BTAT); Questionnaire; and Computer Assisted Instruction (CAI) package were utilized to collect data for analysis in this study. The BTAT consisted of 20 multiple choice items with four options, A, B, C and D to collect data on students' academic performance. A close-ended questionnaire, developed by researchers to collect data from the students on Utilization of Computer Package and Academic Performance (UCPAC) on a Likert Scale, ranging from 1 = Strongly Agree to 4 = Strongly Disagree, was used to encourage respondents to take a specific position on each item presented. The researchers developed and utilized Computer Assisted Instruction (CAI) package as an instructional tool to present content, laden with videos, text and animation, to the students using PowerPoint slides.

Validity and Reliability of Research Instruments

This study was premised on content validity. To further ensure the validity of the instrument, a pilot test involving 18 respondents was conducted in one tertiary educational institution different from LASU, in tandem with the position of Ben (2013). The test-retests conducted to measure the degree of the consistency, stability, predictability and dependability of the instruments, using Cronbach's Alpha Coefficient, yielded 0.768; 0.825

and 0.697 for the three instruments respectively and were relied upon to establish the reliability of the instruments (Bowling, 2007; Bryman & Cramer, 2007 cited in Rattray& Jones, 2017).

Method of Data Collection

Quantitative data were relied upon. The quantitative data were secured through the Basic Teaching Achievement Test (BTAT); Questionnaire; and Computer Assisted Instruction (CAI). Using the quantitative method facilitates the collection of broader information, involving numerical data which help ascertain disparities among variables that have large samples for broader inferences and information (Silverman, 2015).

Method of Data Analysis

Mean, standard deviation, analysis of variance (ANOVA) and t-test are adopted to test the hypotheses. For the purpose of accuracy of findings, the collected data were coded and processed using the Statistical Package for Social Sciences (SPSS), version 22.0. Issues of anonymity, confidentiality and informed consent stipulated by the Research and Ethics Committee of Lagos State University were strictly adhered to throughout the research.

Result Presentation

A total of 90 respondents participated in the study and the 87 students who completed the study were used for analysis. The data gathered from the pre-test and post-test non-equivalent quasi-experimental design were retrieved, sorted and analyzed.

Test of Research Hypotheses

$H_0 1$: There is no significant difference in the academic achievement of students in Drug Use and Abuse in Sports in Lagos State University when taught using CAI and traditional methods of teaching.

Table 17.1 shows that the normality assumption was tested using Shapiro Wilk's *W* test. The outcome showed that for the CAI, the Shapiro Wilk's $W = 0.910$; $\rho = 0.052$ and the Traditional method yielded $W = 0.934$; $\rho = 0.076$. Both techniques showed that the normality assumption was not violated. Also, Levene's test for homogeneity of variance across the CAI and Traditional Method groups showed that; $F\ (1) = 4.040$; $\rho = 0.058$, meaning the homogeneity of variance assumption was not violated. Satisfying the two major assumptions was a precondition to validate the interpretation of the outcome of the independent t-test. Thus, the outcome showed that students taught adopting CAI technique ($M = 8.50$, SD = 1.80) outperformed those taught using the Traditional Instruction Strategy (TIS) ($M = 2.09$, SD = 2.89). Furthermore, independent t-test of CAI and Traditional Methods of teaching was run in Table 17.2 to further authenticate the outcome.

Table 17.2 shows that there existed a significant difference in the academic achievement of students in Lagos State University taught using CAI and traditional method of teaching with $t\ (85) = 12.436$, $\rho < 0.001$ at 95% CI of the Mean Difference [5.38, 7.43] with a Glass' delta, $\delta = 2.214$. This showed that there was 221.4% variance to the advantage of the students taught using CAI over and above those taught using Traditional Instruction Strategy.

$H_0 2$: There is no significant difference between the academic performance of male and female students in Lagos State University when taught Drug Use and Abuse in Sports Using Computer-Assisted Instruction (CAI).

Table 17.1 Group descriptive statistics, normality and homogeneity of variance

Group	*Pre-test*			*Post-test*		*Difference*		*Shapiro–Wilk*		*Levene's test*	
	N	*M*	*SD*	*M*	*SD*	*M*	*SD*	*W*	ρ	*F*	ρ
CAI	44	9.52	1.41	18.02	1.47	8.50	1.80	0.910	0.052	4.040	0.058
TIS	43	9.60	1.31	11.70	2.73	2.09	2.89	0.934	0.076		

Table 17.2 Independent t-test of CAI method and traditional method

T	*df*	*P*	*MD*	*SE D*	*95% CI*	*MD*	*Glass' delta*
12.436	85	<0.001	6.407	0.515	5.383	7.431	2.214

Table 17.3 shows that the normality assumption was tested using Shapiro Wilk's *W* test. The outcome showed that for the male, the Shapiro Wilk's $W = 0.904$; $\rho = 0.063$ and the female $W = 0.903$; $\rho = 0.053$. Both showed that the normality assumption was not violated. Also, Levene's test for homogeneity of variance across the male and female gender taught using CAI showed that; $F\ (1) = 1.098$; $\rho = 0.301$, the homogeneity of variance assumption was not violated. This situation prepared a good platform to validate the interpretation of the outcome of the independent *t*-test. Thus, the outcome showed that male students taught using CAI ($M = 8.68$, SD = 1.91) performed better than their female counterparts ($M = 8.31$, SD = 1.70).

Furthermore, independent *t*-test of academic performance of male and female students taught using CAI was run in Table 17.4 to further ascertain the outcome.

Table 17.4 shows that there existed a significant statistical difference between the academic performance of the male and female students taught using CAI, $t\ (42) = 0.666$, $\rho = 0.509$ at 95% CI of the Mean Difference [−0.74, 1.47] with a Glass' delta, $\delta = 0.214$. This showed that the academic performance of male students was better than their female counterparts when taught with CAI with 21.4% variance.

Table 17.3 Group descriptive statistics, normality and homogeneity of variance

Group	*Pre-test*			*Post-test*		*Difference*		*Shapiro–Wilk*		*Levene's Test*	
	N	*M*	*SD*	*M*	*SD*	*M*	*SD*	*W*	ρ	*F*	ρ
Male	22	9.23	1.602	17.91	1.66	8.68	1.91	0.904	0.063	1.098	0.301
Female	22	9.82	1.140	18.14	1.28	8.31	1.70	0.903	0.053		

Table 17.4 Independent *t*-test of CAI method and traditional method

T	*df*	ρ	*MD*	*SE D*	*95% CI*	*MD*	*Glass' delta*
0.666	42	0.509	0.364	0.546	−0.737	1.465	0.214

Discussion

The outcome of the study reveals that the students taught using Computer Assisted Instruction outperformed those taught using the Traditional Instruction Strategy. The finding is analogous to the finding of Sharma (2017) and Szewczak and Sindgrass (2020). According to them, students lag behind in their learning, and are unable to reach the minimum competency standards planned in the learning design when taught with traditional technique. Sharma (2017) explained that teachers face difficulties in conveying all the materials within the limited time allocation. In contrast, using CAI, students' responses to learning media amount to 73.75%, and students' learning outcomes are often fully achieved (Rampersad, 2012). The current study also corroborates the finding of Scriven (2007) who found that CAI has a significant positive effect on students' academic achievement and retention in Physics. Also, the finding is in line with the finding of Thomas and Knezek (2008) whose findings showed that the use of Computer Assisted Instruction influences the motivation, autonomy, participation, mathematical concepts, results and grade of the students.

Furthermore, the study finds that male students taught using CAI performed better than their female counterparts taught with the same instrument. This finding is in line with the finding of Becta (2013) who studied gender differences in mathematics achievement and found that male students did better than female students in achievement, interest and placement in advanced mathematics courses. Also, the finding of the current study resonates with the finding of Ubogu and Money (2020) that male pupils have a natural affinity towards abstract science, which helps them perform better compared to female pupils.

Conclusion

The use of the teacher-centered method comes with several shortcomings as it is teacher-centered, providing little or no consideration for individual uniqueness, differences and instructional needs of students. The one method fit-all-teaching process where the teacher directs the instructional process leaves many pupils frustrated and unmotivated. The undergraduates are able to interact with the various digital instructional materials. The modern aspects of communication stimulate their sensory organs, facilitating easy retrieval, schema construction and memory consolidation.

Considering the urgent need to effectively educate and rescue the teeming population of our youths from stagnancy, unproductivity, retrogression and intimate partner violence, among others, it is imperative to embrace a more learner-focused teaching approach, Computer Assisted Instruction. The tool, which focuses on each learner's unique ability and learning interest, has the capacity to effectively deliver the content in Drug Use and Abuse in Sports in our universities.

Recommendations

Based on the findings in this study, the following recommendations are made:

1. Government, universities and academics must invest in computer facilities and infrastructures;
2. Universities must facilitate continuous seminars and workshops for lecturers on the use of computer to present animations, produce assessment sheets and teach instructional contents in all academic programmes; and
3. Universities should romance all internet providers in the country to provide internet that will be seamlessly accessible to and utilized by the academics in the course of their pedagogic knowledge and skills development delivery.

References

Adeyemo Florence, O., Beatrice, O., Okpala, P. U., & Oghale, O. (2016). Prevalence of drug abuse among university students in Benin City, Nigeria. *Public Health Research, 6*(2), 31–37.

Adomi, I. A. (2010). Towards effective use of information and communication technology for teaching in Nigerian colleges of education. *Asian Journal of Information Technology, 7*(5), 210–214.

Agburu, J. (2011). *Modern research methodology* (p. 213). The Solid Printing and Publishing Company.

Babajide, A. J. (2012). The role of mass media on behavioural change communication. In *Essays in Honour of Mr. Pius Adekunle George* (pp. 83–93). Joytal Publishers.

Babajide, A. J., & Olatunji, R. W. (2022). Assessing adequacy of corporate social responsibility initiatives of telecommunications companies for tertiary educational institutions development in Lagos State, Nigeria. *LASU Journal of African Studies, 10*(1), 29–47.

Becta. (2013). *What the research says about using ICT in math*. British Educational Communications and Technology Agency.

Brophy, A. K. (2009). *Is computer assisted instruction effective in the science classroom?* Unpublished Master's Thesis California State University, Dominguez Hills.

Çepni, S., Taş, E., & Köse, S. (2006). The effects of computer assisted materials on students' cognitive levels, misconceptions and attitude toward science. *Computers and Education, 46*, 192–205.

Cornu, B. (2015). New technologies: Integration into education. In D. Watson & D. Tinsley (Eds.), *Integrating information technology into education* (pp. 45–55). Chapman and Hall.

Garrison and Anderson in Mlitwa. (2006). Technology of learning in higher education context: AT and ANT Analytical Perspectives. In *Proceedings of the emerge 2006*. net/connect/site/uploadwsc/emerge2006/file103/technology%20for/20teaching%20and%20learning%20in%20higher%20education.pdf.

Ipinmisho, O. (2016). *40% Of Nigerian youths engage in substance abuse*. Statistics of Drug. www.thisdaylive.com

Kosoko-Oyedeko, G. A., & Tella, A. (2010). Teachers' perception of the contribution of ICT to pupil's performance in Christian religious education. *Journal of Social Science, 22*(1), 7–4.

Lafiaji-Okuneye, B. B. (2023). Health education perspective in emerging trends in sexuality and drug addiction in Nigeria. In *A lead paper presented at the 51st National Conference and Workshop of NAPHERSD, held from September 19 to 23, 2023 at Federal College of Education(Technical), Asaba-Delta State*.

Nigerian Drug Law Enforcement Agency. (2007). *Drug data collection and research, Lagos: Drug demand and reduction unit*. National Drug Law Enforcement Agency.

Oliha, J. (2021). Adolescent and drug abuse in tertiary institutions: Implication for counseling. *British Journal of Education, 13*(1), 11–26.

Oshodi, O. Y., Aina, O. F., & Onajole, A. T. (2010). Substance use among secondary school students in an urban setting in Nigeria: Prevalence and associated factors. *African Journal of Psychiatry, 13*, 52–57.

Osuala, E. C. (2011). *Introduction to research methodology* (147 pp.). Africana FEP Publishers Limited.

Rampersad, C. (2012). Teachers' perceptions of the contribution of information and communication technology to the teaching of modern studies, using an integrated system, in an urban secondary school. *World Journal of Advanced Research and Reviews, 19*(01), 174–180.

Rattray, J., & Jones, M.C. (2017). Essential elements of questionnaire design and development. *Journal of Clinical Nursing*, *16* (12): 234–243.

Scriven, M. (2007). *Key evaluation checklist: Evaluation checklists project*. University of Michigan. www.wmich.edu/evalctr/chechlists

Senemoğlu, N. (2003). *Development, learning and teaching*. Gazi Publishing

Sharma, R. (2017). Computer assisted learning—A study. *International Journal of Advanced Research in Education & Technology., 4*(2), 102–105.

Silverman, K. A. (2015). Customer Retention: With special reference to telecommunication in Sri Lanka. *Proceedings of the workshop organized by the Department of Decision Sciences*, University of Sri Jayewardenepura, Nugegoda, Sri Lanka, 186–198.

Szewczak, E. J., & Sindgrass, C. R. (2020). *Managing the human side of information technology: Challenges and solutions*. Idea Group Publishing.

Thomas, L. G., & Knezek, D. G. (2008). Information, communication and educational technology standards for students' teachers and school leaders. In J. Voogt & G. Knezek (Eds.), *International handbook of information technology in primary and secondary education*. Springer.

Ubogu, R. E., & Money, V. (2020). Information and communication technology: A strategic tool in the internationalization of higher education. *International Journal of Education and Practice, 8*(3), 586–598.

United Nations Office on Drugs and Crime. (2018). *Drug use in Nigeria*. https://www.unodc.org/documents/data-andanalysis/statistics/Drugs/DrugUseSurveyNigeria_2019_BOOK.pdf. Retrieved on 13 September 2023.

Watkins, C., & Mortimore, P. (2017). Pedagogy: What do we know? In P. Mortimore (Ed.), *Understanding pedagogy and its impact on learning* (pp. 79–109). Chapman.

Afterword

Comfort Memfin Ekpo

In penning the closing words for this comprehensive exploration of *Educational Broadcasting and Artificial Intelligence: Challenges and Opportunities for Theory and Praxis in Nigeria*, in honor of my scholarship and leadership, I am filled with gratitude and admiration for the collective effort that went into bringing this volume to fruition.

First and foremost, I extend my heartfelt appreciation to the distinguished convener, author/editor, Dr. Unwana Samuel Akpan for the idea of this festschrift in my honor, as I retire from active service in the university. I also appreciate my academic mentee, Dr. Stella Nwosu, the associate editor of this volume for her immense role.

A sincere thank you is also due to the chapter authors who, amidst their demanding research, teaching, and administrative responsibilities, dedicated their precious time to compile the articles that enrich these pages. Your commitment to advancing the discourse on educational broadcasting in the context of AI is commendable.

I must also acknowledge the diverse array of established and emerging scholars scattered across Nigeria whose contributions have shaped the

C. M. Ekpo (✉)
Department of Educational Technology, University of Uyo, Uyo, Akwa Ibom State, Nigeria
e-mail: comforter992000@yahoo.com; commywitgirl@gmail.com

U. S. Akpan (ed.), *Educational Broadcasting in Nigeria in the Age of Artificial Intelligence*,
https://doi.org/10.1007/978-3-031-68530-9

discourse of this volume. Your dedication to exploring the intersection of education and technology has added depth and diversity to the discussions presented here.

As I step back from active academic service, I want to assure all those who have been part of this endeavor that my commitment to mentorship and light-scale research endures. The baton may be passed, but the journey continues, and I am eager to witness the growth and achievements of those who carry it forward.

In reflecting on the content of this book, it becomes evident that we stand at a pivotal moment in the history of education. Never before have we faced technological threats of such magnitude, and the emergence of AI presents challenges and opportunities that demand our careful consideration.

AI, if not embraced and regulated thoughtfully, poses a threat to the educational sector that surpasses even the specter of plagiarism. It is imperative that those entrusted with shaping the future of education acknowledge the transformative power of AI and take proactive steps to harness and regulate its capabilities.

To those who now hold the reins, I offer a piece of advice: do not ignore the digital tool, that is AI; instead, embrace it with a keen understanding of its potential and pitfalls. Through wise regulation and utilization, we can mitigate the negatives and fully reap the benefits that AI brings to the development of the education sector.

Finally, I extend my deepest gratitude to each contributor and participant in this intellectual journey. May your future endeavors be filled with success, innovation, and continued dedication to the advancement of education in the age of AI.

SPRINGER NATURE

GPSR Compliance

The European Union's (EU) General Product Safety Regulation (GPSR) is a set of rules that requires consumer products to be safe and our obligations to ensure this.

If you have any concerns about our products, you can contact us on ProductSafety@springernature.com

In case Publisher is established outside the EU, the EU authorized representative is:

Springer Nature Customer Service Center GmbH
Europaplatz 3
69115 Heidelberg, Germany

The manufacturer's authorised representative in the EU is Springer Nature Customer Service Centre GmbH, Europaplatz 3, 69115 Heidelberg, Germany. If you have any concerns regarding our products, please contact ProductSafety@springernature.com

Printed and bound by CPI Group (UK) Ltd, Croydon, CR0 4YY

01/10/2026

02225898-0005